Free Enterprise and Jewish Law

Aspects of Jewish Business Ethics

THE LIBRARY OF JEWISH LAW AND ETHICS

EDITED BY NORMAN LAMM

Jakob and Erna Michael professor of Jewish philosophy
Yeshiva University

Free Enterprise and Jewish Law

Aspects of Jewish Business Ethics

By

AARON LEVINE

KTAV PUBLISHING HOUSE, INC.
YESHIVA UNIVERSITY PRESS
NEW YORK
1980

Library of Congress Cataloging in Publication Data

Levine, Aaron.
  Free enterprise and Jewish law.

  (The Library of Jewish law and ethics; v. 8)
  Bibliography: p.
  Includes index.
  1. Commercial law (Jewish law) 2. Business ethics.
3. Laissez faire. 4. Judaism and economics.
I. Title.
Law   296.1'8   80-14067
ISBN 0-87068-702-6

Manufactured in The United States of America

Contents

Foreword

It is with a genuine sense of excitement that the Library of Jewish Law and Ethics welcomes its newest offering, Aaron Levine's *Free Enterprise and Jewish Law*. This is the first work we have published in the area of economics, and to my knowledge it is the most exhaustive and knowledgeable volume produced anywhere, on such a scale and in such breadth, on the halakhic and ethical views of Judaism on the subject of free enterprise.

Our author, who is professor of economics at Yeshiva University, is a meticulous scholar in both Halakhah and economics. What he here essays is a synthesis between the "dismal science" and some of the most recondite technical parts of Jewish economic law. His range and scope are quite evident, even from a cursory glance at his notes. This is a one-man interdisciplinary *tour de force* by a young scholar whose self-effacing modesty belies his considerable academic talents.

This is largely a pioneering work, and one should not expect what is, for the most part, the first word on a topic to be the last word on it. Professor Levine has organized the vast halakhic material on the key issues of free enterprise theory in a manner that will make it possible for other scholars, in fields such as law, history, economics, and Talmud, to gain new insights and information, and help advance still further the course of scholarship. The lay reader too will learn much, and the glossaries should prove helpful to readers of all backgrounds.

Norman Lamm
Editor

February 10, 1980

Acknowledgments

The present volume is the product of research I conducted under two separate fellowship grants from the Memorial Foundation for Jewish Culture (1976, 1979) and a research grant from Yeshiva University (1978).

With slight variations, chapter 6 of this volume, "External Benefits," appeared originally in the *Israel Law Review* (Hebrew University, April 1979, vol. 14, no. 2, pp. 184–194). In addition, the present work excerpts small portions from the following articles previously published by the author: "The Free Enterprise Model: A Halakhic Perspective" *(Proceedings of the Association of Orthodox Jewish Scientists,* vol. 5, 1979, pp. 115–151); "The Just Price Doctrine in Judaic Law— An Economic Analysis" *(Diné Israel,* Tel Aviv University Law School, vol. 8, 1978, pp. 7–31); and "Equity in Taxation as Discussed in Rabbinic Literature" *(Intercom,* vol. 16, no. 1, April 1976, pp. 7–28). I would like to thank the editors of the aforementioned periodicals for their permission to reprint the above materials.

Translations of Talmudic texts were adapted from the Soncino edition of the Talmud.

Translations of passages from Maimonides' *Yad* follow the Yale University Press edition.

I wish to acknowledge an intellectual debt to Dr. Shillem Warhaftig's outstanding work, *Dinei Avodah ba-Mishpat ha-Ivri,* vols. 1 and 2. Its influence on chapter 4 of this volume, "Contract Law," extends beyond what is indicated by the references to it in the notes.

To my dear friend Rabbi Dr. Israel M. Kirzner, Talmudist extraordinaire and economist of international renown, I wish to express my deep gratitude for the warm encouragement and stimulating critique he has provided me in my research into the interface of economics and Halakhah.

My heartfelt appreciation to my dear friend Rabbi Dr. Jerome Hochbaum, renowned scholar and outstanding personality in Jewish communal life, for the enthusiastic encouragement and support he has given me throughout this project.

Many thanks to my friend Rabbi Berish Mandlebaum, librarian at the Mendel Gottesman Library at Yeshiva University, for the very patient assistance and direction he has provided me in tracking down biographical vignettes appearing in this work.

To Bernard Scharfstein director of scholarly publications at Ktav Publishing House, Inc. for his encouragement and his editorial guidance. To Robert J. Milch, copy editor for Ktav Publishing House Inc, my sincere thanks for his resourceful technical assistance and advice in the preparation of this work.

My heartfelt appreciation to four very able and devoted students for their technical assistance in preparing this volume for publication: Simon Grunbaum and Shalom Lamm for their thorough work in verifying the sources quoted in chapters 5 and 6; and Elan Sober and David Rabinowitz for their meticulous assistance in the preparation of the indexes of this work.

To the editor of this volume, one of the outstanding Torah scholars and leaders of Orthodox Jewry today, Rabbi Dr. Norman Lamm, President of Yeshiva University, I wish to express a special note of appreciation.

On the occasion of the publication of this volume, I would like to express an appreciation for my dear parents. Their deep affection, steadfast devotion, and constant encouragement have immeasurably enriched my life. Their judicious guidance has cast for me a beacon of light in the byways of life's experiences.

I would also like to express my appreciation for my dear father-in-law and revered rebbe. His abiding love, warm companionship, and inspiring Torah teaching have sublimely uplifted me.

The selfless devotion and warmth my mother-in-law, of blessed memory, showed me remains indelibly impressed in my heart and mind.

To my beloved wife and life companion, Sarah, who has deeply ennobled my life and contributed to this volume in more than intangible ways, no mere acknowledgment will suffice. A fountain of inspiration, she has bestowed the priceless blessings of love, Torah idealism, and grace upon our dear children, may God bless them. To her this book is dedicated.

AARON LEVINE

New York
13 Shevat 5740

For Sarah

· 1

Introduction: The Free Enterprise Model and Jewish Law

The Free Enterprise Model

Production, exchange, and consumption lie at the heart of society's economic activities. Devising a mechanism to organize, regulate, and integrate these activities constitutes the basic economic problem confronting every society. Tradition, authoritative direction, and the free enterprise system are representative of societal approaches to the problem of economic organization.

Under the free enterprise approach, the spontaneous, free interplay of market forces determines the mix of products the economic system produces, its methods of production and exchange, and its patterns of income distribution.

Economic freedom is the salient feature of the free enterprise model: consumers buy what they want, businessmen produce what they can sell, and laborers work for whoever pays most.

Why economic freedom and decentralized decision-making do not produce chaos in the allocation of society's resources is explained by the workings of the price mechanism. In the unregulated marketplace, price will rise when demand exceeds supply at the prevailing norm. What produces this result is the competitive bidding among demanders to secure the available supply. Similarly, when supply exceeds demand at the prevailing norm, competition among sellers to liquidate their inventories will depress market price.

Changes in relative prices act as a powerful stimulus for resource-owners to expand output in those areas where supply is scarce relative to demand, and to contract output where the situation is the reverse.

Within the free enterprise model, abnormal profits in any particular industry would be a transient phenomenon. Alert resource-owners would withdraw from their present endeavors and switch to the advantaged industry. With supply increasing relative to demand in the advantaged area, prices and profit margins would be expected to fall there. Simultaneously, the decrease in supply, *ceteris paribus*, in the disadvantaged sectors would tend to increase prices and profit margins there. These adjustments thus tend to narrow the original differential.

Though the free enterprise model allows man's selfish nature full expression, market forces, paradoxically, harness the selfish motive to serve the social interest. Business establishments are deterred from furnishing adulterated or shoddy goods by the fear that customers may shift their patronage to rivals. Likewise, enterprises which fail to protect their labor force against accidents or industrial disease or which work them unusually hard are penalized by the refusal of workers to work for them except at a higher wage than other employers pay. The workings of the competitive process thus gives rise to the paradox that the pursuit of self-interest results in the maximization of social welfare.

The efficiency of the free enterprise system is predicated on the attainment of certain conditions in each and every microeconomic market. These conditions include the following: (1) a semblance of perfect knowledge on the part of all economic actors; (2) many buyers and sellers in each industry; (3) standardized products in each industry; (4) homogeneity in input markets; (5) freedom of entry in each industry; and (6) perfect mobility of resources.

Realization of the above conditions, according to free enterprise advocates, allows society to maximize its level of satisfaction with the minimum necessary outlay of sacrifice.

The Scope of This Book

The free enterprise approach places a premium on the values of competition, efficiency, and economic freedom. The purpose of this study will be to compare the approaches of free enterprise and of Jewish law (Halakhah) to various economic issues revolving around these three values.

The optimizing character of the self-regulating economy, as discussed above, is predicated on the existence of vigorously competitive forces in each and every microeconomic market. To the extent that the real world departs from the idealized model of perfect competition, the self-regulating market economy will not result in an optimal allocation of resources.

Monopoly and restraint of trade represent major departures from the idealized version of the perfectly competitive model. How these phenomena are dealt with is of vital concern for the advocate of free enterprise. Chapter 2 compares the approaches economic efficiency and Jewish law take in regard to the monopoly problem.

The free enterprise approach places a high premium on the value of competition. Unrestrained rivalry in the marketplace, however, may result in the ruination of the less inventive and efficient firms. To what extent is a competitor entitled to insulation from the aggressive and predatory tactics of a rival? How is the conflict between industrial justice and economic efficiency resolved? Chapter 3 compares the economic and halakhic approaches to the above issues.

Resource mobility provides an essential ingredient in making the competitive process work. Freedom of mobility implies that resource-owners are free to enter into contractual arrangements unencumbered by economic relationships they may have entered into in the past. To the extent that contractual ties inhibit the formation of contemporaneous commitments or otherwise restrain future options, it might well be necessary to make market decisions on the basis of considerations other than efficiency. Chapter 4 discusses Jewish contract law as it relates to the issue of resource mobility.

Economic freedom within the framework of the idealized version of the perfectly competitive model does not always produce an optimal allocation of resources. A case in point is the negative and positive externality phenomena. Chapters 5 and 6 deal with the externality problem from the perspective of economic theory and Jewish law.

Regulation of market conduct in Jewish law is taken up in Chapters 7 and 8. Chapter 7 discusses the regulations Jewish law imposes on the process of value determination and the ethical prescriptions it offers regarding business pricing policies. Chapter 8 discusses regulations of the buyer-seller relationship in Jewish law not specifically related to pricing policy and contract law.

What role should government be assigned in the free enterprise economy? Referred to as the social balance issue, this topic is taken up from the perspective of economic theory and Jewish law in Chapter 9.

Chapter 10 is concerned with the issue of public finance and Jewish law. Its focus is on the impact of the prohibition against interest (*ribbit*) in Jewish law on the efficiency of capital markets and how the prohibition can be reconciled with the need of the modern state to raise capital by means of debt creation.

· 2
Monopoly and Restraint of Trade

The Monopoly Problem in
Economic Theory

Within the framework of the idealized model of the free enterprise system, called perfect competition, market price is driven down to the marginal (extra) cost of producing the last unit demanded. Relatedly, economic rents are competed away in the long run. What this means is that resource-owners earn, in the long run, no more than the rewards they could command in alternative market possibilities. Vigorous price competition among the alternative sources of supply is, in large measure, what is responsible for producing this result.

In the absence of rival sellers, the single seller, or monopolist, can feasibly charge any price he desires for his product. Realizing that the higher the price he charges, the fewer units of his product he will sell, the monopolist will seek out the price that allows him to maximize his profits. Toward this end, the monopolist will extend output up to the point where the marginal revenue *(MR)* earned from the sale of another unit will be balanced by the marginal cost *(MC)* of producing that last unit. Given the assumption that the monopolist cannot engage in price discrimination, the lower price he must charge to induce the sale of the last unit of his product will be the price he must charge to dispose of his entire output. Selling extra output involves, thus, a per unit revenue loss on the previous units produced. This consideration leads to the observation that the per unit price the monopolist charges for his output will always be more than the marginal revenue he realizes on the last unit sold. What follows from the $MR = MC$ optimizing rule is that the monopolist price is always above his marginal cost too.

Given that the *MC* function of the monopolist is either identical to or higher than the corresponding *MC* function of the perfect competitor, monopoly results in higher industry profits, higher prices, and lower output compared to perfect competition.

The misallocative case against monopoly is strengthened further by considering the possibility that the higher monopoly price of X will induce substitution away from it toward Y. Under the assumption that the substitute product Y is produced under competitive conditions, its price will equal the MC of producing the last unit demanded. With the consumption decision between X and Y based on their respective prices rather than on the differences between their marginal costs, consumers will be confronted with false alternatives. Y will seem cheaper to them but in reality may require more of society's scarce resources to produce; i.e., Y's marginal cost of production may be higher than X's. Hence, under monopoly consumer demands are satisfied at a higher cost than necessary.

Regulation of monopoly is desirable from another standpoint. In the absence of legal remedies against monopoly, the opportunity to secure monopoly profits can be expected to attract real resources into efforts by sellers to secure this gain, and by consumers to prevent being charged monopoly prices. Resources used up for these purposes cannot at the same time be used to satisfy consumer wants in the form of goods and services.[1]

Vehicles of achieving monopoly power include internal expansion, buying out rivals, horizontal and vertical mergers, and restraint of trade agreements.

Monopoly Control: The American Experience

Regulation of monopoly and restraint of trade has been part of the American legal system since the enactment of the Sherman Anti-Trust Act of 1890. This act outlawed "conspiracies in restraint of trade." While price-fixing agreements clearly constituted such a conspiracy, it remained for subsequent legislation to delineate specific illegal practices. Tied contracts, exclusive dealerships, predatory price-cutting, and lessening competition by acquiring another firm's stock were included in the specific restraint of trade practices made illegal by the Clayton Act (1914). Acquisition of the assets of another firm when the effect is to lessen competition was prohibited by the subsequent Celler-Kefauver Anti-Merger Act of 1950.

Another form of restraint of trade is the resale-price maintenance contract, commonly referred to as "fair trade" laws. What is involved here is a contractual arrangement between a manufacturer and a retailer whereby the retailer agrees not to sell the product involved below a specified price. The Supreme Court of the United States, in

Dr. Mill Chemical Company v. John D. Parks and Sons, Co., 220 U.S. 373 (1911), held that the fair trade laws violated the federal anti-trust laws. Congress, however, in the depression era passed the Miller-Tydings Act (1937). This act exempted resale-price maintenance contracts from coverage of the anti-trust laws in those states where such agreements were lawful and in the state where the resale was made. The "fair trade" philosophy was further strengthened by the passage of the McGuire Act in 1952. This act permitted the enforcement of fair trade agreements with respect to interstate commerce against persons who were not parties to the contract. Congressional legislation in 1975, however, repealed the Miller-Tydings Act and the McGuire Act. Resale-price maintenance contracts, therefore, are no longer exempt from the anti-trust laws.

Restraint of Trade: An Economic Approach

The American anti-trust experience, according to Richard Posner, has overemphasized the discovery and prosecution of "conspiracies" in restraint of trade. From the standpoint of economic efficiency, the focus should be on the economic effects of restraint of trade.

Notwithstanding the mutual-advantage motive behind restraint of trade arrangements, these agreements do not always produce the desired results. Clearly, no net advantage will accrue to the consorting parties when they comprise only a small segment of the market supply of the product line, service, or labor skill involved. Here, the attempt to sell above the prevailing norm will fail. Consumers will switch their patronage away from the high-priced colluding sellers to lower-priced market alternatives. Similarly, collusion to raise price by limiting supply will also not succeed because nonparticipating firms will expand supply to take up the slack. With the market mechanism penalizing the colluding parties, this sort of restraint of trade agreement presents no problem for economic efficiency.

Restraint of trade will, however, succeed when the nonparticipating firms are incapable of accommodating the market demand below the collusion price. Price-fixing accompanied by an agreement to limit supply has the effect of increasing market price. This variety of restraint of trade agreement is decidedly injurious to third parties, such as consumers and employers. Nonetheless, to the extent that perfect knowledge, resource mobility, and freedom of entry are operative, market forces will in the *long run* weaken the adverse third-party impact of the restraint of trade agreement. Supply in the long run will increase relative to market demand, and the market price will be driven down.[2]

Restraint of Trade in Jewish Law

The distinction between the isolated and the industry-wide varieties of restraint of trade finds expression in Jewish law. Discussions relating to this point find their source in an analysis of the following talmudic passage (*Baba Bathra* 8b):

> There were two butchers[3] who made an agreement with one another that if either killed on the other's day, the skin of his beast should be torn up. One of them actually did kill on the other's day, and the other went and tore up the skin. Those who did so were summoned before Rava [d. 352] and he condemned them to make restitution. R. Yemar b. Shelemiah [4th cent.] thereupon called Rava's attention [to the *baraita* which says] that the townspeople may inflict penalties for breach of their regulations. Rava did not deign to answer him. Said R. Papa [4th cent.]: Rava was quite right not to answer him; this regulation holds good only where there is no Distinguished Person·[*adam chashuv*] in the town, but where there is a Distinguished Person, they certainly have not the power to make such stipulations.

What proceeds from the above talmudic passage is that, subject to the approval of the Distinguished Person, restraint of trade agreements entered into by means of *verbal consent alone* are judicially enforceable. Commenting on this text, early talmudic explicators and decisors emphasized that this applies only when all (a majority)[4] of the members of the trade are party to the agreement. Should the parties to the agreement comprise only a minority of the members of the trade, the terms of the verbal agreement lack legal force.[5] Collectively, the entire local membership of the same craft, product, or service line enjoys the legal status of a Jewish community.[6] While legal obligations cannot generally be created in Jewish law without the performance of an appropriate symbolic act *(kinyan)*, communal legislation becomes effective by means of majority *verbal* approval alone. Likewise, majority-approved policies of trade unions and industry-wide associations acquire legal force by means of verbal consent.[7]

Further insight as to why verbal consent suffices in the latter case is provided by R. Meir b. Baruch of Rothenburg (1215–1293) et alia. What *kinyan* usually accomplishes is to make the intent of the parties involved to carry out the terms of the agreement objectively evident. While communication of intent of this nature is generally not produced by verbal consent alone, it does obtain in the case at hand.

Given the certainty of mutual advantage proceeding from the agreement, verbal consent generates satisfaction to each participant. It is this mutual satisfaction that creates a presumption that the level of intent embodied in *kinyan* obtains here by virtue of verbal consent alone.[8]

R. Meir of Rothenburg's analysis clarifies the difference in legal status between the isolated and industry-wide varieties of restraint of trade agreements. Whereas mutual advantage proceeds, at least temporarily, in the industry-wide case, net gain is problematic in the isolated case. In the latter instance, the aggregate activity of the nonparticipating firms may very well make it impossible for the colluding parties to realize their anticipated gains. Given this possibility, verbal consent alone does not make it *objectively evident* that the parties intend to honor the terms of the agreement.

Restraint of trade agreements of the isolated variety apparently have no legal force in Jewish law even if the terms were either put in the form of a properly witnessed written document or the parties involved obligated themselves to adhere to the terms by means of *kinyan sudar*.[9] *Kinyan*, according to many talmudic decisors, can give legal force to commitments only when the obligations involved are concrete in nature.[10] What follows is the unenforceability of restraint of trade agreements involving mutual commitments to refrain from certain competitive practices.

Illustrative of the treatment of restraint of trade agreements in the responsa literature is the exclusive local dealership case discussed by the Hungarian decisor R. Solomon Leib Tabak (1832–1908). Here, a distributor entered into an exclusive local dealership with a baker. Though the agreement had been put in written terms *(kinyan shetar)*, R. Tabak ruled it judicially unenforceable. The court could not disallow the baker from violating the terms and selling his baked products to other local outlets.[11]

While *kinyan* cannot impart legal force to an isolated restraint of trade agreement, the solemn-oath method can. Mechanically, each party simply agrees to adhere to the terms by force of an oath.[12]

The terms of a restraint of trade agreement entered into by means of an oath are also binding on the heirs of the principals.[13]

Consummating a verbal agreement by means of a "handshake" imparts to the commitment a solemn-oath character in Jewish law.[14]

While the *form* of the isolated restraint of trade agreement determines whether or not it is judicially enforceable, such arrangements present several moral issues. Entering into a verbal restraint of trade agreement with no intention of fulfilling its term violates the "good faith" moral imperative.[15] Moreover, reneging on a verbal commitment entered into in good faith may stigmatize the violator as "untrustworthy." This occurs when the oral commitment generates expectations of fulfillment on the part of the other participants to the agreement. Hence, should A retract from his announced intent to confer B with a small gift, A would be called "untrustworthy." In contrast, no such appellation would be attached to A should he retract from his announced intent to confer B with a magnanimous gift, as B presumably never relied on this commitment.[16]

Short-Run Remedies Against Restraint of Trade

Restraint of trade, in the final analysis, reduces social welfare only when its impact is to limit the market alternatives of third parties. Concern with restraint of trade focuses, therefore, mainly on the industry-wide case. It is here, ironically, that the mechanics of restraint of trade find few legal complications. What protection, then, does Jewish law afford third parties against the adverse consequences of restraint of trade? Countervailing measures against a restricted section of the public dichotomize into short- and long-term stratagems. Let us first examine short-term measures. These include: (1) the Distinguished Person's approval; (2) communal anti-monopoly legislation; (3) countervailing power exercised by adversely affected third parties; (4) monopoly pricing power constraint; and (5) protection against predation.

Approval of the Distinguished Person

Restraint of trade agreements do not acquire legal force unless they are approved prior to their enactment by the local Distinguished Person (*adam chashuv*).[17] This individual must combine in himself both halakhic expertise and recognized leadership in public affairs.[18] Outside approval of this nature is required for any industry-wide ordinance which is disadvantageous to third parties.[19]

Requiring restricted sections of the public to submit their resolutions for approval to a scholar-leader effectively assures that the economic and social ramifications of these policies will be considered from an equity standpoint.

The practical significance of this constraint is, however, limited, as no outside approval is required should such a scholar-leader not reside locally.[20]

Anti–Restraint of Trade Legislation

Monopoly power can be directly checked by means of communal

price and wage legislation.[21] Restraining monopoly power could also be accomplished by means of communal legislation directed at changing the relative scarcity of the product or service involved. R. Levi Chaviv (ca. 1483–1545), for instance, approved a communal edict which made it unlawful for a dry-cleaning establishment to be closed for more than two months of a year. By minimizing allowable idle capacity, the edict rendered nugatory a price-fixing arrangement among members of the trade.[22]

Countervailing Power

A remedy available to parties adversely affected by restraint of trade is countervailing power in the form of organized economic strength. To illustrate, consumers could organize a boycott against a high-priced seller. Similarly, employers could organize into employers' associations to reduce the bargaining strength of labor unions.

Countervailing power finds approval in the responsa literature as a means of curbing a monopoly position. R. Krochmal (1600–1661), for instance, gave explicit sanction to the use of the consumer boycott by the town of Nikolsburg, Moravia, against its non-Jewish local fishmongers. These vendors, "having seen that the Jews were not deterred by expensive prices from buying fish for the Sabbath," decided to charge an exorbitant price for their product. Rejecting the notion that the boycott in some measure slighted the honor of the Sabbath, R. Krochmal ruled that in order to enable the poor "to honor the Sabbath by [eating] fish," it would be better not to buy fish for a few Sabbaths so as to bring down the price.[23] Similarly, R. Joseph Saul Nathanson of Lemberg (1810–1875) legitimized a consumer boycott against local butchers who were raising their prices.[24]

Indeed, faith in the self-regulating nature of countervailing power led R. Chayyim Halberstam of Sanz (1793–1876) to reject a plea for judicial intervention against a restraint of trade agreement between wool suppliers and clothing manufacturers. More vigorous and imaginative competition, insisted R. Chayyim, would allow them to recoup their lost business with the clothing manufacturers.[25]

Monopoly Pricing Constraint

Vendors dealing in commodities essential to human life are subject in Jewish law to a one-sixth profit constraint.[26] Intervention of this sort may produce a disequilibrium in the marketplace; i.e., demand may exceed supply at the profit-constraint price level. Under these conditions automatic market forces will force price above the profit-constraint level. While price and wage controls fall within the legislative prerogative of the Jewish community, imposing a *disequilibrium* ceiling price consistent with the one-sixth profit constraint would necessitate rationing as a device for clearing the market. Should the community regard rationing as an unacceptable allocational device, market price would be allowed to settle to its natural level.

Within the framework of an unregulated market price, vendors in the Necessity Sector are not restrained from selling their wares at the *current* market price, notwithstanding any additional windfall above the one-sixth profit constraint they may realize thereby.[27]

While selling at the current market price presents no moral issue in the Necessity Sector, *conspiring* to increase the market price and raise profit margins above the one-sixth rate violates the regulation set for this sector.

Collapse of the market mechanism may leave a particular seller with a monopoly position to exploit. What catapults the seller to his monopoly position here is not contrivance on his part, but rather events outside his direct or indirect control. Selling here at whatever price the market will bear, as the following talmudic text indicates, may present a moral issue in Jewish law:

> It has been taught, R. Judah b. Bathyria [mid 1st cent.] said: The sale of a horse, sword and buckler on [the field of] battle are not subject to *ona'ah*, because one's very life is dependent upon them.[28]

Given the life-threatening environment of the battlefield, the vendor of implements of war enjoys a captive market. The buyer, for all intents and purposes, will not hazard to investigate market alternatives amidst a raging battle. The vendor therefore enjoys a monopolistic position here.

With the vendee's demand for a horse or weapon in the battlefield zone described as perfectly inelastic, he certainly receives subjective equivalence for whatever price he agreed to pay for these articles. This is the reasoning of R. Judah b. Bathyria. Whether his ruling represents mainstream talmudic thought is a matter of dispute among the early decisors. R. Hai ben Sherira of Pumbedita (939–1038)[29] and R. Isaac ben Jacob Alfasi of Algeria (1013–1103)[30] ruled that R. Judah b. Bathyria's opinion represented a minority view and should therefore be rejected. R. Chananel b. Hushi'el, an eleventh-century North African decisor, however, ruled in accordance with R. Judah b. Bathyria.[31]

The acceptability of R. Judah ben Bathyria's opinion, according to R. Moses ha-Kohen of Lunel, a thirteenth-century decisor, hinges heavily upon the validity of assimilating his battlefield case with the fugitive-ferryman case discussed in *Baba Kamma* 115a. Here, the Talmud relates that in the event an absconding criminal agreed to pay a ferryman an above-market price to provide him with conveyance across a river, he is entitled to recoup from the ferryman the differential involved.[32]

The point of similarity between the two cases is obviously that in both instances the buyer's interest in the product involved is price-inelastic; i.e., he would agree, for all intents and purposes, to pay any price the seller insists on. In the ferryman-fugitive case, since the conveyance averts the fugitive's imminent capture, the latter certainly receives subjective equivalence in his transaction with the ferryman. Nonetheless, if his fugitive status were removed, this same individual's demand for the conveyance would properly be described as price-elastic and he would presumably not valuate the service above market price. With his price-inelastic demand reflecting transitory subjective value, the fugitive is entitled to recoup from the ferryman any amount he paid him above the competitive norm. Similarly, remove the condition of war and the vendee would presumably not agree to pay the price he paid for the implements of war.

Though R. Moses ha-Kohen advances no specifics as to why the assimilation should be rejected, two points of dissimilarity, in our view, stand out. Firstly, whereas the demand-inducing factor in the battlefield case affects all market-demanders equally, causing the *aggregate* demand schedule for implements of war to shift upward, no such similar upward *shift* of the demand schedule occurs in the fugitive-ferryman case. In the latter case, the demand-inducing factor uniquely affects the fugitive's subjective evaluation of the ferryman's services, leaving the aggregate market demand for the service unaffected. Secondly, whereas a competitive norm exists for the services of the ferryman at the time the fugitive contracted for his services, no competitive norm exists when an individual transacts for weapons on the battlefield.

What proceeds clearly from the school of thought that accepts the analogy between the fugitive-ferryman case and the battlefield case is the general principle that exercise of monopoly power, when the relevant aggregate demand schedule is price-inelastic, is ethically immoral.

Selling at whatever price the market will bear when the relevant demand the monopolist faces is price-elastic, however, presents no moral issue in Jewish law. This is evidenced from the long-standing sanction given to the communal practice of auctioning the privilege of performing a public ceremonial function of a religious character to the highest bidder.[33] With the ceremonial honor put up for sale unavail-

able elsewhere, the competitive bidding among the auction participants *determines* value. Hence, no moral issue is raised here.
Capitalizing on "site value,"[34] auctioning a rare painting, and selling
the patent rights of a new invention to the highest bidder provide
other examples of monopoly pricing under conditions of elastic
demand.

Protection Against Predation

Restraint of trade frequently occurs as a result of the initiative of an
aggressive firm. Suppose A, for example, sees the possibility of
monopoly profits if only his rivals B and C would join with him in a
cartel agreement to limit supply and raise price. Suppose further that
B and C refuse to join in the cartel. To induce his uncooperative rivals
to sign the cartel agreement, A subjects them to physical violence or
threatens to sell below cost as a means of driving them out of
business. Restraint of trade agreements arrived at by means of coercive tactics are not judicially enforceable.[35]

Acquiring the stock or assets of another firm by means of strong-
arm tactics is, however, another matter. The element of duress per se
does not invalidate a sale contract in Jewish law. Provided A pays B
the "fair market value" of the article he seeks, forcing him to sell the
said property by means of physical violence or credible threats does
not invalidate the sale. Notwithstanding Jewish law's requirement
that intent of transfer must be *objectively evident*, given the pressure
the seller faces, and his acceptance[36] of the purchasing price, we may
presume that he makes up his mind to transfer the object. Failure on
the part of A to offer "fair market value" for the property involved,
however, renders the duress transaction null and void.[37]

A variation of the above case occurs when A snatches away B's
article but leaves him with its "fair market value." With the duress
element absent here, B's acquiescence to the exchange does not
become objectively evident until B explicitly verbalizes his consent.[38]

While a fair market price duress sale is legally enforceable, it is
morally objectionable. Pressuring an individual to sell his article
violates the biblical injunction[39] against "coveting" a neighbor's
property. The prohibition is violated even if the initial resistance of
the seller is overcome by offering him more than the market price for
his asset.[40] Indeed, even scheming in the heart to change the attitude
of a recalcitrant seller violates the biblical prohibition[41] against "desiring" a neighbor's property.[42]

Jewish law protects society against the predatory tactics of cartels.
Illustrating the nature of this protection is the distiller-tavern case
dealt with by R. Tabak. Distillers in the local area banded together

into a cartel for the purpose of raising the wholesale price of whiskey for the tavern-owners. The cartel whiskey was inferior to the cheaper alternative sources of supply. To induce local tavern-owners to enter into an exclusive arrangement with them, the cartel members set up a new tavern in the area which undercut the competition by selling below cost. Noting the predatory tactics used by the cartel, R. Tabak issued a cease and desist order against them.[43]

Long-Run Remedy Against Restraint of Trade

Monopoly profits, in the absence of artificial barriers, can be expected to attract new entry. By expanding market alternatives, new entry fosters competition of various forms, including price reduction. Analysis of the following talmudic passage indicates Jewish law's attitude toward freedom of entry.

> R. Huna b. R. Joshua [4th cent.] said: It is quite clear to me that the resident of one town can prevent the resident of another town [from setting up a competing outlet in his town]—not, however, if he pays taxes to that town—and that the resident of an alley cannot prevent another resident of the same alley [from establishing a competing outlet in his alley]. R. Huna b. R. Joshua then raised the question: Can the resident of one alley prevent the resident of another [from competing with him]—This question remains unresolved.[44]

What follows from R. Huna b. Joshua's accepted view[45] is that enjoining a new entrant is legitimized only when the plaintiff is an out-of-town tradesman who does not pay taxes in the complainant's town. Given the moot entry status of a resident of a different alley, the Jewish court would not enjoin him from entering the complainant's alley. (Rabbinical courts in Israel today have understood the modern "neighborhood" to correspond to the talmudic "alley.")[46]

Jewish law's freedom-of-entry stance emerges even in connection with the out-of-town intrusion case. This is evidenced from the following considerations.

Freedom of Entry for Wholesale Trade

Protection against nonlocal competition is limited to the retail-trade level. The Jewish community may not, however, place any restrictions on foreign wholesale-trade activities.[47] Allowing the community to regulate foreign wholesale trade would, in effect, disrupt intercommunity trade.[48]

Out-of-Town Price Competition

Should locally available merchandise be offered by out-of-town merchants at a lower price, the latter group, according to R. Joseph Ibn MiGash (1077–1141), may not be barred from competing for local patronage. Insofar as competition here decidedly benefits local consumers, protectionist pleas of local merchants must be resisted.[49]

Citing the following talmudic passage in *Baba Metzia* 60a, Nachmanides (1194–1270) disagrees with the above ruling of R. Joseph Ibn MiGash:

> R. Judah said: Nor may he reduce the price, but the Sages say, he is to be remembered for good. What is the Rabbis' reason? Because he lowers market price.

Though the Sages regard price-cutting as a fair business tactic, they would not permit a non-taxpaying outsider to employ this stratagem as a means of gaining entry into the town. How can such vendors be permitted to generate losses to local merchants? If the townspeople feel that local prices are too high, legitimate means to reduce them are readily available. Encouraging local merchants to compete with the high-priced local vendors would be one approach. Alternatively, price reductions could be mandated directly through the legislative process. Given that the community has the power to fix local prices, this body may not allow outside merchants to effectively usurp this function by causing local prices to go down.

Furthermore, argues Nachmanides, should out-of-town merchants be guaranteed entry whenever they offer to undersell the local competition, the community would *never* be able to block foreign entry. This follows from the fact that an increase in supply, *ceteris paribus*, will always exert a downward pressure on price. Hence, regardless of whether foreign merchants initially offer to undersell local vendors, their competitive presence will nonetheless force local prices down.[50]

Understanding the anti-protectionist stance of R. Joseph Ibn MiGash to refer only to the circumstance where the out-of-town merchants offer to undercut the local competition by a significant margin, R. Joseph Chabib (14th cent.) finds R. Joseph Ibn MiGash's view to converge closely with Nachmanides' position.[51] Other commentators, however, find the two views diametrically opposed: Nachmanides' protectionist view is advanced even when the proposed price cut is significant, and R. Joseph Ibn MiGash's freedom-of-entry view is held even when the price cut involved is slight.[52]

The implication of the above conflicting views for Jewish law is that the Jewish court would not enjoin out-of-town merchants when they offer to undercut the local competition by a significant margin. Accordingly, R. Chiyya Abraham b. Aaron di Boton (ca. 1560–1609) refused to issue an injunction against an out-of-town tailor who offered his services at 50 percent the local price.[53]

Freedom of Entry on Market Days

Restrictions against out-of-town merchants must be suspended on "market days" (*yoma dishuka*).[54] On these days the marketplace expands to include consumers from nearby towns as well as the local population. Given that foreign retail trade at this time cannot be said as a matter of certainty to attract local customers away from local merchants,[55] Tosafot (12th–14th cent. French commentators) and R. Asher b. Jechiel (1250–1327) would allow the out-of-town merchants to cater to the nonlocal portion of the market on these days.[56] A still broader view of the trading rights of out-of-town merchants on market days is taken by R. Joshua ha-Kohen Falk of Lemberg (1555–1614). According to his view, out-of-town merchants on these days may sell their wares indiscriminately to local and nonlocal customers alike.[57] The presumptive claim of local merchants to the local market, according to R. Falk, is apparently lost entirely on market days.

Retail trading privileges on these days allow nonlocal merchants only to sell their wares in the marketplace. Peddling their merchandise from door to door in the local community is a privilege not extended to them even on market days.[58]

Freedom of Entry in the Debt and Loan Connection Case

Debt or loan connections with members of the local community provide the nonlocal merchant with another legitimate basis for gaining business entry to a town. Until such time that the out-of-town merchant collects or pays off his debts, as the case may be, the community may not interfere with his subsistence-generating business activities.[59] Though not a bona fide member of the community, the out-of-town merchant must participate in some measure in the burden of local taxation for the duration of his stay. His tax liability is assessed proportional to his business profits.

Individuals forced to leave their own communities to avoid impending harm may enter another community on the same terms outlined above.[60]

Cosmetic Salesmen

By virtue of a special enactment by Ezra (5th cent. B.C.E.), foreign cosmetic salesmen are conferred with special status. To afford women with easy access to beautification aids, the community must allow these salesmen to peddle their wares from door to door. These nonlocal peddlers may, however, be prevented from marketing their wares in a retail outlet. When the peddler is a rabbinical scholar, the latter privilege must be extended to him as well.[61]

Substitute Products

Increasing the supply of substitute products represents another means of weakening a monopoly position. Should the out-of-town vendors offer for sale merchandise unobtainable locally, the community may not obstruct their entry. Heterogeneity of product, in R. Joseph Caro's view, is what is crucial in generating free trading rights. Hence, should the out-of-town merchants offer to sell a product available locally, but superior or inferior in quality, the outsider's freedom of entry is vouchsafed.[62] Loss of local profits due to the substitution effect apparently provides no grounds for excluding the nonlocal merchants.

Competition in the Field of Torah Education

Primary-school religious teachers (*melamdei tinokot*) are offered access to any community they might desire to enter. The free movement of the primary-school teacher is guaranteed even when he desires to enter a town where a competitor is firmly entrenched. Competition in this profession is very favorably viewed. The Talmud's approving attitude toward rivalry here finds expression in the adage, *kinat soferim tarbeh chokhmah* ("jealousy among scholars increases wisdom").[63]

Freedom of movement for instructors of Mishnah and Talmud, according to R. Joseph Saul Nathanson of Lemberg (1810–1875), follows from the above argument with equal force. Indeed, he advances an even more fundamental basis for guaranteeing freedom of movement to the latter group. Compensation for teaching Mishnah and Talmud is prohibited.[64] Earnings for such instruction are justified only as an inducement not to seek employment elsewhere. New entry in the secondary-school sector, therefore, does not *directly* reduce the livelihood of the established teacher. Any reduction of the established teacher's earnings occasioned by the new entrant merely imposes to the former a loss in the form of opportunity cost, i.e., *income* he could have earned had he spent his time outside the secondary educational field. Now, preventing someone from earning his livelihood incurs liability only when the loss in earnings can be *directly traced* to the action of the offender. Locking someone in his home, thereby preventing him from going to work, qualifies as such a direct action.

When the link between the plaintiff's loss of earnings and the action of the offender is not direct, no liability is incurred. Insofar as the new entrant in no way initiated any action that prevented the established teacher from earning income outside the secondary educational field, the established teacher has no legal claim against the new entrant.[65]

R. Moshe Sofer (1762–1839) would extend freedom of movement to any religious ministrant, provided the resulting competition would produce the same beneficial consequences as rivalry in Torah education.[66]

Ruinous Competition and Monopoly Profits

Competitive pressures produced by freedom of entry may, in some instances, not only reduce the monopoly profits of the established firm, but deprive it of its livelihood entirely. In the deprivation-generating case, restraining the rival allows the monopoly profits of the established firm to persist, while allowing freedom of entry ruins the established firm. Whether Jewish law entitles an established firm to restrain a rival from locating in its neighborhood when such location would ruin its livelihood is disputed among talmudic decisors.[67] What follows from the protectionist school of thought is that freedom of entry cannot be relied upon, in the deprivation-generating case, to compete monopoly profits down. Countervailing power or communal price regulation would have to be relied upon here to accomplish the desired price reduction.

Union Strikes and Jewish Law

An extreme form of restraint of trade is the union strike. The use of this tactic is given legitimacy in Jewish law, according to R. Abraham I. Kook (1865–1935), only as a means of forcing an employer either to submit a labor grievance or demand to arbitration or to adhere to a labor arbitration decision.[68] Ruling in a similar vein is R. Ben Zion Uziel (1881–1953).[69]

A majority vote by members of a union to strike, according to R. Moshe Feinstein, binds the decision on all members of the union, including the dissenting minority. While both union demands and the decision to strike are not binding on non–union members, the striking union workers are entitled to judicial protection against the intrusion of strikebreakers. Offering to work for less advantageous terms than the demands of the striking workers amounts to encroaching upon the latter's livelihood and is therefore prohibited.[70]

Since the codes rule in accordance with the freedom-of-entry advocacy of R. Huna b. Joshua, R. Tchursh regards the enjoinment of strikebreakers as outside the scope of the Jewish court. Nonetheless, striking workers are entitled to make use of any means available to them, including recourse to the non-Jewish authorities, to prevent the strikebreakers from taking away their jobs. This follows from the ruling of R. Joseph Colon (ca. 1420–1480)[71] regarding the recourse open to a community to exclude taxpaying outsiders. While the Jewish court will not enjoin taxpaying outsiders from entering, members of the community who feel that the new entrants pose an economic threat may make use of any means available to them to place impediments in their path and frustrate the new entry.

Strikes endangering the public health and safety, according to R. Tchursh, cannot be countenanced under any circumstances. Labor disputes in such industries must, therefore, be settled by means of compulsory arbitration.[72]

Natural Monopoly in Economic Theory and Jewish Law

The competitive norm is not regarded as the ideal market structure when a single firm can provide for the entire market demand under conditions of decreasing marginal cost. Electric power, telephone, and urban transit provide examples of this circumstance. Allowing competitive forces free rein in these industries effectively divides the market demand among the rival firms, forcing marginal cost above what it would be under monopoly. With the ability to lower marginal cost by expanding market share, the competitive arrangement could very well degenerate into cutthroat rivalry. In the absence of such aggressive conduct, the competitive arrangement would likely be characterized by relatively high output prices and would encourage reductions in quality as a means of increasing profits. Here, the optimal organizational structure is the conferring of monopoly status to a single firm, but subjecting it to government regulation as a means of protecting the public interest.

The natural monopoly phenomenon finds explicit expression in Jewish law in the writings of R. Moshe Sofer. In a responsum dealing with exclusive publication rights, R. Sofer ruled that it was appropriate for the Jewish court to confer this privilege to publishers of Talmud. Given the decreasing-cost nature of the industry and the very low per capita income in the target market, profits are predicated on the ability of publishers to sell their books in large quantities. Allowing unbridled competition in this industry would thus increase the risk factor and reduce the profit motive. With the wide dissemination of essential religious books endangered by competitive forces, a legitimate basis for conferring monopoly status is established. To avoid financial loss to other would-be publishers, R. Sofer required the individuals conferred the monopoly status to adequately publicize their privilege.[73]

Conclusion

Moral concern with restraint of trade and monopoly finds its major focus in Jewish law in the ethics of exercising economic leverage. Most striking, in terms of direct interference with the free interplay of market forces, is the one-sixth profit-rate constraint imposed on industries dealing in necessities. Jewish law's notion of industrial justice affords little protection against new entry to an established firm when the expected impact is merely to reduce the complainant's monopoly profits.

Rabbinic literature reflects a faith in the long-run workings of countervailing forces as a means of curbing monopoly power. Nonetheless, should society desire to control a monopoly directly, it may do so through communal legislation.

At the other extreme, the desirability of limiting competition in the "natural" monopoly phenomenon finds explicit recognition in the responsa literature.

Monopoly market structure per se is neither condemned nor regulated by Jewish law. Vertical and horizontal integration achieved by means of acquisition of stock or assets is judicially enforceable. Provided "fair market value" is paid, acquisition of stock or assets by means of duress is legally recognized, albeit morally reprehensible. Predatory tactics as a means of achieving a monopoly position is, however, subject to judicial restraint.

Freedom of contract allows isolated parties to enter into restraint of trade agreements. Though Jewish law generally finds no moral objection to these agreements, restraint of trade of the isolated variety is judicially enforceable only if it is entered into by means of the solemn-oath method. Subject to the approval of the Distinguished Person, industry-wide restraint of trade agreements become judicially enforceable by means of verbal consent alone. Should such a scholar-leader not reside locally, countervailing power and communal legislative authority would have to be relied upon to curb the economic leverage proceeding from the agreement.

Restraint of trade designed to circumvent the one-sixth profit-rate constraint set for industries dealing in necessities is morally objectionable and legally invalid.

· 3
Ruinous Competition

Introduction

Unrestrained rivalry in the marketplace in the form of competition for choice location, competitive price-cutting, or aggressive salesmanship and advertising may result in the ruination of the less inventive and efficient firms. Survival in the marketplace may also become very difficult when legitimacy is given to the practice of selling below cost for the purpose of driving out a competitor.

The legal treatment of unfettered competition may present a conflict between common notions of industrial justice and consumer welfare. Industrial justice demands that the businessman be protected against overaggressive and unsavory business conduct by a rival. Overprotection of firms against the unpleasantness of competition, on the other hand, runs counter to economic efficiency and is decidedly injurious to consumer welfare.

Ruinous Competition in Economic Theory

One basic criterion economic efficiency offers in assessing the legitimacy of a business tactic is its exclusionary impact in the relevant market. Should the tactic effectively eliminate or impede entry of firms as efficient or more efficient than the firm employing the tactic, the practice should be disallowed. Let us illustrate this general principle in relation to predatory pricing and other exclusionary practices.

In assessing what constitutes predatory pricing, it is necessary, as a preliminary matter, to identify the concepts of fixed and variable costs. Costs that are independent of the level of output of a firm are called fixed costs. These costs may include depreciation allowances on fixed plant and equipment, insurance, rent, and property taxes. Variable costs are costs that vary directly with the level of output. Raw material and labor costs are typical examples of variable costs. When output is zero, variable costs are, by definition, zero.

When a firm can select the price it charges for its product, profit maximization obtains when it extends output up to the point where the marginal (extra) revenue it earns by the sale of its last unit is just equal to the marginal (extra) cost it incurs in the production and sale of that last unit. The price it can charge at the optimal-output level will always exceed the marginal revenue earned on the last unit sold. This follows from the standard assumptions that the firm faces a downward-sloping demand curve and it is forced to sell its entire output at a unified price. These assumptions indicate that in order to sell another unit of the product, the firm must not only reduce its price to induce purchase of the last unit but must also lose revenue on that part of its output that would be demanded at a higher price. The increase in total revenue realized on the sale of the last unit, therefore, will always fall short of the per unit price of the entire output.

Since fixed costs do not enter into the marginal-cost calculation, total cost, including fixed costs, may exceed total revenue at the marginal revenue equal marginal cost level. Nevertheless, provided total revenue (TR) exceeds total variable cost (TVC) at the optimal output level, staying in operation and producing at the $MR = MC$ level is preferable to shutting down. Shutting down means to the firm a loss equal to its fixed costs. Let us suppose this loss is equal to $100. Staying in operation incurs for the firm additional costs in the form of variable costs, but at the same time generates for it revenue from the sale of its product. Now, suppose that total revenue at the $MR = MC$ output level is equal to $80 and TVC at this output level is equal to $60. Staying in operation here minimizes for the firm the maximum loss it can incur in the short run as TR exceeds TVC by $20. This sum reduces the firm's loss from $100 to $80.

Areeda and Turner identify predatory pricing as selling below short-run marginal cost.[1] Measurement problems, as Posner points out, make this definition operationally difficult. A firm may be offering its product below cost as a method of sales promotion. In such a case the real sale price can be calculated only by including at least some of the future revenues generated by the sale. Furthermore, since long-run marginal cost is always above short-run marginal cost, the Areeda-Turner rule theoretically allows a price-cutter to drive out a rival whose long-run cost of production is lower than his.

In the light of these difficulties with the Areeda-Turner criterion, Posner identifies predatory pricing as selling below long-run marginal cost, with intent to exclude a competitor. *Intent* is a very important element of the definition. In the event that the development of new technology makes it evident that the subject firm will not replace its plant and equipment when they depreciate, no social purpose is served by forcing the firm to include in its price a charge for depreciation allowances. Here, entry of the more efficient firms will be postponed until the plant and equipment of the existing firm depreciate entirely.

Measurement problems also present themselves in connection with the long-run marginal cost rule, for it is difficult or even impossible to make a non-arbitrary allocation of marginal costs to an individual product or market.

Average balance-sheet costs serve, according to Posner, as a workable proxy for long-run marginal cost. Proof of sales below average balance-sheet costs with intent to exclude establishes, therefore, a prima facie case of predatory pricing.[2]

An implication to be drawn from the long-run marginal cost rule, in our view, is that a pricing policy that does not allow the firm to recoup the marginal opportunity costs of all the resources it employs in its enterprise should be regarded as predatory. Included in this calculus is not only the next-best market alternative of the resource-owners provided with explicit rewards, but the competitive market return of owner-furnished labor, capital, and other resources. This procedure may very well require an adjustment of the accountant's calculation of cost. To illustrate, suppose the owner assigns himself an inflated salary, i.e., a salary above what he could command working for someone else; then, only the value of his services in his next-best opportunity would enter the short- and long-run cost functions of the firm. Similarly, the return the firm could earn on the capital it has tied up in its plant, equipment, and inventory would be regarded as a cost, rather than as profit.

The economist's conceptualization of cost in terms of opportunity cost leads, in our view, to the necessity of transforming the raw data on costs and profits recorded in the balance sheet in terms of opportunity cost in assessing whether the firm's pricing policy is predatory. Transforming accountancy data into opportunity-cost data may uncover a concealed predatory pricing policy. This would occur when the owners assign themselves salaries considerably below their opportunity costs. Here, though price is above average balance-sheet costs, it may be below the long-run opportunity costs of the firm.

Economic efficiency offers the exclusionary-impact criterion as one basic test in assessing the legitimacy of nonpricing business tactics. If the conduct tends to increase entry costs relative to the long-run costs of the firm employing the tactic, the conduct should be disallowed. To illustrate, suppose a manufacturer were to buy up all the retail outlets for the product of his industry in order to foreclose his competitors from access to the market. In the event vertical integration of this sort imposed higher entry costs on would-be competitors relative to the long-run costs of existing firms, the tactic would be regarded as exclusionary.[3]

Ruinous Competition in Jewish Law

The attitude of Jewish law toward ruinous competition reflects a mediation between the social values of economic efficiency and industrial justice. The following amoraic dispute, appearing in *Baba Bathra* 21b, provides a basic source for the legal discussions in Jewish law surrounding this issue:

> R. Huna [d. 296] said: If a resident of an alley sets up a handmill and another resident of the alley wants to set up one next to him, the first has the right to stop him, because he can say to him "You are interfering with my livelihood.". . .
> R. Huna b. Joshua said: It is quite clear to me that the resident of one town can prevent the resident of another town [from establishing a competing outlet in his town]—not, however if he pays taxes to that town—and that the resident of an alley cannot prevent another resident of the same alley [from establishing a competing outlet in his alley]. R. Huna b. Joshua then raised the question: Can the resident of one alley prevent the resident of another [from competing with him]?—This question remains unresolved.

Talmudic decisors rule in accordance with R. Huna b. Joshua's view. What follows from this advocacy of freedom of entry is that an established firm is entitled to protection against intrusion into its territory only when the potential entrant is an out-of-town tradesman who does not pay taxes in the complainant's town. Given the moot entry status of a resident of a different alley, the Jewish court would not enjoin him from entering the complainant's alley.[4] (Rabbinical courts in Israel today have understood the modern "neighborhood" to correspond to the talmudic "alley.")[5]

The Deprivation-Generating Criterion

While R. Huna's protectionist philosophy is apparently rejected, several rishonic rulings indicate that his view is not entirely discarded. R. Eliezer b. Joel ha-Levi of Bonn (1140–1225) confers monopoly status to a store located at the extreme end of a closed alley. Allowing another firm to locate immediately in front of the established firm would effectively ruin the livelihood of the original competitor as passersby would be blocked from its view and take all their business to the new entrant.[6]

Commenting on R. Eliezer b. Joel ha-Levi's ruling, the Polish codifier R. Moses Isserles (1525 or 1530–1572) suggests that whenever the expected impact of a competitive tactic is to financially ruin an established rival, the tactic must be disallowed in accordance with the protectionist philosophy of R. Huna. Price-cutting that an established firm cannot match without undergoing financial ruin is, according to R. Isserles, analogous to R. Eliezer b. Joel ha-Levi's closed-alley case.[7]

Another Rishon following a protectionist philosophy is R. Joseph Ibn MiGash (1077–1141). His protectionist advocacy is clearly seen by his comments on the following talmudic passage in *Baba Bathra* 21b:

> May we say that this view [R. Huna's] is supported by the following: Fishing nets must be kept away from [the hiding place of] a fish [which has been spotted by another fisherman] the full length of the fish's swim! And how much is this? Rabbah son of R. Huna [d. 322] says: A parasang?—fish are different because they look about [for food].

Why a fisherman is conferred a territorial preserve while a tradesman is not similarly treated is explained by R. Joseph Ibn MiGash as follows: A fisherman's design to capture a large fish he sights is effectively frustrated when another fisherman places his net between this fish's hiding place and the bait. The second fisherman's action has the effect of intercepting the swarm of little fish that surround the large fish. Insofar as the large fish will change direction as soon as he notices that the small fish have been caught, the action of the intruder effectively deprives the first fisherman of his catch. In contrast, the arrival of a new firm on the competitive scene in no way *forces* customers to discontinue their patronage of the entrenched firm. With the new entry generating no deprivation effects on the established firm, the latter is denied a territorial monopoly.[8]

The foregoing leads the Hungarian decisor R. Moses Sofer (1762–1839) to reconcile the dispute between R. Huna and R. Huna b. Joshua: R. Huna's protectionist philosophy is restricted to instances where the effect of the new entry would ruin, not merely reduce, the livelihood of the established firm. The free-entry advocacy of R. Huna b. Joshua, on the other hand, is confined to instances where the effect of the new entry would be merely to reduce the profit margin of the entrenched competitor and not deprive him of his livelihood entirely.[9]

The complainant's wealth level and the number of sources of his livelihood are, according to R. Moses Sofer, irrelevant in considering the merits of a ruinous-competition case. To qualify for judicial intervention, a complainant need only demonstrate that a particular source of his livelihood is cut off as a result of his competitor's action.[10]

Concurring with R. Sofer's deprivation-generating criterion, R. Moses Feinstein (b. 1895), a leading contemporary decisor, would enjoin a new entrant whenever its expected impact is to reduce the established competitor's earnings below the mean earnings of his socioeconomic peer group.[11] Deprivation, in R. Feinstein's formulation, is not associated with below-subsistence earnings. A complainant, depending upon his socioeconomic status, may aspire for protection of an earnings floor above the margin of subsistence.

The foregoing, in our view, indicates that the distinction between deprivation of livelihood and reduction of earnings can be formulated in terms of opportunity cost. Provided the competitive tactic does not entirely ruin a rival's particular source of income, the court will not enjoin a business initiative unless the complainant's livelihood, as a result, is driven below his opportunity-cost earnings. Here, the direct impact of the rival's initiative is to force the complainant to withdraw from his present employment. The complainant's protectionist plea would be rejected, however, when it is assessed that he can maintain his opportunity-cost earnings within the framework of the new competitive environment.

Suspension of the Umbrella Protection Obligation When the Complainant Can Become More Efficient

Protecting a competitor's opportunity-cost earnings in no way guarantees that the subject product or service will be produced at its lowest possible social cost. This clear-cut conflict between efficiency, on the one hand, and industrial justice, on the other, is somewhat lessened by the consideration that the complainant's protectionist plea is rejected when the means are objectively available to him to counter his rival's initiative and maintain thereby his opportunity-cost earnings. This point emerges from the following talmudic passage in *Baba Bathra* 21b:

> Said Ravina [d. 422] to Rava [d. 352]: May we say that R. Huna adopts the same principle as R. Judah? For we have learnt: R. Judah says that a shopkeeper should not give presents of parched corn and nuts to children, because he thus entices them to come back to

him. The Sages, however, allow this!—You may even say that he is in agreement with the Rabbis also. For the ground on which the Rabbis allowed the shopkeeper to do this was because he can say to his rival: "Just as I make presents of nuts so you can make presents of almonds"; but in this case they would agree that the first man can say to the other: "You are interfering with my livelihood."

Given the permissibility of business promotional activities in Jewish law, in accordance with the Sages' view,[12] the import of the Talmud's question, "May we say that R. Huna adopts the same principle as R. Judah?" is that R. Huna's protectionist philosophy is rooted in R. Judah's minority view and should therefore be rejected. What follows is that the distinction the Talmud draws in its rejoinder between ability to counter a rival's initiative and inability to do so is critical in rationalizing R. Huna's protectionist philosophy. To qualify for protection against a competitive tactic, a complainant must demonstrate to the court's satisfaction that it is not within his means to counter the tactic without falling below his opportunity-cost earnings.

Within this framework, the court would deny a complainant umbrella price protection whenever it assessed that it was within his means to reduce cost by improving the efficiency of his operation. To illustrate, suppose A and B are rival leather-bag manufacturers. A sells at a profit but his price falls below B's per unit cost. Examination of their respective enterprises reveals, however, that A's operation is much more efficient than B's. While B tolerates sloth on the production line, A does not. Similarly, B's cutting technique wastes relatively more leather than the technique A employs. Since it is within B's means to modify his operation and reduce costs, he is not entitled to umbrella price protection.

Efficiency-based Pricing

Efficiency-based pricing rooted in economies of scale and new technology is, however, another matter. A large-scale enterprise often has inherent cost advantages over a competitor operating on a smaller scale. These advantages may include the ability to substitute capital for labor, making use of division of labor, taking advantage of bulk discounts, and pooling risk by diversifying the product line. Given these advantages, the profit-seeking larger firm can easily undersell a smaller rival and drive it out of business. Similarly, the use of new technology may allow a firm to price its product above cost, yet sell below the per unit cost of a rival.

What characterizes both cases is the complainant's inability to become competitive by means of short-term adjustments. It is not within the resources of the small firm to achieve the improvement in efficiency inherent in large-scale operation. Similarly, it may not be profitable for a firm to introduce new technology into its operation until its presently employed plant and equipment depreciate entirely. Within the framework of the deprivation-generating criterion, the complainant, in the above cases, as it appears to us, would be entitled to umbrella price protection.

Suspension of the Umbrella Protection Obligation When the Rivals Are Geographically Separated

R. Warhaftig's survey of rabbinic literature concludes that the deprivation-generating criterion would not call for umbrella price protection when the competitors involved are located in different towns.[13]

Illustrating this principle is the tavern case dealt with by the Hungarian decisor R. Chayyim Sofer (1821–1886). A and B owned taverns situated in adjacent towns. The price difference between the competitors was insignificant, and each was able to capture his local market. Now C opened a tavern in a nearby third town. Realizing that the local market was not large enough to allow him to earn a livelihood from his enterprise, C tried to expand his market by significantly undercutting A and B. Attracted by C's low price, many customers switched their patronage from A and B to C. Protesting that their livelihood was threatened by C's pricing policy, A and B petitioned R. Sofer to require C to increase his price to a level that would allow them to recapture their original local customers. Noting that C charged the same low price to both his local and nonlocal patrons alike, and that ordering C to raise his price would make it impossible for him to attract a sufficient clientele to support his livelihood, R. Sofer refused to order umbrella price protection.[14]

A variant of the above case came to the court of the Lemberg decisor R. Isaac Aaron Ettinger (1827–1891): A and B owned taverns situated in adjacent towns. Both A and B paid license fees to their respective local noblemen. While A's fee was nominal, B's fee was very high. Since the other cost conditions were similar, the license fee differential allowed A to sell his whiskey profitably at a price B could not match. B's petition for umbrella price protection was rejected by R. Isaac Aaron Ettinger. What entitles a complainant to umbrella price protection is the inevitable loss of customers to his lower-priced rivals. Inevitable loss of customers on account of price difference can only be said to occur when the competitors involved are situated in the same local area. Geographic separation, however, frees a competitor of an umbrella price obligation even according to R. Huna's protectionist view.[15]

Noting that R. Huna's protectionist stance refers to the right of a firm to exclude a rival from locating in its closed alley, the Swiss contemporary decisor, R. Mordechai Jacob Breisch, posits that R. Huna would not entitle a firm to enjoin a rival from locating outside its closed alley, despite its deprivation-generating effects.[16]

What is critical in making operational the above exception to the umbrella price rule, in our view, is *market* separation of the rivals, rather than mere geographic separation on the basis of political jurisdiction.

Relating this criterion to the modern urban product market, the extent of umbrella protection afforded an individual competitor would depend on the nature of the market he serves. Standing at one end of the continuum is the firm serving exclusively its local neighborhood. Here, only rivals located inside the neighborhood are subject to the deprivation-generating constraint. Competitors located outside the neighborhood, however, need not restrain their competitive conduct so as to insure the viability of firms located inside the neighborhood. Clearly falling into this category are retail grocery, drug, and dry-cleaning stores. Should the customer market extend beyond the neighborhood area, umbrella protection would be extended up to the boundary of the relevant market. Firms dealing in the wholesale trade and consumer durables provide examples of product markets extending beyond the immediate neighborhood of the firm's location.

Given that a firm is not entitled to umbrella protection from firms outside its product market, a sequence of events can be imagined wherein the umbrella obligation is dropped entirely. Suppose A operates a small-scale grocery store in his local neighborhood. Now, B makes known his intent to open a supermarket in the same area. While the competitive presence of B per se would not reduce the livelihood of A below his opportunity-cost earnings, underpricing him would drive him out of business. The Jewish court would, accordingly, allow B to locate in the neighborhood but would impose an umbrella protection constraint on him. At this point in time C establishes a supermarket outside the neighborhood. Economies of scale allow C to operate his enterprise profitably and yet significantly undersell A and B. Attracted by C's low prices, many customers desert A and B in favor of C. While B is capable of avoiding ruination by matching C's prices, small-scale competitor A cannot meet the challenge and faces bankruptcy. Since A faces ruination regardless of what B will do, the Jewish court, in our view, would, at this point, remove the umbrella protection obligation from B.

The Protection Against Encroachment Confined to Permanent Income Source

Protection against encroachment obtains only when the subject firm's permanent source of income is threatened. Should a firm operate under a negotiated government license, protection against encroachment is no longer extended at the termination of the license. Accordingly, the court would not enjoin B from his efforts to secure an exclusive license to deal in a certain product line effective when A's exclusive license for this product expires. Nonetheless, given that business licenses are routinely renegotiated and renewed, B's interference amounts to an encroachment of A's anticipated gain. While not subject to judicial restraint, B's conduct is morally objectionable.[17]

The Predation Criterion

Another school of thought in Jewish law conceptualizes industrial justice in terms that call for much less insulation from the unpleasantness of competition than proceeds from the deprivation-generating rule. The anti-protectionist school views the dispute between R. Huna and R. Huna b. Joshua as irreconcilable and rules in accordance with the free-entry advocacy of R. Huna b. Joshua.

R. Eliezer b. Joel ha-Levi's view is regarded as being rooted in the protectionist philosophy of R. Huna and therefore not consonant with mainstream thought.

Similarly, R. Joseph Ibn MiGash's explanation of the preserve rights of fishermen must be regarded as expressing a minority viewpoint since it is not in conformity with the mainstream interpretation of this right offered by R. Solomon b. Isaac and Nachmanides. What qualifies the first fisherman for a territorial preserve, according to R. Solomon b. Isaac, is not the deprivation effects of the interloper's action, as R. Joseph Ibn MiGash would have it, but rather the *anticipation of gain* he enjoyed prior to the arrival of the interloper. Casting bait in the fish's hiding place assures the fisherman that he will be able to lure fish into his net. With his catch thereby assured, another fisherman may not spread his net at the same spot, since doing so would deprive the former of an anticipated gain. In contrast, a firm may locate in close proximity to another firm, since the entrenched competitor was never *guaranteed* a clientele. Each firm sets up shop on its own premises, and customers decide to patronize the firm of their choice.[18]

Elaborating on R. Solomon b. Isaac's position, R. Mordechai Jacob Breisch maintains that even if the original firm was the only firm of its kind in the entire town prior to the arrival of the new entrant, nevertheless, the former monopolist's clientele cannot be regarded as guaranteed. This follows from the fact that the original firm, even in R. Huna's view, could not prevent a competing firm from locating in an adjacent closed alley. Hence, its clientele could have, at any time, been lured away to a distant competitor. In contrast, casting bait at a safe distance from the first fisherman would in no way affect the latter's catch. Casting bait in a particular location, therefore, establishes for the fisherman a territorial preserve.

Another difference between the cases, according to R. Breisch, is that the anticipated gain of the fisherman, the catch of fish, is existent at the time the intruder arrives on the scene. In contrast, the anticipated gain of the storekeeper, the patronage of his long-standing clientele, is nonexistent (*davar shelo ba la'olam*) at the time the rival competitor sets up shop. With the anticipated gain in the latter case nonexistent at the time of the intrusion, the entrenched competitor is denied the right to treat his former clientele as his exclusive preserve.[19]

Nachmanides offers a different rationale for the preserve rights of a fisherman. What the second fisherman is prohibited from doing is to spread his net in close proximity to the net of the first fisherman, because such action could result in directly depriving the first fisherman of what is rightfully his. Fish already captured in the first fisherman's net could, at times, spring into the second fisherman's net. With only this fear accounting for the privileged status of the first fisherman, an entrenched competitor does not qualify for similar treatment unless his degree of anticipation of gain parallels the confidence level of the first fisherman. Such parallelism, obviously, cannot be demonstrated by the monopolist tradesman in presenting his case against the interloper.[20]

Moreover, the fisherman case is omitted in the codes of R. Isaac Alfasi, Maimonides, R. Jacob b. Asher, and R. Joseph Caro.

Finally, an inconsistency is noted in the writings of R. Moses Isserles in regard to his adoption of the deprivation-generating rule. In his responsa work,[21] R. Isserles protected the right of R. Meir b. Isaac Katzenellenbogen (1473–1565) to disseminate Maimonides' work against the encroachment of a competing publisher. R. Joel ha-Levi's ruling is cited in support of the decision. Yet in his gloss in the *Shulchan Arukh* (the *Rema*), R. Isserles rejects R. Joel ha-Levi's view.[22] Noting that R. Joel ha-Levi's ruling was only *one* of many *factors* in the R. Katzenellenbogen case and that the *Rema* is a later work, R. Breisch posits that R. Isserles, in reality, rejects the deprivation-generating rule.[23]

Noting the controversy surrounding the deprivation-generating rule, the highest rabbinical tribunal in Israel expressed the view that it would not enjoin a religious teacher from enrolling children from the neighborhood of a competitor.[24] Similarly, in a case involving an alleged breach of contract between a newspaper and a publisher of Talmud, the court refused to enjoin the newspaper from entering into a distributorship agreement with a competing publisher of Talmud, notwithstanding the deprivation effects the arrangement would generate to the first publisher.[25]

While rejection of the deprivation-generating rule considerably emasculates the social value of industrial justice, the businessman is protected in Jewish law against the predatory tactics of rivals. Specific forms of predation discussed in the rabbinic literature include price discrimination and selling below cost.

Price discrimination in the form of selling the same article at a higher price to local patrons and at a lower price to customers residing outside the local area is prohibited. With the motive clearly to entice nonlocal customers to desert their neighborhood outlets, the tactic violates Jewish law's notion of industrial justice.[26]

Selling below cost, according to R. Tabak, places the initiator in the category of a tort-feasor. Selling below cost is, hence, subject to judicial restraint.[27]

What constitutes predatory pricing does not, however, find precise definitional form in the rabbinic literature. The economic criterion of predation, discussed earlier in this chapter, is suggested here as a possible guideline. Following this criterion, predation would be defined as selling below long-run marginal opportunity cost.

· 4
Contract Law

Contract Law in Economic Theory

Contract law provides an essential ingredient for the efficient functioning of the economic system. By furnishing prospective transacting parties with information regarding the consequences of commitments, including the contingencies that may defeat an exchange, contract law fosters voluntary exchange. Besides maintaining appropriate incentives, contract law reduces the costs of entering into voluntary exchange by supplying a set of normal terms, which, in the absence of contract law, the parties would have to negotiate themselves.

Without contract law, parties would be discouraged from entering into exchanges in which performance by one party is deferred.[1]

Contract law also profoundly affects resource mobility.

Economic resources, it can be expected, will be employed in their highest market use when the marketplace is characterized by perfect mobility. Freedom of mobility implies that resource-owners are free to enter into contractual arrangements unencumbered by economic relationships they may have entered into in the past. To the extent that contractual ties inhibit the formation of contemporaneous commitments or otherwise restrict future options, it might be necessary to make market decisions on considerations other than efficiency.

The degree of resource mobility an economy attains is greatly affected by the legal framework under which it operates. How society chooses to define the reciprocal obligations a contract generates to its parties assuredly affects the future economic options of the principals involved. Similarly, the penalties the legal system imposes on a reneging party determine the strength of the *economic* disincentive to break a contract.

In this chapter we will discuss Jewish contract law as it relates to the issue of resource mobility. While the discussion will occasionally broaden to Jewish voluntary-exchange law, the main focus will be on Jewish labor law. The topics of investigation include: (1) the criterion

Jewish law adopts in deciding when contractual arrangements become legally and morally binding on the parties concerned; (2) what
constitutes just cause for breaking a labor contract; (3) the penalty
consequences for breaking a labor contract without just cause; (4)
tenure and seniority rights in the private sector; (5) tenure and
succession rights for positions of communal authority; (6) restrictions
on the length of labor contracts; (7) restrictions on outside work for
the worker.

Contractual Obligations
in Jewish Law

Voluntary exchange does not acquire legal force in Jewish law until it
becomes objectively evident that the parties involved have firmly
resolved to conclude the arrangement at hand. This requirement,
called the *gemirat da'at* condition, applies both to the transfer of
proprietary rights and to the creation of obligations.

Evidence of *gemirat da'at* usually obtains when the transaction
involved is consummated by means of a formal symbolic act (*kinyan*).

While Jewish law prescribes the form of *kinyan* to be used for
various transactions, acceptable forms of *kinyan* expand to include
local mercantile custom. In this regard, the Talmud records that it was
the custom among wine merchants to mark the barrels they had
purchased (*sitamta*).[2] Accordingly, a barrel of wine is regarded as
legally sold when the purchaser affixes a mark to the barrel.

The underlying purpose of *kinyan* is to establish *gemirat da'at*
between the parties concerned.[3] When *gemirat da'at* is established by
means of verbal consent alone, the *kinyan* requirement is dropped.
Several talmudic cases will be cited to illustrate this point.

1. A paid bailee may change his status to that of a *sho'el* (borrower)
   by means of oral stipulation alone. The consequence of his
   change in status is that he becomes liable for the bailment even
   in the event of accidental loss. Why *kinyan* is not needed to effect
   this change in status is explained by R. Yochanan (ca. 180–279)
   on the grounds that the presumption of *gemirat da'at* obtains here
   by means of oral consent alone. Owing to the pleasure of
   becoming reputable as a trustworthy person, the bailee firmly
   makes up his mind to increase his responsibility for the bailment
   on the basis of oral stipulation alone.[4]
2. Similarly, a suretyship obligation given at the time of the creation of the debt is established orally. Owing to the pleasure of
   knowing that the *very* loan is given on the strength of his

guarantee, the suretor firmly makes up his mind to undertake his responsibility by means of oral consent alone.[5]

3. Promises regarding a dowry, provided the property involved is in the possession of the promisors, become binding by means of oral consent alone. Owing to the pleasure of forming mutual family ties, the parties involved firmly resolve to obligate themselves in accordance with their stipulations by means of verbal consent alone.[6]

4. Conferring *kinyan* status to local mercantile custom results in the dispensation of the formal *kinyan* requirement if local custom regards a particular transaction as concluded when the parties reach oral consent alone.[7]

While formal *kinyan* is not indispensable in establishing *gemirat da'at*, *kinyan* does not always establish *gemirat da'at*. The discussion below provides a description of the form of *kinyan* Jewish law prescribes for various particular transactions, and the circumstances under which the *kinyan* does not consummate the transaction because of the presumption of the absence of *gemirat da'at*.

A commonly used *kinyan*, efficacious for both movable and immovable property, is *kinyan sudar* (*kinyan* of the kerchief). Mechanically, the alienator draws to himself an article belonging to the acquirer, and the latter acquires thereby the subject of transfer. Resembling barter, *kinyan sudar* is in actuality only token barter as the acquirer's article need not be equal in value to the subject of transfer and, in addition, may be returned to him at the conclusion of the ceremony. Customarily, *kinyan sudar* is performed with a kerchief: the alienator merely grasps at the acquirer's kerchief, and the latter acquires thereby the subject of transfer.[8]

A unique feature of *kinyan sudar* is that it does not effect transfer as long as the parties are still discussing the details of their deal.[9] Since the *kinyan* entails a simple act and is not performed on the subject of transfer, *gemirat da'at* does not objectively emerge until the parties have completed their discussions regarding the deal.[10]

By pentateuchal law, *kesef* (money) effects transfer for both movable and immovable property. (Out of fear that the seller would be less than diligent in extricating from fire and other dangers merchandise on his premises belonging to the purchaser, the Sages enacted that *kesef* does not effect transfer for movables.)[11]

Kesef consists of payment by the vendee of at least part of the purchasing price. While payment of a *perutah*, the smallest coin, suffices for this purpose, part payment does not effect *kinyan* when there is a presumption of an absence of *gemirat da'at* on the part of the seller. This occurs when the latter refuses to allow the balance to stand as a loan and, in addition, is either known to be desperate for liquid assets at the time of the sale or seeks out the purchaser twice on the due date or twice on the day before the due date to extract payment from him.[12]

Shetar (deed) is a form of *kinyan* prescribed for the transfer of immovable property. Mechanically, this *kinyan* effects title for the vendee when he receives a deed in which the vendor writes: "My field is sold [given] to you." Receipt of the deed establishes title for the vendee even in the absence of witnesses. *Shetar* alone effects *kinyan* for immovable property only when the property involved is unproductive or the seller is moving to a different neighborhood. In both these instances the owner is anxious to sell his property and presumably makes up his mind to transfer it on the basis of the purchaser's receipt of the deed alone. In the absence of the above circumstances, the purchaser acquires legal title to the property only at such time that the agreed-upon price is paid in full.[13]

Kinyan does not effect transfer when it fails to create a presumption of *gemirat da'at* on the part of the purchaser. Accordingly, in the case of immovable property, should it be local custom to record such transactions in the form of a deed, full payment of the purchase price does not make the property pass. Here, the property does not pass until the purchaser receives the deed because his *gemirat da'at* is not evident until then.[14]

The *gemirat da'at* condition is apparent in other aspects of Jewish voluntary exchange law too. Proprietary rights are transferred by means of *kinyan* only if the acquirer executes the *kinyan* at the instruction of the alienator. Departing from the alienator's instructions invalidates the *kinyan* even if the *kinyan* actually executed is normally valid for the transaction at hand.[15]

Moral Obligations in Jewish
Voluntary Exchange Law

While verbal consent alone usually does not produce *legal* consequences in Jewish law, verbal commitments entail various moral obligations.

The "good faith" imperative requires an individual to fully intend to execute any commitment he orally makes.[16]

Not fulfilling a commitment of the heart which has not yet been verbalized usually presents no moral dilemma in Jewish law.[17] More stringent, however, is a resolve involving charity. A resolve to donate charity of a specific amount must be fulfilled, according to the Polish codifier R. Moses Isserles (1525–1572), even if the commitment was not yet verbalized.[18]

Retracting from a verbal commitment made in "good faith" is morally objectionable when the said commitment induced reliance. Reneging on a promise which induced reliance is regarded as a "breach of faith" and stigmatizes the violator as an untrustworthy person.[19] Accordingly, reneging on a promise to confer someone with a small gift is morally objectionable because the promise induced reliance.[20] Similarly, retracting from a sales negotiation at the verbal-consent stage incurs moral sanction even if the retraction is prompted by a change in market price.[21]

Charitable pledges, it should be noted, generate not only a moral obligation but legal consequences as well. Once verbalized, a pledge to charity is subject to judicial enforcement.[22]

Retracting from a promise made in "good faith" which did not induce reliance, however, presents no moral issue. Relating this rule to the gift example cited above, no moral condemnation results for the individual who retracts from a promise made in good faith to confer someone with a large gift.[23] The presumption of nonreliance on the part of the promisee in the case of a large gift is, however, invalid when the promise is made by a group. Hence, it is morally objectionable for a group to retract from its oral commitment to confer someone with a large gift.[24]

While retraction from an oral commitment that did not induce reliance does not amount to a "breach of faith," the injured party may have cause for legitimate grievance. Jewish labor law illustrates this point.

In the absence of *kinyan*, labor contracts are not *legally* consummated until the worker begins his assigned work.[25] Given that verbal consent alone in a labor contract negotiation does not produce mutual reliance,[26] withdrawal at this juncture by either of the parties does not amount to a breach of faith. Nevertheless, should the unilateral canceling of the contract generate to the other party an inconvenience of sorts, the injured party has legitimate grounds for grievance. Accordingly, the worker's complaint is just when he can find alternative employment only with difficulty in consequence of the employer's retraction from their oral agreement. Similarly, legitimacy would be given to the employer's complaint in the event he could find replacement workers only with difficulty in consequence of the worker's cancellation.[27]

When legitimacy is given to a grievance in Jewish law, the complainant, according to R. Israel Salanter (1810–1883), is permitted to demand from the offender a monetary settlement in exchange for pardoning the grievance.[28]

More stringent is the moral condemnation levied against retraction after the purchasing price has been paid. Such conduct becomes a *moral* rather than a legal issue in instances where *kesef* does not effect *legal* transfer. The transfer of proprietary rights in both movable and immovable property illustrates this point.

By dint of pentateuchal law, *kesef* effects transfer of movable property. Payment therefore confers title to the purchaser even if the merchandise remains on the premises of the seller. Out of fear that the seller would be less than diligent in extricating from fire and other dangers merchandise on his premises belonging to the purchaser, the Sages enacted that *kesef* does not effect transfer for movables. Legal transfer of movables is therefore customarily effected by either *hagbahah* (lifting), *meshikhah* (pulling), or *mesirah* (grasping). Which of these modes of *kinyan* is to be used for a particular transaction depends upon the domain where the *kinyan* takes place and the nature of the article of transfer.[29]

Now, suppose a sale negotiation involving movable property advances beyond verbal consent to the actual payment of the purchasing price. Since the mode of acquisition proper to the transaction has not yet been observed, the purchaser does not acquire legal title to the subject of transfer. Nevertheless, retraction by either party at this juncture incurs the judicial imprecation, "He who punished the generation of the Flood and of the Dispersion will exact payment from one who does not stand by his word." This extreme sanction is referred to as *me'shaparah*.[30]

Since *kesef* does not legally effect transfer for immovable property when it is local custom to record the transaction in the form of a deed, retraction after payment is made would incur the *me'shaparah* sanction for the offending party.

Grounds for Discharging a Worker

Focusing on Jewish labor law, we will here investigate what constitutes legitimate grounds for dismissing a worker before the expiration of his contract. This subject has profound implications for both job security and resource mobility.

The circumstances under which the employer's dismissal right is recognized in Jewish law is discussed in the following talmudic passage (*Baba Bathra* 21b):

Rava [d. 352] further said: A teacher of young children, a planter, a [ritual] slaughterer, a bloodletter, and a town scribe are all liable to be dismissed immediately [if inefficient]. The general principle is that anyone whose mistakes cannot be rectified is liable to be dismissed immediately [if he makes one].

What proceeds from the above passage is that malfeasance resulting in irretrievable loss provides legitimate grounds for an employee's dismissal. Rishonic elucidation of the above text clarifies the "irretrievable loss" criterion as it applies to each of the above cases.

Teacher malfeasance of the irretrievable sort occurs when a teacher either fails to provide his pupils with their full lesson time[31] or misinstructs them.[32] Knowledge the pupils lost during their forced idleness can never be restored to them.[33] Similarly, erroneous instruction, rooted in teacher incompetence,[34] will not be corrected and therefore represents for the pupils an irretrievable loss.[35]

Irretrievable loss of another sort occurs in the planter case. Failure to plant saplings in accordance with professional standards reduces the proprietor's crop yield from what it could have been had the job been done properly. While the incompetent planter is held culpable for the saplings he ruins, the potential loss in crop yield is speculative and therefore not subject to collection. Since part of the proprietor's loss cannot be recovered, the planter's malfeasance is regarded as generating an irretrievable loss.[36]

In a similar vein, R. Vidal Yom Tov of Tolosa (fl. 14th cent.) explains the irretrievable-loss element in the ritual slaughterer malfeasance case. While the slaughterer is held culpable for the value of the animal, he cannot be made responsible to pay for the embarrassment of the proprietor and his disappointed guests. Since the entire loss is not recoverable, malfeasance on the part of the ritual slaughterer is characterized as irretrievable loss.[37]

In the bloodletting case, irrecoverable loss, according to R. Solomon b. Isaac (1040–1105), occurs when the bloodletter's malpractice results in the death of his patient.[38] R. Abraham b. David of Posquières (1125–1198), however, understands irretrievable loss to occur even if the patient does not die as a result of the malpractice. Since the unnecessary suffering the patient sustains as a result of the malpractice is not subject to monetary claim, the practitioner's malfeasance represents an irretrievable loss.[39]

Finally, malfeasance by the town scribe in the form of inaccurate preparation of legal documents results in an irretrievable loss because such errors may cause the users of the documents financial loss. Since the scribe cannot be held legally responsible for the losses his errors may cause, his malpractice results in irretrievable loss.[40]

While the potential loss inherent in retaining an inept worker is usually much greater when he is a public servant rather than employed by a private individual, dismissal on the grounds of malfeasance resulting in irrecoverable loss is recognized in the latter case too.[41] Nonetheless, an isolated incident of malfeasance does not provide legitimate ground for immediate discharge without warning. Summary dismissal is justified only if the worker is guilty of malfeasance of the irretrievable form on three separate occasions. In addition, it must be proved in the worker's presence that he was indeed failing in his duties.[42]

Suspicion of dishonesty, according to the German codifier R. Mordechai b. Hillel (1240–1298), provides another ground for summary dismissal.[43] The responsa literature has, however, limited the dismissal right here to instances where the suspicion is either rooted in a persistent rumor impugning the worker's integrity or is based on his present pattern of behavior, observed by the employer.[44]

Transgression of religious law, evidenced by testimony admissible in court, provides ground for dismissing a religious ministrant. Proper repentance on the part of the wayward ministrant entitles him, however, to be restored to his position.[45]

Out of concern for the morals of the household, R. Jair Chayyim Bacharach (1638–1702) legitimized the summary dismissal of a woman housekeeper on the grounds of the discovery of her past history of promiscuity.[46]

Evidence of sexual immorality, according to R. Warhaftig, does not provide grounds for the summary dismissal of an individual who is not employed as a religious ministrant.[47] His position is presumably taken only when retention of the sexually immoral worker would not endanger the morals of co-workers.

The Disincentive Effect of Breaking a Contract

Focusing on Jewish labor law, we will now investigate the strength of the disincentive effect of breaking a contract in Jewish law.

A labor contract is legally consummated, according to Nachmanides (1194–1270), once the worker begins his assigned work.[48] Breaking the contract without just cause at this point incurs a penalty for the reneging party. We will first investigate the penalty consequences for the employer.

Penalty Consequences for the Employer
While an individual cannot be forced to employ someone against his

will,[49] breaking a legally consummated labor contract, without just cause, incurs for the employer a compensation obligation to the worker for the broken portion of the contract. Critical in assessing the degree of responsibility the reneging employer faces is the nature of the immediate employment opportunities available to the worker in consequence of the retraction. Several variants are discussed in the rabbinic literature.

In the event employment is not available to the worker at the time of the retraction, the employer bears compensation responsibility to the worker not only for the work he has done but for the time of the unfulfilled labor contract as well. Insofar as the breaking of the contract affords the worker the consolation of spending his day in leisure, a discount is applied to the wages that corresponds to the unfulfilled part of the contract. Application of the discount element reduces compensation for the broken part of the contract to the sum the worker would demand if asked to abandon his work for the broken portion of the contract in favor of leisure (*k'poel bateil*).[50] This sum, according to R. Solomon b. Isaac's general rule, amounts to one half the stipulated wage for the relevant period.[51]

In instances where we are certain that the worker would have preferred work to leisure, the above discount element is not applied. Agricultural workers and hard-laborers fall within this category since even short layoffs exert a debilitating effect on their health. Consequently, a reneging employer would be obligated to compensate these workers by the full amount of prorated wages he originally stipulated.[52]

Similarly, an employer seeking release from his contractual responsibilities to a religious teacher must compensate him by the full amount of wages he originally stipulated. Since idleness blunts the mental sharpness of the teacher and erodes his pedagogical skills, we are certain he prefers teaching to idleness.[53]

Another variant occurs when the only employment available to the worker at the time of the retraction consists of work identical to the type called for by the broken contract, but at a lower wage rate. Compensation responsibility here, according to the disciples of R. Solomon Adret (1235–1319) and the codifier R. Jacob b. Asher (1270–1343), allows the employer the choice of exercising either of the following options: he may (a) require the worker to accept the lower-paying job and make good on the loss in the wage differential, or (b) require the worker to accept the sum he would demand if asked to abandon the work called for by the broken contract in favor of leisure.[54]

The choice of the above options rests, according to the Polish decisor R. Joel Sirkes (1561–1640), not with the employer, but with the worker.[55] R. Abraham Isaiah Karelitz (1878–1953) ruled in accordance with R. Sirkes' view.[56]

Still another variant occurs when the only employment opportunity available to the worker at the time of retraction consists of work that is more difficult but not higher-paying. Compensation responsibility here, according to R. Shabbetai b. Meir ha-Kohen (1621–1662), depends entirely on the course of action the worker takes. Should the worker decide to accept the more irksome work, the reneging employer escapes thereby any compensation responsibility in regard to the broken portion of his contract. Notwithstanding that the effect of the retraction is to force the worker into more irksome work at the same pay as the original work, the court will not force the employer to pay the worker any premium on this account. Alternatively, the worker may opt to reject the more irksome work and spend his time in idleness. Selection of this option allows the worker to exert a claim on the reneging employer in the amount of *poel bateil.*[57]

Should only work less irksome but lower-paying be available at the time of the retraction, the compensation due the worker, according to R. Aryeh Loeb b. Joseph ha-Kohen (1745–1813), extends only to the sum he would demand if given the opportunity to abandon the original work in favor of the lighter work.[58]

In the event identical work at the same wage rate is available to the worker at the time of the retraction, the reneging employer is free from any compensation responsibility in regard to broken portions of the contract.[59] Whether the worker has claim here to a legitimate grievance is, however, a matter of rishonic dispute.[60]

Retraction at the point of verbal consent, it should be noted, may entail for the employer compensation responsibility. This occurs when alternative sources of employment were available to the worker at the time of verbal consent, and in consequence of the retraction the worker is either shut out of work entirely or can only secure a lower-paying job. In the former instance, the liability of the employer is fixed at the sum the worker would demand if asked to abandon the work stipulated in the broken verbal agreement in favor of leisure. In the latter instance, the reneging employer must make good on the difference between the wage rate he originally stipulated and the lower wage rate now available to the worker.[61]

Retraction Due to Unavoidable Circumstances (O'nes). The penalty consequences for the employer described above obtain only when his retraction is due to negligence or fault. No compensation obligation for the broken portion of the contract is imposed on the employer, however, when the retraction is due to circumstances he could not anticipate. The latter instance is referred to as the *o'nes* condition.[62]

Illustrating the *o'nes* condition is the breaking of a teacher's contract on account of an illness the pupil developed. If the sickness could not have been reasonably anticipated at the time the contract was entered into, the employer bears no compensation responsibility for this unfinished part of the term of services.[63]

Similarly, should A's contract to water B's field be made superfluous by the previous night's rainfall, B bears no compensation responsibility to A, provided B inspected the field the night before.[64]

Moreover, should both the employer and the worker have anticipated an event which makes execution of the contract impossible, the former is free of any compensation liability for the unfulfilled portion of the contract.[65]

Illustrating the above principle is a variant of the stricken-pupil case discussed above. Suppose it is commonly known that the child is prone to illness and the teacher is a local resident. Here, the burden is on the teacher to stipulate before entering into the contract some arrangement in the event the pupil is taken sick during the term of the agreement.[66]

Makkat Medinah. A special case of *o'nes* occurs when the unforeseen event not only makes A's contract with B impossible to execute, but identically affects all employers in the same situation. Pandemic *o'nes* of this sort, referred to in the rabbinic literature as *makkat medinah*, occurs when, for instance, the government suddenly prohibits religious instruction. With *all* religious instruction contracts affected by the decree, the *o'nes* qualifies as *makkat medinah*. Given the pandemic nature of the *o'nes*, R. Meir b. Baruch of Rothenburg (1215–1293) held the employer liable for the entire term of the contract.[67] R. Joshua ha-Kohen Falk (1555–1614), however, entitles the teacher here to only one half of his wages for the broken portion of the contract.[68]

Liability for the employer in the pandemic *o'nes* case, according to R. Jechiel Michael Epstein (1829–1908), is limited to the instance where the worker is ready and able to perform the stipulated work, but due to the unforeseen event is unable to do so. The anti-religion decree case cited above meets this specification. Should it be *physically* impossible for the worker to perform the stipulated work, he loses his advantage, despite the pandemic nature of the *o'nes*.[69]

Following the above line is the military draft case dealt with by the Lithuanian decisor R. Aaron Walkin (1865–1942). Induction into military service at the outbreak of war forced a ritual slaughterer (A) to leave his communal post before the term of his employment was over. A sued for the salary he would have earned for the duration of his contract on the ground that military induction constitutes an *o'nes* of the *makkat medinah* variety. Rejecting the plea, R. Walkin pointed out that *makkat medinah* confers an advantage to the non-performing worker only when he is *physically* ready and able to perform the stipulated work, but due to the pandemic, unforeseen event cannot do so. With the military draft making it *physically* impossible for A to perform his job, he has no claim for the wages of the unfulfilled portion of his contract, despite the pandemic nature of his *o'nes*. [70]

Liability for the employer in the pandemic *o'nes* case, according to R. Mordechai Birdugo, is limited to the instance where the event forcing cancellation of the contract could not have been anticipated by either the employer or the non-performing worker. Should it have been possible for both to have anticipated the event which forced cancellation of their contract, the worker loses his claim, despite the pandemic nature of the *o'nes*. [71]

Penalty Consequences for the Retracting Worker

Inexcusable refusal on the part of a *public* servant to execute his contractual responsibilities may subject him to a judicial order to remain on the job until he supplies a replacement. [72]

While an individual may not be forced to work for a private employer against his will, [73] a worker incurs a penalty consequence for quitting a job before the term of the contract expires. Several factors are relevant in determining the nature of this penalty. Foremost of these factors is the condition of the labor market. For the employer's compensation claim against the worker to be valid, the following double condition must be satisfied: (1) alternative sources of labor supply must have been available to him at the time the labor contract was entered into, and (2) replacement workers could not be secured at the time of the retraction. Should the above double condition fail to obtain, the employer's claim against the worker extends only to legitimate cause for grievance. [74]

Once the above double condition obtains, several factors become relevant in determining the degree of financial obligation the reneging worker faces. These factors include the manner in which the worker hired himself out and the type of work he was engaged to perform.

The Distinction Between the Day-Laborer and the Piece-Worker. In Jewish law a worker is legally classified as either a day-laborer *(poel)* or a piece-worker *(kabbelan)*. The day-laborer is either hired for a specific period of time or is required to work at fixed hours. The piece-worker, in contrast, is hired to perform a specific task, with no provisions made regarding fixed hours. [75]

The day-laborer has the legal right to withdraw from a labor contract at any time. This right is regarded as a necessary safeguard to his personal freedom. Denying him this right would have the effect of relegating him to the status of a chattel, bound to his employer against his own inclination. This right is exegetically derived from the verse, "For unto Me the children of Israel are servants . . ." (Lev. 25:55)—"They are My servants but not servants to servants."[76] Retraction rights place the *poel* in an advantageous position relative to the employer should he decide to quit his job before completing a full day of work. The nature of this advantage will be discussed below.

Insofar as retraction rights are conferred to the day-laborer only as a means of assuring that his status would not be characterized as servitude, the piece-worker is not conferred with similar rights.[77] This, according to R. Joshua ha-Kohen Falk, follows from the fact that the status of a piece-worker is intrinsically not akin to servitude. Unlike the *poel*, who is *continuously* bound to his employer to perform his work, the *kabbelan* is free to perform the stipulated work at his own discretion and at his own pace, and hence not "tied" to his employer.[78]

Retraction on the part of the piece-worker places him at a disadvantage. The nature of the disadvantage will be discussed below.

Another consideration in assessing the penalty consequences for the reneging worker is the type of work he was engaged to perform. Other things being equal, the retracting worker is treated more harshly when the task at hand requires immediate attention, postponement of which results in irretrievable loss for the employer. This circumstance is referred to as the *davar haavud* case.

An example of *davar haavud*, cited in the Talmud, is the hiring of a worker to take out flax from its steeping. If the task is not performed immediately, the employer will suffer material loss. Another example is the hiring of a worker to bring litter-carriers and pipers to a wedding ceremony. Since the litter-carriers and pipers are sent with the purpose of enhancing the ceremony, delay in their dispatch will defeat the purpose of the sender because they will arrive after the ceremony is already over.[79]

Religious instruction, according to authorities cited by R. Mordechai b. Hillel, qualifies as *davar haavud*.[80] Codified by R. Moses Isserles, [81] this ruling is rationalized on the grounds that children suffer irreparable loss when their studies are interrupted.[82]

Domestic work, according to R. Israel Isserlein (1390–1460), may also qualify as a *davar haavud*. This occurs when the householder is wealthy and not accustomed to performing domestic chores himself.[83]

What proceeds from the above is that the day-laborer engaged to perform work not classified as *davar haavud* enjoys a relative advantage should he quit his job before the end of his term of employment. An arithmetic example will illustrate the nature of this advantage. Suppose labor market conditions are such that employer A can secure the services of any number of day-laborers at a per diem wage of $8. A hires B at the competitive wage of $8 per diem. After working for only one half of the workday, B quits his job. At this point, the cost of hiring a replacement to work for the remainder of the workday must be calculated. Should this cost be equal to more than $4, B is nevertheless entitled to his prorated wage of $4.[84] In the instance where the competitive wage went up at the time of the retraction, A does, however, have cause for legitimate grievance.[85]

How B is treated in the event the competitive wage went down at the time of the retraction is disputed among talmudic decisors.

R. Jacob b. Asher entitles B to his entire originally stipulated per diem wage minus the cost of completing the day's work. Extending the illustration cited above, suppose the competitive wage went down to $4 per diem at the time of the retraction. Since the cost of completing the remaining half-day's work is only $2, B is entitled to $6 for the half-day of work he put in.[86] Ruling in accordance with R. Jacob's opinion is R. Aryeh Loeb Joseph ha-Kohen.[87]

Disputing R. Jacob's view on the grounds that the latter's formulation allows the worker to parlay his retraction into a profit, R. Shabbetai b. Meir entitles B only to the prorated share of the *original* stipulation. Following this formula entitles the worker to $4 in the example cited above.[88]

Varying the above example, suppose B is a piece-worker instead of a day-laborer. This places him at a disadvantage should he quit his job before completion. To illustrate, suppose a tailor is commissioned to manufacture a suit. Compensation for the job is fixed at $8. Now, after completing only one half of the required work, the tailor quits his job. The compensation due him for services rendered is determined as follows. First, the cost of completing the job is calculated. Should this cost exceed the $4 payment the employer would have had to pay for the job to be completed, the $4 wage due the tailor for his work can theoretically be reduced down to zero. On the other hand, should the cost of completing the suit be less than $4, the reneging tailor does not gain from this circumstance and is entitled to only $4. The compensation due the reneging tailor, therefore, can theoretically *range* from zero to $4.[89]

In cases not involving *davar haavud*, the retracting day-laborer, according to most authorities, is conferred the advantage described above, even when his labor contract was consummated by means of *kinyan*.[90]

Instances Where the Retraction Right Is Not Recognized. Retraction rights for the day-laborer are, however, not absolute. In instances where the withdrawal right is not recognized, as discussed below, the retracting day-laborer is treated in the same manner as the reneging piece-worker. Instances where the withdrawal right is not recognized include the following:

1. The day-laborer, according to R. Meir b. Baruch of Rothenburg et alia, does not enjoy retraction rights when his labor contract was consummated by means of a solemn oath or handshake.[91]
2. Withdrawing from his present employment for the purpose of securing higher-paying work elsewhere places the retracting day-laborer in the disadvantaged position of a piece-worker.[92]
3. Since the favored treatment of the retracting day-laborer is rooted in the concern that his employment should not be characterized as servitude, teachers of religious instruction, according to R. Jechiel of Paris (d. ca. 1265) et alia, do not enjoy retraction rights. Compensation for providing religious instruction is prohibited in Jewish law. Earnings for such instruction are justified only as an inducement not to seek employment elsewhere, so denying religious teachers withdrawal rights does *not* amount to "tieing" them to their instructional activity.[93]
4. In the event the day-laborer received his wages in advance of the work he was engaged to perform, many authorities, on the interpretation of R. Ephraim Nabon (d. 1735), suspend the retraction right until the advance is returned to the employer. Other authorities, on the interpretation of R. Nabon, however, regard the withdrawal right as remaining intact even while the worker is still in possession of the advance.[94]

Davar Haavud (Irretrievable Loss). The reneging worker is subject to the severest sanctions when he withdraws from work classified as *davar haavud*. No distinction is here made between a day-laborer and a piece-worker regarding the penalty consequences of nonperformance.

The tactics open to the disappointed employer in the *davar haavud* case are described below.

Faced with the prospect of a work stoppage in the *davar haavud* case, the employer may promise the recalcitrant worker a raise as an inducement to complete the work. Should the tactic succeed, the employer bears no responsibility to pay the differential,[95] and is entitled to recovery of the "extra wage" in the event he paid it out.[96]

Should the above tactic fail, the employer is entitled to hire a replacement worker to complete the work and charge this expense, at least partly, to the reneging worker. Liability for the reneging worker here cannot, however, extend beyond forfeiting the wages already due him and an out-of-pocket fine equal to the additional wages he would have earned had he finished the job.[97]

Another variant of the *davar haavud* case occurs when the worker's work tools or other property is deposited with the employer.[98] Here, to prevent his loss, the employer is entitled to hire workers against the value of the worker's deposit.[99] The charge against the worker, however, may not exceed the sum employers, in the given situation, would customarily pay to have the work at hand completed.[100]

In the event replacement workers cannot be secured, the reneging worker bears full responsibility for any material loss his employer suffers. For *davar haavud* cases not involving material loss, no compensation claim is recognized in the latter instance.[101]

The penalty consequences for the reneging worker in the *davar haavud* case, it should be noted, apply even if the broken contract was not consummated by means of *kinyan*.[102]

Retraction Due to Unavoidable Circumstances. Penalty consequences of the nature described above obtain for the worker only when his retraction is due to fault or negligence.[103] Should unavoidable circumstances beyond the worker's control (*o'nes*) force him to interrupt the work at hand, he is entitled to payment for the work he has done and is not assessed any amount in connection with the expense of completing the job.[104]

Justifiable grounds for interrupting work, mentioned in the Talmud, include the sickness of the worker and the death of one of the worker's relatives.[105] R. Israel Isserlein adds illness of a spouse as a valid reason for work stoppage.[106]

Interruption of work for any reason, according to R. Jechiel Michael Epstein, provides the employer with legitimate grounds to hire replacement workers immediately for the purpose of completing the job. The employer here is under no obligation to hold up completion of the job until the retracting worker is ready to resume.[107]

The above prerogative is not available to the employer in the event the retracting worker is *kabbelan*. Insofar as the piece-worker is not hired to complete the work within a specified time frame, the work may not be taken away from him and given to someone else. If, however, it is evident that the employer requires completion of the work by a particular time and the indisposed *kabbelan* cannot meet the deadline, the work may be taken away from him and given to a replacement.[108]

In the event replacement workers cannot be secured and the work already performed is in itself of no use to the employer, the retracting worker forfeits thereby the wages due him, despite the legitimacy of his work stoppage.[109]

Tenure Rights in the Private Sector

While Jewish law protects a worker from summary dismissal before the expiry date of his contract, the private employer, according to the Hungarian decisor R. Moshe Schick (1807–1879) et alia, bears no responsibility to renew his contract at the termination date.[110]

A different view here is, however, expressed by one of the leading contemporary decisors, R. Moshe Feinstein. Renewal rights depend most basically, in his view, on whether the position the worker was originally hired for was temporary or permanent in nature. In the former case, the employer bears no responsibility to renew the worker's contract. In the latter case, however, provided the position is still open, the employer may not deny the worker renewal of his contract without just cause. Just cause is established when the employer sustains an irrecoverable loss as a result of the worker's malfeasance.

Since contracts are customarily renewed provided there is no cause for dismissal, the renewal privilege for the worker is an implied condition of employment. It follows that inclusion of an explicit clause reserving to the employer the option of rehiring at the expiration date nullifies the worker's renewal right.[111]

What follows from the above line is that, in the absence of just cause, contract flexibility can be achieved by the employer only by means of hiring workers as provisionals.

Seniority Rights

Another job security issue is the treatment of seniority rights in Jewish law. Analysis of this topic is found in the responsa work of R. Moshe Feinstein. In the two cases he deals with, R. Feinstein rejects seniority as an operational principle governing layoff procedure in Jewish law. The elements of the first case are as follows: A hires B to perform a *specific* work load in his factory. Subsequently, responding to an increased demand for his product, A adds C to his labor force. Now, experiencing a slack period, A finds it necessary to lay off one of his workers. According to R. Feinstein, the layoff procedure in this case hinges on the nature of the legalistic relationship established between the employer and employee in consequence of the labor contract. Several views regarding the nature of the relationship have been advanced.

R. Meir b. Baruch et alia regard the employer as acquiring a lien on the person of the worker (*kinyan haguf*) at the point the labor contract is entered into.[112] While simple logic rejects the notion that the labor agreement acquires for the worker a similar type of lien on the person of the employer, two possibilities present themselves. One approach would be to view the labor agreement as acquiring for the worker an obligation on the part of the employer to provide him with work. Alternatively, assuming no such obligation is generated, consummation of the labor agreement requires the employer to compensate the worker provided the latter performs the work stipulated.

Rejecting the view that the labor agreement generates a lien to the employer on the person of the worker, Tosafot et alia maintain that what the employer acquires as a result of the agreement is only an obligation on the part of the worker to perform the work stipulated.[113] What constitutes the essence of this obligation lends itself to two alternative interpretations. One possibility is to view the obligation as interpersonal in nature. What occurs in consequence of the labor agreement is the generation of reciprocal obligations for the parties involved. The employer acquires an obligation on the part of the worker to perform the work stipulated, while the employee acquires an obligation on the part of the employer to provide this work. Another possibility is to view the above mutual obligations as *separate self-requirements (chiyuv metzad atzmo)* rather than as interpersonal in nature. What forces the employer to provide work is the fulfillment of a self-requirement and not a need to satisfy his obligation to the employee. Similarly, what compels the worker to perform work is the necessity of fulfilling a self-requirement and not a need to satisfy any obligation to the employer.

Explicit subscription to the self-requirement view of the labor contract is taken by R. Jacob Lorberbaum.[114]

Subscription to the reciprocal-obligation view of the labor agreement leads to the conclusion that seniority in service entitles the worker to employment preference. Given the interpersonal nature of the employer's obligation, implementation of any subsequent labor contract to perform the same task must be held in abeyance until sufficient work is available to justify expansion of the labor force beyond the senior worker. It follows that contraction in the amount of work available generates layoffs in reverse order of seniority.

Viewing the labor agreement as generating only a requirement to the employer to compensate the employee should he perform the work stipulated leads, however, to the conclusion that all workers currently employed enjoy equal rights to continued employment. With the *labor agreement itself* generating a requirement to the employer to compensate the worker should the work be performed, the actual performance of the work is what concretizes this abstract obligation. The work itself, from the perspective of the employees, is not merely a condition to fulfill in order to obtain compensation, but is a means of concretizing an abstract obligation already in existence in consequence of the agreement itself. With each worker demanding that the work at hand be furnished to him, does the senior employee enjoy employment preference, or are all currently employed workers invested with equal rights in this matter? An analogous circumstance occurs when creditors converge all at once upon a debtor to secure repayment. Here, the majority view is that all creditors enjoy equal rights to the immovable property of the debtor. Nachmanides, expressing a minority viewpoint, rules that the antecedent creditor has a prior claim to the immovable property of the debtor.[115] Following the majority view, all currently employed workers would enjoy an equal claim to the available work. The available work would, therefore, be divided equally among them.

Should the obligation the labor contract generates for the employer merely consist of a duty to furnish the worker with the specified work, Nachmanides' viewpoint would become irrelevant to the matter at hand, for his ruling refers to the resolution of competing *creditor* claims against a debtor and not to competing claims against a prospective employer. The available work would then, according to all disputants, be divided equally among the currently employed workers.

Finding the self-requirement formula most plausible and noting that the seniority privilege as a definite matter proceeds only from the reciprocal-obligation formula, R. Feinstein rejects the seniority principle in the specific work load case as a method of governing layoff policy. By the strict letter of the law, the available work should be divided among the competing workers. Nevertheless, since the seniority rule does proceed from Nachmanides' minority viewpoint within the context of the compensation-responsibility formula, R. Feinstein recommends an accommodation between the competing workers, calling for three fifths of the available work to be assigned to the senior worker and the remaining two fifths to the other workers.

A variation of the above circumstance occurs when a worker is hired explicitly to perform *all* the available work of the employer. Subsequently, an increase in the work load forces the employer to hire an additional worker. Suppose, now, the work load diminishes to such an extent that two workers are no longer needed. How is the work load to be divided at this point among the workers? Given the above explicit stipulation with the senior worker, R. Feinstein posits that the second worker must be considered in essence as the hired hand of the senior worker as well as an employee of the proprietor. Consequently, the second worker may exert a legitimate claim to the senior worker to provide him with work. The available work should, therefore, be divided between the two workers equally.

In the event the work, as a practical matter, cannot be divided, each worker must submit a bid to buy off his competitor's share of the work load. In exchange for his tender, the highest bidder is entitled to exclusive title of the contested job.[116]

Tenure Rights and Job Competition for Positions of Communal Authority

Special job security is conferred to individuals occupying positions of public authority (*serarah*). Exegetical interpretation of the verse, " . . . to the end to prolong his kingdom he and his children, in the midst of Israel,"[117] establishes the principle that the kingship is vested as an inheritance to the son of the incumbent. The phrase "in the midst of Israel" is taken to extend succession rights to the son of anyone occupying a position of communal authority.[118]

Life tenure rights for positions of communal authority follow, according to R. Moses b. Joseph Trani (1500–1580), from the above inheritance aspect. Given the power to cause succession, the life tenure rights of the incumbent follow *a fortiori*.[119]

Assimilating a position of communal authority with an object of sanctity, R. Isaac b. Sheshet Perfet (1326–1408) derives the life tenure rights of an incumbent from the prohibition against degrading the importance of an object of sanctity. This interdict finds expression in the oft-quoted talmudic adage: *maalin bakodesh veein moriden* (*Yoma* 9b)—"we may promote in [a matter] of sanctity, but not degrade."[120]

Another rationale for the job-security rights of the *serarah* officeholder is offered by R. Solomon Adret. Dismissal of an individual occupying a position of public authority subjects him to speculation that his removal was due to immoral conduct. To forestall suspicions of this sort, the *serarah* officeholder may not be dismissed without just cause.

Should it be local custom to appoint people to positions of communal authority only for fixed periods of time, the *serarah* officeholder may be replaced at the termination of the customary time, even if his contract did not specify an expiration date. Since it is the custom to rotate the office, removal does not give rise to speculation of moral misconduct.[121]

Finding an individual more suitable for the position does not allow the community to replace the incumbent. In addition, hiring another individual to perform the same duties as the incumbent is also prohibited as doing so effectively forces the incumbent to share his duties with another person.[122]

Malfeasance resulting in irretrievable loss provides a basis for dismissing the *serarah* officeholder.[123]

Transgression of religious law, evidenced by court-admissible witnesses, according to Maimonides, provides grounds for removing the *serarah* officeholder. Rumor of misconduct does not suffice to effect the incumbent's removal. Should the offense have been committed in public view, the testimony removes the incumbent even if he is willing to accept his due punishment. Commission of the religious violation in private, however, allows the incumbent to extricate himself from removal by accepting his due punishment.[124]

Tenure and succession rights, according to R. Jekuthiel Asher Zalman Ensil Zusmir (d. 1858), are conferred only to individuals occupying public positions of authority, but do not extend to all public servants. Accordingly, tenure and succession rights would not be conferred to the publicly employed ritual slaughterer and sexton.[125] R. Isaac Yehuda Schmelkes (1828–1906), however, includes the ritual slaughterer and sexton in the category of *serarah*.[126]

Appointment to a communal position of authority for a fixed period of time, according to R. Solomon Zalman Lipschitz (1765–1839) et alia, allows the community the option of refusing to renew the contract at the expiration date.[127] R. Joseph Raphael b. Chayyim Joseph Chazzan (1741–1820), however, regards tenure for the *serarah* officeholder as a divinely bestowed prerogative which cannot be taken away by a term or option clause.[128]

Following R. Chazzan's line is the contemporary decisor R. Moshe Feinstein. In a responsum dealing with the authority of a yeshiva's board of directors to terminate the services of a member of its religious staff, R. Feinstein rules that as long as the teacher performed his duties diligently and adequately, he may not be replaced, notwithstanding the fact that no commitment was made to him at the time he was hired that his contract would be renewed. Moreover, even if the teacher's contract explicitly specified that renewal of his services would be at the board's discretion, the condition may very well have no validity. This follows from the fact that the board is elected to conduct the affairs of the yeshiva in a manner that would sanctify the name of Heaven (*leshem shamayim*). Refusing to renew a contract without just cause violates all canons of equity and is, therefore, not an action that would foster santification of God's name. Since the board exceeds its authoritative limits with a stipulation of this nature, the option clause to renew the teacher's contract could very well have no legal validity.[129]

Succession Rights for a Position of Communal Authority

Another factor that limits competition in the job market for positions of communal authority, as mentioned above, is the succession right enjoyed by the son of the incumbent. The son's claim to succession must be honored even if he does not measure up to his father in all respects. As long as the son is his father's equal in piety, though not in wisdom, the community must give him preference in filling the vacant position.[130]

The community is required to honor the succession claim of the incumbent's son, according to R. Solomon Adret, only when the other competing candidates are not vastly superior to the aspiring heir. Should the incumbent's son be eclipsed by the other aspirants, he is given no preferential claim to succession.[131] Other authorities, however, require the community to give preferential consideration to the *qualified* heir, notwithstanding the availability of candidates vastly superior to him.[132]

Unlike inheritance of material wealth, succession rights become applicable even in the lifetime of the incumbent. As soon as the father leaves his position, his son becomes eligible to succeed him.[133]

Should the son be a minor at the time his father's communal position of authority became vacated, the community may fill the position on a competitive basis. Filling the position in this manner permanently disentitles the son of the predecessor to any future preferential right to the position.[134]

Insofar as local custom overrides religious *civil* law[134a], the succession claim to a position of communal authority is denied when it is local custom to fill such a position by means of the competitive process. Given the awareness of the custom, the occupant presumably waives his right to vest the position to his son.[135]

Succession Rights in the Rabbinate

Whether the rabbinate is subject to inheritance is disputed in the responsa literature. Assimilating the rabbinate to other positions of communal authority, R. Isaac b. Sheshet Perfet et alia regard it as subject to inheritance.[136] Citing the following talmudic passage in *Yoma* 72a, R. Samuel b. Moses de Medina (1506–1589) et alia deny succession rights for this position:

R. Johanan [ca. 180–279] said: there are three crowns: that of the altar, that of the table, and that of the ark. The one of the altar Aaron deserved and received it. The one of the table, David deserved and received. The one of the ark is still lying and whosoever wants to take it may come and take it.

What proceeds from the above passage is that the crown of Torah is not an inheritance. Hence, when a rabbinical position becomes vacant, it is filled by means of the competitive process. [137]

Narrowing the differences between the schools of thought, R. Joseph Saul Nathanson (1810–1875) posits that all disputants agree that the succession right for the rabbinate position is not denied when the son is at least equal to his father in piety, though not in scholarship. [138]

An alternative rationale for denying succession rights in the rabbinate is offered by R. Moshe Sofer (1762–1839). What is subject to inheritance is only a communal position of authority, but not a *communal position of holiness.* Insofar as a rabbinical position involves teaching Torah and interpreting Jewish law, the rabbinate is intrinsically a communal position of holiness and therefore not subject to inheritance. Nevertheless, the rabbinate nowadays, according to R. Moshe Sofer, is subject to inheritance. This follows from the fact that today the rabbi is *formally hired* by the community to cater to its spiritual needs. Because of the professional nature of the rabbinate today, the position is akin to any other position of communal authority and should, therefore, be subject to inheritance. [139]

The Duration of Labor
Contracts

In this section we will investigate the degree of freedom parties to a labor contract enjoy in setting the length of their arrangement.

The pentateuchal interdict against contracting into a status of servitude, [140] according to R. Meir b. Baruch of Rothenburg, prohibits an individual from contracting the continuous provision of his labor services for more than three years. The three-year limit follows from an examination of the following biblical verse dealing with the master's obligation to bestow his Hebrew bondservant with gifts upon his release: "And this shalt not seem hard in thine eyes when thou sendest him away from thee, for double the amount of wages of a hired day servant he earned for six years . . . " (Deuteronomy 15:18). What is clearly intimated by the above verse is that six years is double the normal contractual obligation of the hired hand. Given this intimation, contracting to provide continuous labor services for more than three years, though not constituting servitude, nonetheless places the worker in a classification inferior to that of the hired hand. Included in the interdict against contracting into servitude is the prohibition of contracting into a stature inferior to that of a hired hand.

Blanket prohibition of long-term labor contracts, cautions R. Meir b. Baruch, does not, however, follow. To be akin to servitude, the labor contract must call for the worker to live in the employer's home and accept his board for the duration of the contract. Such an arrangement "ties" the employee and is akin to servitude. Absence of the room-and-board provision frees the labor contract from any restrictions regarding its length.[141]

Rejecting the assimilation of a labor contract with servitude, Tosafot in *Baba Metzia* (10a) find no reason to object to long-term labor contracts. R. Moses Isserles, however, follows R. Meir b. Baruch's view.[142]

Following R. Meir b. Baruch's ruling, the responsa literature has further limited its application.

1. A three-year labor contract, according to R. Chayyim b. Israel Benveniste (1603–1673), may be renewed any number of times for another three-year period. Notwithstanding the cumulative tieing effect of such successive contracts, the arrangement is not objectionable because each contract individually falls within the permissible time limit.[143]

2. Insofar as the interdict against contracting into servitude does not apply to an individual entering such an arrangement out of financial desperation, a destitute individual, according to R. Shabbetai b. Meir ha-Kohen, may enter into a long-term labor contract with a room-and-board provision.[144]

3. Rabbinical contracts in the time of R. Moshe Sofer were commonly extended for three to five years. Since the spiritual leader is required to live within the community of his employment, rabbinical contracts should apparently be limited to three years. Defending the prevailing practice, R. Sofer posits that the prohibition against long-term labor contracts is violated only if the length of the contract is six years. Moreover, the three to five year clause is incorporated solely to allow the rabbi the option of leaving the community at the expiration date. With the term clause included solely for the benefit of the rabbi, the community may not refuse renewal of the contract at the expiration date without just cause.[145]

Regulation of Outside Working Hours

Because it is regarded as a form of robbery, an individual may not work at night while under contract as a *poel* during the day.[146] Similarly, a *poel* may not refuse to use his wages to provide himself with minimum nourishment, even if the money saved is used toward the support of his family.[147] In both instances, the conduct reduces the *poel's* productivity while performing his contracted work and is therefore prohibited.[148]

Accordingly, a schoolteacher may not stay up late at night or rise very early as such conduct reduces his efficiency during teaching hours.[149]

Insofar as the *kabbelan* is paid for the completed job, rather than by the hour, the prohibition against outside night work, according to R. Jechiel Michael Epstein, does not apply to him.[150]

R. Warhaftig posits that the prohibition against outside night work applies only when the workday extends from sunrise to sunset. Outside night work here makes it well-nigh impossible for the worker to recharge himself overnight and discharge his duties with any vigor the following day. Nowadays, with the workday typically extending only eight hours, outside night work cannot be said to exert a debilitating effect on the performance of the worker in his daytime job.[151]

Blanket liberalization of the outside-work interdict on account of the shortened workweek, in our view, does not follow. What is crucial in determining the appropriateness of relaxing the interdict is not the amount of leisure time available to the worker today compared to previous times, but the *impact* the extra work exerts on the efficiency level of the worker in his regular job. Should the extra work reduce the productivity of the worker in his regular job, the outside work should be disallowed. An area of questionable ethics occurs, in our view, when the outside work does reduce the efficiency level of the worker in his regular job, but not below the performance level of co-workers in identical jobs.

An express stipulation in the labor contract allowing the worker the option of undertaking extra work outside regular hours is, however, recognized in Jewish law and presents no moral issue.[152]

· 5
External Costs

Introduction

Neoclassical economic theory views man in his economic activities as a monetary maximizer. Efficient pursuit of economic gain requires an economic unit to evaluate his market alternatives by balancing anticipated marginal gains against anticipated marginal losses. Relevant for the initiating agent in this calculation is the amount of benefits he can anticipate to capture against the costs society's legal system force him to take into account. External benefits and external costs—benefits and costs to other parties generated by his actions, but not falling within this calculus—are assumed to play no motivational role in his market conduct. To the extent that society's legal system fails to provide adequate incentives to allow the initiating agent to be compensated for the full extent of the benefits his actions generate, and fails to charge economic actors for the full extent of the detriment their actions impose on others, a misallocation of economic resources will occur. From a social standpoint, too much will be produced by enterprises involving external costs, while less than the optimal amount will be produced by industries involving external benefits.[1]

External Costs in Economic Theory

From the standpoint of economic analysis, the elimination of negative externalities involves both equity and efficiency considerations. These issues, as the following example will illustrate, can be considered separately. Suppose the smoke emitted by a steel factory destroys a neighboring farmer's wheat. Suppose further that the damage can be avoided either by growing smoke-resistant wheat or by installing a smoke-control device in the factory. Which of the two, the farmer or the factory-owner, should be charged with the responsibility of eliminating the negative externality? Equity clearly demands that the expense of internalizing the negative externality be borne by the economic unit that generates it. What follows is that the factory-owner, in our case, would, on equity grounds, be held liable.

While the principle of equity is promoted by the selection of appropriate liability rules, economic efficiency is realized when the negative externality is eliminated by the *least-cost* method. Hence, should it be less costly to avoid crop damage by growing smoke-resistant wheat than by installing a smoke-control device, the former method should be adopted. Whether the farmer or the factory-owner should bear the additional expense of eliminating the negative externality is entirely irrelevant as far as the efficiency question is concerned. Internalizing the negative externality by means of the least-cost method allows society to maximize its product with its given resources.

Assuming zero transaction costs and economic rationality, Coase, in his seminal work, demonstrated that the market mechanism is capable of eliminating negative externalities without the necessity of governmentally imposed liability rules. Coase's assertion can be illustrated with the aid of our above example. What we will demonstrate is that regardless of the liability rule adopted, bargaining between the farmer and the factory-owner is capable of producing a result that is economically efficient. Let us, first, suppose that the factory-owner is made liable for the crop damage his enterprise causes. With the liability rule against him, the factory-owner is forced to enter the marginal cost of avoiding crop damage explicitly into his cost function. Profit-maximization considerations would tell him to extend his output up to the point where his marginal cost of production, including the marginal cost of avoiding crop damage, is equal to his anticipated marginal revenue. Assuming that growing smoke-resistant wheat is the least-cost method of avoiding crop damage at the output level that maximizes profits, the factory-owner would rationally offer the farmer a payment equal to the differential cost of growing smoke-resistant wheat as compensation for allowing him to operate his factory at its profit-maximizing level. Rearranging the liability rule in favor of the factory-owner is capable of yielding the same resource-allocation result. This follows from the fact that with the liability rule working against the farmer, the latter must take action to minimize his loss. Passivity on the part of the farmer generates to him a loss equal to the market value of the portion of the crop that is destroyed by the operation of the factory. To minimize his loss, the farmer would rationally offer the factory-owner a payment up to the differential cost of growing smoke-resistant wheat as a bribe not to run the factory, guaranteeing no crop loss. The factory-owner would view this offer as the opportunity cost he sustains as he expands output. Bargaining between the parties involved hence internalizes the negative externality, regardless of the liability rule assumed. The least-cost method of eliminating the negative external-ity is always taken into account by the factory-owner, either in the form of an *explicit* cost or in the form of an opportunity cost, depend-ing upon the liability rule.[2]

Coase's proposition that the market mechanism itself is capable of eliminating a negative externality without recourse to governmentally imposed liability rules finds general acceptance among economists when the negative externality affects only a few parties. This cir-cumstance is referred to in the economic literature as the small-numbers case. Here, the assumptions of zero transaction costs and economic rationality appear reasonably valid. When the negative externality affects large numbers of people, however, the above assumptions are less tenable. Bargaining is not likely to emerge when the only thing the victims share is their common suffering from the negative externality. Elimination of negative externalities in the large-numbers case, therefore, requires the legislation of *amenity rights*, i.e., laws protecting society against the noxious side-effects of economic activity.[3]

Exemplifying the economic approach to the large-numbers nega-tive externality case is Ruff's effluent fee scheme for pollution abate-ment. The plan calls for those that produce and consume goods which cause pollution to pay the costs involved. All that is needed to implement such a plan is a mechanism for estimating the pollution output of all polluters, together with a means of collecting fees. Under such a system, anyone could emit any amount of pollution as long as he pays the price which the government sets to approximate the marginal social cost of pollution. If pollution consists of many com-ponents, each with its own social cost, there would be different prices for each component. Prohibitive prices would be set for pollutants that endanger human life. Once the prices are set, polluters could adjust to them in any way they choose. Because they act on self-interest, they will reduce their pollution by every means possible, up to the point where further reduction would cost more than the price. Should the initial price scheme prove to be too low to accomplish the desired amount of pollution abatement, the prices could be increased to effect the desired reduction.[4]

Society's legal approach to the problem of negative externalities has usually taken the form of granting the complainant an injunction against the offender. Such an approach, as Coase points out, often ignores the reciprocal nature of the problem at hand. Granting the complainant relief harms the offender, while refusing relief harms the complainant. From an economic standpoint, the objective of such intervention should be to avoid the more severe harm. Citing the 1879

British court case *Sturges v. Bridgman,* Coase illustrates the divergence between the legal and the optimal economic approaches to the problem of negative externalities. In this case, a doctor sought an injunction against a neighboring confectioner, claiming that the noise and vibrations caused by the latter's machinery made it impossible for him to conduct his medical practice. The court's decision established that the doctor had the right to prevent the confectioner from using his machinery. From the standpoint of promoting resource allocation efficiency, the objective of the court's intervention should have been the avoidance of the more severe harm. Securing more doctoring is at the expense of a reduced supply of confectionery products. Which one of these activities merits the right to displace the other should be determined by comparing the total product obtainable under alternative arrangements of rights for the parties involved. In the absence of a liability rule, the parties involved, through the process of negotiation, could arrive at an agreement that would be consistent with resource allocation efficiency. Through the process of bargaining, the activity yielding the higher market value would displace the activity of the lower market value. To illustrate, suppose the doctoring services are valued at $100 per hour, while the corresponding value of the confectionery product is $50. By mutual consent, the confectioner would rationally accept a payment of $50 as an inducement to desist from his enterprise. A voluntary transfer of $50 from the doctor to the confectioner thus eliminates the negative externality and maximizes the total product.[5]

This chapter will investigate the treatment of negative externalities in Jewish law in both the small- and large-numbers cases. Conclusions will be drawn regarding the degree to which Jewish law's approach to this problem converges with the economic efficiency approach.

Small-Numbers Negative Externalities

The amenity right finds recognition in Jewish law, but its recognition is by no means absolute. Consideration of the nature of the harm involved as well as how it was produced forms the basic criterion Jewish law adopts in deciding whether the amenity right should be invoked.

When an adverse side-effect is legally classified as a negative externality, the initiator, by force of a biblical interdict, must refrain from the activity generating it.[6] In the absence of voluntary compliance, the courts will enjoin the activity by petition of the party that stands to be injured.[7] An actionable negative externality is thus dealt with in Jewish law by means of the restraining-order technique.

Jewish amenity law is characterized by the following general features:

1. A negative externality is generally not actionable unless a direct link between the adverse effect and the action of the initiator can be established. This condition is referred to as the *gi'ri de'lei* criterion; i.e., the adverse effect must be akin to the shooting arrows of the initiator.[8]
2. The amenity right enjoys limited recognition when the adverse effect consists of a potential, as opposed to a concrete, harm.[9]
3. To be actionable, the harm the plaintiff stands to sustain as a result of the defendant's activity must consist of actual or potential bodily harm or property damage. We will refer to this condition as the *destructive-effect* criterion.[10]
4. The amenity right against a nuisance externality enjoys limited recognition.[11]
5. In some instances the relevant criteria in adjudicating the negative externality case widens beyond the narrow interests of the litigants themselves to a consideration of how compatible the disputed activity is with social and religious objectives.[12]

The Gi'ri De'lei Criterion
The Talmud deems various degrees of linkage between the adverse effect and the initiator's action as sufficiently meeting the *gi'ri de'lei* (direct link) criterion. Illustrating *gi'ri de'lei* in its strongest form is the talmudic case involving a vibration-producing enterprise. Papi Yona'ah, relates the Talmud, was able to obtain an injunction against sesame oil producers in his neighborhood on the grounds that the crushing action involved in their enterprise caused his villa to shake.[13]

For all cases analogous to the above, should the plaintiff sustain loss as a result of the defendant's failure to refrain from his forbidden activity, the latter incurs liability.[14]

A weaker form of linkage falling under the *gi'ri de'lei* criterion involves a delay of time between the adverse effect and the activity that generates it. Accordingly, an individual may be enjoined against establishing a bakery, a dyer's shop, or a cattle stall under his neighbor's storehouse,[15] for the heat produced by such enterprises would harm the produce in the storehouse.[16]

Whether the plaintiff's recovery-of-loss claim is recognized in the above category of negative externality cases is disputed among talmudic decisors.[17]

By extension, a non–*gi'ri de'lei* action whose effect is to *trigger* an immediate bodily harm or property damage is prohibited. Illustrating this case, called *gerama d'gi'ri* in the rabbinic literature, is the requirement that a flax-production enterprise must be safely distanced to prevent flying tow from injuring neighbors. Though the tow cannot inflict damage without the aid of an ordinary wind, the flax-production enterprise must be properly distanced because its operation triggers an inevitable harm.[18]

The plaintiff's claim for recovery of losses sustained is not recognized in *gerama d'gi'ri* cases.[19]

Negative Externalities Imposing Potential Harm

Drawing an illustration from the talmudic literature, a *potentially* harmful negative externality occurs when A places lime in close proximity to his common boundary with B. Though the initiator's action generates no immediate harm to B, the lime placement represents to the latter a potential harm. The potential harm follows from the fact that should B subsequently build a wall within three handbreadths of his boundary, his construction would sustain damage from A's lime. With A's action not regarded as a major normal use of his property, talmudic decisors differ as to whether it is subject to restraint.[20] Nonetheless, should the initiator's action represent a major normal use of his property, all disputants agree that the potentially harmful negative externality he generates is not subject to restraint. Hence, A may open a dyer's shop in the lower level of a house, though his action is potentially harmful to the upper-story occupant (B) in the event the latter would establish a storehouse there.[21] Insofar as A's action generates no concrete harm to B, denying him the right to establish a productive enterprise on his own premises is tantamount to revoking his property right altogether. B's petition for a restraining order is therefore rejected here. Moreover, B's petition is denied even at such time that he actually sets up a storehouse in his upper-story premises. Having acquired his right to conduct his enterprise in the lower story, A may not be forced to withdraw.[22]

Legitimacy in invoking the amenity right in the potentially harmful adverse-effect case is not universally recognized unless the defendant derives a benefit from the plaintiff's property at the time he generates the negative externality to him. This aspect of amenity law emerges from R. Jacob Lorberbaum's (1760–1832) analysis of a point in *hezek re'iyah* (privacy invasion) law. Privacy invasion law prohibits A from installing a window facing B's courtyard because the latter would thereby be exposed to his view.[23] Here, A's window-installing activity may be restrained even if it merely poses a potential harm to the plaintiff (B). This would occur when the window faces a neighbor's ruin. Insofar as private activities are not customarily performed in a ruin, the window presents no immediate harm to the owner of the ruin (B). Nonetheless, credence is given to B's claim that he plans to eventually renovate the ruin. Should A be allowed to maintain his window, B would suffer at once at that time from A's visual penetration of his domain. B's request to have the window walled up immediately is therefore acceded to. Given the predilection of most people to secure what is rightfully theirs with a minimum amount of litigation and nuisance, the plaintiff's petition here is not regarded as Sodomitic in character (i.e., denying someone a benefit when it involves no cost to oneself).[24] Installing a window facing a neighbor's ruin allows the initiator to benefit from the latter's air space. Given the presumption that the ruin will eventually be renovated, A's benefit inevitably generates a harm to the owner of the ruin. Insofar as the owner of the ruin is within his rights to object to someone benefiting from his air space when he would inevitably sustain a loss thereby, the defendant may be forced to close his window, though it poses no immediate threat to the owner of the ruin.[25]

The Destructive-Effect Criterion
To be actionable, the adverse effect must be in the form of bodily harm or property damage. Should the defendant's action merely prevent the plaintiff from using his property in a particular manner, the defendant's action is not subject to restraint. That a forced misallocation effect is not actionable in Jewish law proceeds from the following rishonic rulings:[26]

1. The lower-story occupant of a house (A), according to R. Solomon Adret (1235–1319), may not restrain his upper-story neighbor (B) from establishing a storehouse on his premises. Though the effect of the action is to restrict A from conducting any enterprise that would harm the produce of the storehouse, the misallocation effect A suffers is not actionable, for building a storehouse generates no destructive effect.[27]

2. A may build his wall, according to R. Solomon b. Adret and Tosafot (12th–14th cent. school of French and German talmudic commentators), adjacent to B's boundary. Given that the strengthening of the foundation of a wall requires treading by passersby on both its sides (*davsha*), the effect of A's action is to preclude B from building a wall within four cubits of his wall. A's wall building is, nevertheless, not actionable, for his wall

building merely prevents treading from occurring, but in itself generates no destructive effect to B.[28]

Commenting on the above Tosafot, R. Aaron Kotler (1892–1962) derives the general principle that a negative externality is not actionable when the adverse effect consists of disallowing the plaintiff from conducting income-producing activities on his premises.[29]

That a forced misallocation effect is not actionable is further bolstered by an analysis of why a privacy-intruding act is subject to restraint. What is the nature of the damage we presume B will suffer if A is allowed to open a window facing his courtyard? Two alternative approaches present themselves. One possible approach would be to view the installation of the window as inevitably causing B the embarrassment and humiliation of having his courtyard activities observed by A. Anticipated *invasion* of privacy, in this view, is what directly enjoins the initiator's activity. But, perhaps, installation of the window cannot be enjoined on this basis as the courts would find sympathy with A's protest that he would exercise caution not to observe B's courtyard activities. Rather, the restraining order is legitimized on the presumption that A's window would inevitably render B's courtyard unfit for use. Out of fear of being spied on by A, B would refrain from conducting private activities in his courtyard. What legitimizes the restraining order in this approach is the property-use restriction A's window imposes on B. Addressing himself to this question, R. Yechezkel Abramsky (1886–1976) demonstrates that mainstream thought in Jewish law legitimizes the restraining order on the basis of the first approach outlined above. What disallows A from installing his window is the privacy-*invasion* effect it would impose on B. B's complaint that A's window would force him to refrain from using his courtyard for private activities would not, however, provide sufficient grounds to enjoin A from building his window.

The privacy-invasion effect theory is bolstered by consideration of the following stringent aspect of *hezek re'iyah* law: The plaintiff's petition to force B to barricade his window is upheld even when the visual penetration into his domain was not triggered by the defendant's direct action. This would occur when a wall originally separated A's window from B's courtyard and the wall subsequently fell down. With the defendant's action not tortious in Jewish law unless it meets the *gi'ri de'lei* criterion, the above law would not be understandable under the property-use restriction approach. Insofar as the window-installation activity *itself* can in no way be said to directly render B's courtyard unusable, A would not be required to barricade his window when the wall separating the courtyard from the window falls down. Why the plaintiff's petition is upheld here is, therefore, comprehensible only under the privacy-invasion rationalization. Given that the separating wall has fallen down, B will now inevitably suffer embarrassment from having his courtyard activities *observed* by A. The latter is therefore ordered to wall up his window under the *gi'ri de'lei* interdict.[30]

Conducting an enterprise that restricts a neighbor from using his property in a particular manner undoubtedly reduces its market value. Given the nonrecognition of the amenity right when the adverse effect is solely misallocative in nature, loss of property value *alone* does not provide sufficient grounds to restrain an activity. The defendant's action is not actionable unless it is regarded as tortious, notwithstanding the loss in the property's market value that the plaintiff suffers thereby.

Nuisance Externality

The amenity right finds limited recognition in Jewish law when the adverse effect consists of a mere nuisance and involves no real damage to the person or property of the plaintiff. Supportive of the above assertion is the treatment of smoke pollution in Jewish law. The strength of the amenity right here, as R. Jechiel Michael Epstein (1820–1908) points out, depends on the nature of the damage the smoke generates. The widest recognition of the amenity right is found when the damage involved consists of bodily injury, e.g., eye irritation. In this instance, the Jewish court will enjoin the harmful enterprise at any time on the request of an injured party. Injury of this sort is regarded as an obnoxious damage. Having conducted the enterprise in the past unprotested, therefore, does not entitle the defendant to continue it should his neighbors object. The amenity right in the smoke pollution case becomes somewhat attenuated when the enterprise inflicts no bodily injury, but merely blackens the surrounding buildings. Here, delay in the lodging of the protest for a period of time sufficient to establish for the defendant a prescriptive right to continue his enterprise,[31] establishes for the latter a right to continue his smoke-generating activity. Finally, should the smoke-generating enterprise inflict no bodily or property harm, the amenity right is not recognized at all. Between the conflicting interests of indulging the aesthetic sensibilities of the complaining neighbors and allowing the factory-owner to conduct his commercial enterprise unobstructed, the latter is given precedence.[32]

Further evidence of the attenuated status of the amenity right against the nuisance externality in Jewish law is seen by the halakhic treatment of noise and traffic externalities.

Residents of a courtyard may not enjoin residents of a neighboring courtyard from conducting noise- or traffic-generating commercial activities on their premises.[33] The noise externality is actionable only in the instance where the plaintiff is an invalid or known to be hypersensitive. Here, the noise externality causes actual suffering and not just an annoyance.[34]

More expansive is the amenity right residents of the *same* courtyard enjoy against each other. Here, any resident may invoke his amenity right to restrain a fellow resident from establishing a traffic-generating commercial enterprises in his home. As examples of commercial enterprises qualifying for restraint on this account, the Talmud specifically mentions a weaving concern, a bloodletting enterprise, and a trade school.[35] Broadly interpreted, the amenity right allows residents of the courtyard to restrain each other from selling or renting their apartments to professionals of the types mentioned above.[36] Moreover, should a resident obtain permission from the other members of the courtyard to conduct a traffic-generating commercial enterprise on his premises, the approval may be revoked at any future time by means of the registration of a veto by any single member. Insofar as traffic congestion is regarded as an obnoxious nuisance, a prescriptive right to continue the activity is not recognized. Credence is given to the plaintiff's claim that while he was able to endure the traffic congestion in the past, he is unable to tolerate it anymore.[37]

Standing at the basis of the amenity right against a traffic-generating activity, according to R. Meir Abulafia (1170–1244), is the right of a resident of a courtyard to prevent a fellow resident from engaging in an enterprise on his own premises that would, as a side-effect, radically alter the character of the courtyard. Insofar as conducting a traffic-generating commercial activity on his premises effectively converts the courtyard into a marketplace, any resident may object to this activity.[38]

Traffic congestion generates two distinct annoyances to the residents of a courtyard, namely noise and time delay. R. Solomon Adret et alia posit that noise-generating activities alone do not provide adequate grounds for the issuance of a restraining order. Time delay as a consequence of the traffic congestion is what provides the residents with a legitimate basis for obtaining a restraining order. Hence, should a resident of the courtyard desire to carry out on his premises noise-generating activities not involving traffic congestion, i.e., hammering and grinding activities, complaining residents are denied a restraining order.[39]

Maimonides (1135–1204) et alia, however, regard noise-generating activities alone as adequate grounds for the issuance of a restraining order. Noise externalities, according to this school of thought, are classified into two categories: those involving traffic congestion, and those not involving the latter nuisance. In the former instance, a restraining order is issued at the request of any resident of the courtyard even if the activity had previously gone unprotested for an interval normally sufficient to establish a prescriptive privilege for the perpetrator.[40] A prescriptive right is not recognized here because the nuisance itself, time delay, cannot be directly linked to the violator's actions. Moreover, traffic congestion occurring on a particular day is independent of traffic congestion occurring on another day. With each instance of time delay treated as a new and independent event, a request by a resident of the courtyard for a restraining order is honored at any time, despite his previous lack of protest.

In sharp contrast, noise externalities not involving traffic congestion are linked directly to the actions of the perpetrator and are, therefore, properly regarded as his continuous action. Hence, should the residents have allowed the noise externality to go on unprotested, the violator establishes thereby a prescriptive right to continue his enterprise.[41]

Social and Religious Goals
Consideration of the compatibility of the disputed activity with social and religious objectives finds illustration in Jewish law in the following two negative externality cases.

1. Out of fear that small cattle (sheep, goats, etc.) would wander into neighboring fields and destroy crops there, the Sages prohibited the breeding of small cattle in the land of Israel except in the deserts. The importing of small cattle for consumption purposes was permitted under controlled conditions. What the ordinance did was not merely hold the cattleman responsible for crop damage inflicted by his herd, but outlawed the breeding of small cattle altogether.[42] The former approach would force internalization of the negative externality but allow bargaining between the cattlemen and farmers to determine the land-use pattern. The latter approach, however, dictates a land-use pattern in the form of farming, regardless of the implications for economic efficiency.

Why the Sages did not find it sufficient to impose a liability rule against the cattleman is explained by Maimonides on the basis of the inevitability of the crop damage that would result from the cattle-breeding enterprise. Dealing with the negative externality by merely imposing a liability rule would be tantamount to licensing the cattle-man to destroy the farmer's crop while calling for compensation for damages as they occur.[43]

Standing at the basis of the ordinance, according to R. Solomon b. Isaac (1040–1105), however, is a desire to stabilize Jewish settlements and promote population growth.[44] What follows, in our view, is the inadequacy of the liability-rule approach. A liability rule allows subsequent bargaining between the parties involved to determine the land-use pattern, regardless of the impact on population growth. To insure that the narrow interests of the parties involved do not produce a bargaining result that would subvert the social goal of population growth, the Sages prohibited outright the breeding of small cattle in the land of Israel.

2. Notwithstanding the amenity right residents of a courtyard enjoy against traffic-generating activities, a resident may not be restrained against opening or operating a Torah school on his premises. Between the conflicting interests of upholding the amenity rights of residents of a courtyard and allowing Torah education to go on unhindered, the latter is judged to be more important. Establishing a religious school promotes the viability of Torah education and is consistent with the intent of R. Joshua b. Gamala's (d. 69/70 c.e.) ancient ordinance requiring local communities to maintain religious-educational institutions for the young.[45]

Assimilating any enterprise of a religious character to Torah education, R. Jacob b. Asher (1270–ca. 1343) and R. Joseph Caro (1488–1575) extend the traffic disamenity right to any enterprise of a religious purpose.[46]

Though residents of a courtyard have no choice but to tolerate the disamenities associated with enterprises of a religious character, joint owners of a home may restrain each other from conducting traffic-generating religious activities on their jointly owned property. Unless they originally stipulated to the contrary, we may presume that they entered their partnership with the understanding that neither partner should use the premises in a manner that would inflict a disamenity to the other partner.[47]

Large-Numbers Negative Externalities

Negative externalities affecting a large number of people are discussed in the Talmud in connection with the amenity rights of the residents of a town. Actionable negative externalities are dealt with here, as in the small-numbers case, by means of the restraining-order technique. Mandated zoning, at appropriate distances, is accordingly prescribed for harmful activities falling under the *gi'ri de'lei* and *gerama d'gi'ri* interdicts.

Local zoning ordinances designed to protect the town residents from a variety of damages include the following: A permanent threshing floor must be zoned fifty cubits from the town's limits, as operating it at a closer distance would expose the townspeople to the danger of flying chaff particles.[48] Similarly, to protect the town residents from smoke damage, furnaces must be distanced fifty cubits from the town.[49] With the objective of minimizing the damage foraging pigeons would inflict to the gardens of the town residents, dovecots are zoned the same distance from the town.[50]

Halakhic concern for the welfare of the town residents also finds expression in the zoning ordinance requiring a tannery to be distanced fifty cubits from the town[51] and to be located only on its east side.[52] Standing at the basis of this ordinance, according to R. Solomon b. Isaac (1040–1105), is a concern to spare the town residents from the offensive odor involved in this enterprise. Similarly rooted, according to R. Solomon b. Isaac, is the fifty-cubit zoning ordinance applying to cemeteries.[53] R. Mordechai b. Abraham Jaffe (1535–1612), however, rationalizes the latter ordinance as reflecting a concern to spare the town residents the trauma and anguish close contact with the cemetery would arouse in them.[54]

Preservation of the aesthetic quality of the town[55] stands at the basis of the local zoning ordinance forbidding the growing of a tree within a distance of twenty-five cubits from the town, or fifty cubits if it is a carob or sycamore tree.[56] Majority opinion in Jewish law views the latter ordinance, however, as applying only to the land of Israel when it is under Jewish control.[57]

Compared to the small-numbers case, halakhic recognition of the amenity right in the large-numbers case is more expansive. In the small-numbers case, as will be recalled, a concretely harmful *gi'ri de'lei* activity is not subject to restraint provided it was only potentially harmful at the time it was initiated and also represented for the initiator a prime use of his property. This is not so in the large-numbers case. Here, the amenity right is invoked against any concretely harmful *gi'ri de'lei* enterprise, irrespective of its only potentially harmful origin.

Illustrative of the above aspect of the broadened amenity rights of the residents of a town is the talmudic ruling that a tree planted within twenty-five cubits of the town is subject to removal even if its planting preceded the establishment of the town.[58] Similarly, the residents of a town may insist upon the removal of a permanent threshing floor the prescribed distance, even if the enterprise was in operation before the town existed.[59]

Though operating a *gi'ri de'lei* enterprise prior to the formation of the town does not fortify the entrepreneur's right to continue his enterprise once the town is established, he is entitled, in the above instance, to indemnification for losses he sustains as a result of removing his enterprise. No compensation, however, is due him in the event formation of the town preceded the establishment of his enterprise.

When compensation is due the owner, the enterprise must first be removed and only then may the owner of the enterprise exert his claim for indemnification. This is defended by the Talmud on the grounds that a prepayment procedure would subject the removal of the dangerous enterprise to inordinate delay. With people in general in no hurry to part with their money, each resident of the town would rely upon his neighbor to initiate the necessary collection. In the interest of expediting the removal of the dangerous enterprise, the prepayment scheme is rejected in favor of the procedure described above.[60]

The Halakhic and Economic Approaches to Small-Numbers Negative Externalities

Assuming along with Coase that judicial nonintervention in the small-numbers negative externality case allows the parties affected to negotiate an economically efficient bargain, the halakhic and economic approaches to the above problem converge in the whole range of cases where the amenity right is not recognized in Jewish law. Here, the party that stands to be injured would rationally offer the initiating party a payment to discontinue his enterprise up to the amount he valued the elimination of the adverse effect. This amount would then enter into the calculus of the injuring party as the opportunity cost he incurs should he decide to continue his enterprise. With the negative externality internalized in this manner, resource-allocation efficiency is obtainable. It should be noted, however, that the rationale behind halakhic nonintervention in a negative externality case is not the promotion of economic efficiency, but rather a commitment to the principle that the property right must not be interfered with when the activity involved is not tortious.

Highlighting the area of convergence between the halakhic and economic approaches to the problem of negative externalities is the nonintervention stance Jewish law would take in the *Sturges v.*

Bridgeman case, cited earlier in this chapter. The plaintiff's complaint in that case, as will be recalled, was that the pounding of the confectioner's equipment made it impossible for him to conduct his medical practice. Such a complaint does not demonstrate sufficient cause to enjoin the defendant's enterprise. The confectioner's action generates to the doctor merely a misallocative effect but causes him no actual or potential bodily or property damage. Should the plaintiff base his complaint on the nuisance element of the noise externality, his petition would also be rejected since the amenity right is halakhically not recognized against a noise externality, as discussed above, when plaintiff and defendant reside in separate courtyards. Sympathy would be found with the plaintiff's petition only in the event that he is an invalid or known to be hypersensitive. Here, the noise generated by the confectioner's machinery would presumably inflict to him actual suffering and not just a mere annoyance.

The halakhic and economic approaches to the problem of negative externalities, however, diverge in the whole range of cases where the amenity right is given recognition in Jewish law. An actionable negative externality in Jewish law, as will be recalled, is dealt with by means of the restraining-order technique. By no means does this technique guarantee that the activity having the highest economic value will displace the one having the lower value.

Highlighting the above divergence is the halakhic treatment of the reciprocal externality case. A reciprocal externality occurs when the concurrent operation of A's and B's enterprises on their neighboring premises generates harm to each other. To illustrate, suppose A and B desire, at the same time, to construct on their own premises cisterns adjacent to their common boundary. Given that a cistern requires a wall of at least three handbreadths wide, it would be impossible for *both* A and B to construct their cisterns within three handbreadths of their common boundary. Some accommodation between them must be made. What arrangement of rights is appropriate here? Promotion of economic efficiency clearly requires a consideration of the opportunity cost involved in alternative arrangements of distributing the six-handbreadths distance between the cavities of the cisterns. Judicial nonintervention would allow bargaining between the litigants to achieve an efficient solution along these lines. In sharp contrast, Halakhah entitles each of the disputants with equal rights here. Accordingly, A may force B to distance his cistern at least three handbreadths from their common boundary, and B may force A to do likewise.[61] Whether this *initial* arrangement of rights allows the combined output of the litigants to be maximized is, as far as Halakhah is concerned, entirely irrelevant in deciding the merits of this case.

That resource allocation efficiency assumes no halakhic relevance in the reciprocal externality case is further evidenced by an examination of a point in law in connection with the sapling-vineyard externality case. Suppose the owners of two neighboring fields, A and B, desire, at the same time, to plant a sapling and a vineyard, respectively, on the adjacent ends of their common boundary. Concurrent operation of their intended enterprises obviously imposes a reciprocal harm, for A would be exposed to B's plow intrusion and B would be exposed to A's plow intrusion. The reciprocal harm inherent in this intended spatial arrangement is, however, not symmetrical. While plow intrusion represents the only harm the vineyard poses to the sapling, the sapling generates this harm to the vineyard, and, in addition, exposes it to damage from foraging birds. The latter injury follows from the presumed attractiveness birds would find in flying down from their perch atop the sapling to the vineyard below, inflicting damage in the process. Given this asymmetry, the distancing requirement is disproportionately imposed on the sapling-owner (A). Disputing the view of R. Joseph Ibn MiGash (1077–1141), Nachmanides (1194–1270) rules that the disproportionality principle applies even in the instance where the vineyard field (B's enterprise) is best suited to growing something else. Relieving A of any additional distancing requirement on account of B's misallocative use of his land, as R. Joseph Ibn MiGash would have it, effectively allows A to dictate to B "either employ your field in its highest market use or suffer damage from my enterprise."[62] Here, again, the combined output levels obtainable under alternative arrangements of distributing the distancing requirement between A and B is halakhically irrelevant in judging the merits of a reciprocal externality case.

Notwithstanding the general halakhic nonrelevance of economic-efficiency considerations in deciding reciprocal externality cases, R. Asher b. Jechiel (1250–1327) explicitly relied upon this criterion in deciding the cistern-cellar case. In this instance, the accumulated water in A's drainage ditch seeped into B's property, putrifying his cellar and courtyard. R. Asher ordered A to desist from operating his drainage ditch. Though A's action, the construction of the drainage ditch, can in no way be regarded as a *gi'ri de'lei* action, prevention of the greater harm clearly calls for A to discontinue his enterprise. Here, it is impossible for B to put himself out of reach of damage without abandoning his home. In contrast, requiring A to discontinue his enterprise would not inflict upon him a severe harm, as maintaining a drainage ditch on his property is not a vital need.[63]

It should be noted that the restraining-order technique merely establishes an *initial* arrangement of rights between the litigants. Nothing precludes the disputants from altering this initial arrange-

ment of rights through the process of bargaining. Economic rationality would impel the injuring party to offer the plaintiff a payment to
allow him to continue his enterprise. His payment would extend up
to the point where the marginal cost of continuing his enterprise
would be equal to his anticipated marginal revenue. The plaintiff
would rationally accept the payment as long as it would at least cover
his anticipated loss.

Though the restraining-order technique does not preclude the
attainment of an efficient bargain, the plaintiff would be within his
rights to reject an effluent-charge proposal by the defendant. Jewish
law clearly prohibits an individual from damaging his neighbor's
property even if he promises to compensate the victim for losses
sustained.[64] What follows is that unless voluntarily negotiated, the
plaintiff may insist that the court impose a restraining order on the
defendant's activity.

The Halakhic and Economic Approaches to
Large-Numbers Negative Externalities

Convergence between the halakhic and economic approaches to the
problem of large-numbers negative externalities is readily apparent in
all cases where Jewish law recognizes the indemnity right. Here, the
community is forced to consider the opportunity cost it would incur
should it decide to enjoin the harmful enterprise. Economic rationality demands that the community carefully weigh the losses it would
incur should it allow the enterprise to continue against the financial
cost of the indemnity. Such a calculus leads to an economically
efficient decision on the part of the community.

Divergence between Halakhah and economics in the large-
numbers case is, however, identifiable in the range of cases where the
negative externality is actionable but the indemnity right is not
recognized. Here, the community is not forced directly to consider
the opportunity cost involved in its decision to enjoin the harmful
enterprise. This noncorrespondence is, as discussed below, from one
standpoint heightened and from another standpoint lessened. Given
the substantial transaction costs associated with eliminating a large-
numbers externality by means of a negotiated arrangement, the
likelihood that a negotiated arrangement would supersede the
restraining order is small. Nonetheless, should the community decide
by majority vote to waive its right to enjoin the harmful activity and
instead enter into an arrangement with the defendant, the ability of a
dissenting minority to veto this arrangement is limited. In the small-
numbers case, as will be recalled, the plaintiff is within his rights to

reject an effluent-charge plan. In contrast, the ability of a minority to veto a majority-approved effluent-charge plan is limited. Let us elaborate on this point with the aid of an illustration. Suppose, at the injunction hearing against a local industrial polluter, it is pointed out that enjoining the harmful enterprise would adversely affect the local economy. Not only would the local jobs provided by the factory be lost, but the resultant drop in income would hurt the community's retail trade. Finally, with the enjoined product no longer produced locally, those interested in the product would have to obtain it elsewhere, at additional expense. Suppose, now, that the residents of the community are thoroughly persuaded by the above arguments and decide that it is not in their best interests to press for the relocation of the factory. Consultation with experts further convinces them that the effluent-charge approach represents the most efficient means of allowing the enterprise to continue and at the same time forcing its owners to internalize the damage the enterprise inflicts on the community. Insofar as the effluent-charge approach licenses the defendant to inflict damage, if he so chooses, and first face penalties after the damage is already done, can a minority reject this procedure and insist that the enterprise be enjoined? Assuming that the community maximizes its income within the effluent-charge approach, minority insistence that the negative externality be dealt with by means of the restraining-order technique imposes a financial burden on the community. It thus seems clear that majority rule should determine how the negative externality is to be dealt with.

The aforementioned thesis is bolstered by the following ruling of R. Moses Isserles (1525–1572). Reviewing the indemnity procedure prescribed by talmudic law in negative externality cases, R.Moses Isserles derives the principle that should it be necessary for individuals to sustain a loss in order to prevent the community from incurring harm, the individuals must suffer their loss and only then may they exert an indemnity claim on the community. Hence, should a duke threaten his Jewish subjects with expulsion unless their co-religionists, living in the countryside under another potentate, agree to come under his dominion, the countryside Jews must uproot their homes and comply with the duke's directive. Should they demand satisfaction of their indemnity claim as a prior condition to their acceptance of the directive, their petition is rejected.[65] Emergent in R. Isserles' ruling is the principle that the individual's responsibility to sustain an indemnifiable loss in order to prevent the community from suffering harm extends even to the circumstance where the source of the communal harm is entirely outside his present or past initiatives.

An effluent-charge scheme that compromises the health standards of the community does, however, encounter a variety of halakhic problems. An indication of the complexities involved follows. Suppose the community incorporates in its effluent-charge scheme a schedule of fines to be levied on those responsible for generating levels of pollution that increase the incidence of curable respiratory diseases. Mechanically, victims of pollution-related respiratory diseases would be entitled to recoup associated medical expenses and losses in earnings sustained during their period of convalescence.

Attaching fines to health-threatening pollution levels, instead of prohibiting such levels outright, amounts to a health-defying scheme analogous to the self-infliction of a wound (*chovel be'atzmo*). The self-infliction of a wound is prohibited[66] even when the wound is inflicted for a purpose.[67] Nonetheless, the Talmud (*Baba Kamma* 9lb) relates that whenever R. Chisda (ca. 217–309) had to walk between thorns and thistles, he used to protect his garment by picking it up. Acting in this manner exposed R. Chisda to bodily injury from pricking thorns. He defended his conduct by observing that whereas nature would heal his injury, the garment once torn would become useless. Citing this passage, R. Zvi Beer (late 19th cent.) posits that the interdict against the self-infliction of a wound does not apply when it is done for the purpose of avoiding monetary loss.[68] Analogous to the R. Chisda incident is the case at hand. Prohibiting outright pollution levels that would tend to increase the incidence of curable respiratory diseases generates a financial loss to the community in the form of higher prices, increased unemployment, and reduced business profits. Given this opportunity cost, the effluent-charge scheme would be permissible despite its health-defying character.

A further halakhic complication for the effluent-charge scheme occurs when the plan does not enjoy unanimous communal approval. May a dissenting minority object to this scheme and insist that the community prohibit outright any level of pollution that would create a health problem of any sort? Given this opposition, the majority-approved effluent scheme may be invalid as it contracts out of Torah law by permitting polluters to inflict disease, an action Halakhah prohibits.[69] But perhaps primacy should be given to the consideration that acceding to the minority demands here imposes a financial loss on the community? Under the assumption that the majority decision may not be blocked by a minority, what indemnity rights do the dissenting minority enjoy? Does the community's responsibility to them extend no further than the compensation arrangement it provides for other victims of pollution-related diseases? Or does any member of the dissenting group have a legitimate claim to indemnification for relocation expenses he incurs, necessitated by his refusal to be exposed to the health hazard the majority-approved effluent-charge scheme entails?

Clearly contracting out of the law of the Torah, however, is an effluent-charge scheme that attaches fines to pollution levels that would endanger human life or permanently lower the community's health standards. By not prohibiting such pollution levels outright, such legislation would appear to violate the pentateuchal interdict "Take ye therefore good heed unto yourself . . . " (Deuteronomy 4:15).[70]

Conclusion

Jewish law's treatment of the negative externality case takes into account the reciprocal nature of the problem. In contrast to economic theory, which weighs the economic interests of the parties involved, Jewish law focuses on the conflict between the property right, on the one hand, and the amenity right, on the other.

Dealt with by means of the restraining-order technique, a negative externality is generally not actionable in Jewish law unless both the direct-link and destructive-effect criteria are met.

Preventing the greater economic harm, however, does explicitly enter as Jewish law's criterion in deciding the negative externality case when disallowing the disputed activity would impose a minimal harm to the initiator, while its continuation would generate a major harm to the plaintiff.

Consideration of the compatibility of the disputed activity with social and religious goals also enters as a criterion in adjudicating the negative externality case.

While the amenity right enjoys limited recognition against the nuisance externality in the small-numbers case, it enjoys wider recognition in the large-numbers case.

Modification of the original arrangement of rights by means of bargaining is possible in the vast number of negative externality cases.

· 6
External Benefits

An Economic Approach

The external benefit case represents another area where the unregulated marketplace will not produce an optimal allocation of resources.

External benefits occur when the benefits of an expenditure extend to parties other than the individual that incurred the expense. Education is often cited as a good example of the external benefit phenomenon.

Expenditures on education economically benefit individuals other than the direct recipients of the educational services. First, education ultimately may affect the productivity of persons other than the recipients, and it may affect expenditures on other services made necessary by a lack of education. Through the process of emulation and work association with more educated workers, individuals may improve their communication skills, develop flexibility, and learn reliability and maturity. Beyond raising productivity and bringing greater returns to both the educated and the less-educated co-worker, education may also serve to promote a minimum standard of citizenship, and to preserve and even enlarge the cultural heritage of a community.[1]

Under the assumption that the external benefit element does not enter into the calculus of the economic decision-maker, an economic unit's spending on a particular good or service would extend only to the point where the marginal private benefit would be balanced by the marginal private cost. If the *total* marginal benefit, both private and external, exceeds the marginal cost at this point, the expenditure is extended *below* its socially optimal point.[2]

Correction of the above misallocative effect apparently calls for government subsidization of goods and services involving external benefits. Recipients of the external benefits would be taxed to finance the subsidy, for benefiting from someone else's expenditure gratis amounts to unjust enrichment. Such action promotes the expansion of the external benefit good to its socially optimal level.

Recognition of the reciprocal nature of the external benefit problem necessitates, in our view, qualification of the above approach. Categorizing the capture of an external benefit as unjust enrichment and calling for a compensation rule generates for the benefit recipient an opportunity cost in the form of less income to save or spend elsewhere. Hence, while a compensation rule allows the enterprise generating the external benefit to expand, it *may* be at the expense of reduced saving or reduced output elsewhere. The pattern of resource allocation occasioned by a compensation rule cannot be deemed an improvement unless we are reasonably certain that the benefit recipient would have, in any case, expended his resources to secure the said benefit. Here, the compensation rule merely eliminates the "free rider" problem. Should the said benefit not represent a preferred item for the recipient, requiring him to compensate his benefactor on the basis of the advantage he derives alone has the effect of deflecting his expenditure pattern away from its intended direction. Optimality is attained by the individual in his expenditure pattern when the marginal utility he derives per last dollar spent on the various items in his budget is brought into equality. Forcing an individual to compensate an external benefit he captures without being certain that the said advantage represents a preferred item, lowers the level of satisfaction the benefit recipient could have otherwise attained with his given level of resources.

Insofar as the "free rider" motive is what stands at the basis of the external benefit problem, bargaining between the parties involved cannot be relied upon to eliminate the externality. The imposition of a compensation rule to deal with the external benefit problem is therefore indicated.

This chapter will explore the treatment of external benefits in Jewish law. Conclusions will be drawn regarding the degree to which the halakhic approach to this problem converges with the economic efficiency approach.

External Benefits in Jewish Law

Jewish law's approach to the problem of external benefits can be derived from its legal discussions relating to unjust enrichment and quasi-contract law. We will first delineate the general propositions Jewish law offers relating to these issues and then proceed to discuss a specific talmudic case of direct bearing to the external benefit problem.

Benefit Acceptance Responsibility in the Quasi-Contract Case. In Jewish law, an individual may not be forced to *accept* a benefit he did not expressly contract for. Accordingly, should A enter B's field and plant it without permission, B may demand that the saplings be removed at A's expense. Insofar as B did not explicitly contract for the saplings, credence is given to his protest that he would have preferred to put his field to some other use. B's protest is honored even if orchard cultivation represents the highest market use of his land.[3]

Similarly, A's advance declaration that he has no interest in a proposed benefit and is not prepared to make any payment to acquire it exempts him from any financial obligation should the benefit subsequently be provided for him in an unsolicited fashion.[4]

In the event the said benefit cannot physically be removed from the proprietor's domain without destroying its value, as would be the case when A dyes B's garment, the latter, according to R. Jacob Moses Lorberbaum (1760–1832), cannot escape liability by simply declaring that he would not have spent money to acquire the unsolicited benefit.[5]

R. Abraham I. Karelitz (1878–1953) posits that the compensatory obligation of the benefit recipient here is equal to the minimum sum we are reasonably certain he would have spent to acquire the said benefit. In the absence of this certainty, the court would free the benefit recipient from any financial obligation in the matter on the basis of his sworn denial that he would not have spent any money to acquire the said benefit had it not been provided for him in an unsolicited fashion.[6]

Quasi-Contract Law and the Loss Condition. Securing a benefit from another man's property does not generate compensation responsibility in Jewish law unless the property-owner sustains a *loss* in consequence of the capture of the benefit. A's benefit from B must entail a loss for B. This requirement must be met even if A secures the benefit by means of his own initiative.[7]

For the claim of unjust enrichment to be valid, according to R. Meir Simcha ha-Kohen of Dvinsk (1843–1926), not only must B sustain a loss, but A's benefit must be the cause of it. In the absence of this causative link, the compensation claim is not honored. Illustrating this point of leniency in unjust-enrichment law is the following case: Suppose A flees from his town and the government wrongfully expropriates his home, making it available to B gratis. Though B derives a benefit from A's property, he bears no compensation responsibility to him, as his occupancy is not what caused A's loss.[8] Disputing this view, R. Ephraim Nabon (d. 1735) interprets rishonic[9] opinion to hold B responsible to pay A rent for the period of his occupancy. For the claim of unjust enrichment to be valid, the condition of a causative link need not be satisfied. Whether or not A causes B's loss, benefiting from his loss carries for A compensation responsibility.[10]

Nonetheless, should A's benefit not entail any loss for B, the capture of the benefit is not regarded as unjust enrichment. Illustrating this point is the following case: Suppose A's field is bounded on one side by the public domain and on the other side by B's field. Now, A fences in his property from the public domain. Self-interest in the form of prevention of trespass is what motivates A's project. Completion of the project incidentally secures B's property, too, from trespass emanating from the public domain. B, however, bears no compensation responsibility to A, for the latter undertook his project entirely out of self-interest and his expenditure was not increased at all on account of B.[11]

The Public Tax Levy Case and the Loss Condition. In the public tax levy case, the loss condition, according to R. Meir of Rothenburg (1215–1293), need not be satisfied. Accordingly, A may not escape his share of a public levy by claiming that the effective demand for the project emanating from the rest of the community is sufficient to finance the expenditure. Assimilating the law of unjust enrichment in the private expenditure case with the public levy case effectively legitimizes the "free rider" motive and frustrates the emergence of communal projects entirely. Each member of the community would rely on the initiative of his neighbors to create the communal project. Once it was completed, the nonparticipating member would claim exemption from financial responsibility on the grounds that the sponsors' financial commitments would have taken place in any case and were not increased on his account. Widespread maneuvering of this sort obviously frustrates altogether the emergence of communal projects.[12]

Unjust Enrichment and the Initiating Condition. Making use of an unsolicited benefit gratis is generally not regarded in Jewish law as unjust enrichment. For compensation responsibility to devolve upon the benefit recipient, the benefit must be captured by either his own initiative or the initiative of his livestock.[13] Three important exceptions to this general rule should, however, be noted.

1. When A's benefit entails a *loss* for the property-owner (B), A incurs liability whether or not the initiating condition is met.[14]
2. The initiating condition, according to Tosafot (12th–14th cent. school of French and German talmudic commentators) and R. Asher b. Jechiel (1250–1327), need not be met when the benefit consists of corporal pleasure. Accordingly, should A force B to swallow C's food, B incurs liability for the value of his benefit.[15]
3. The initiating condition, according to many authorities, need not

be satisfied when the benefit consists of tangible property deposited in the domain of the benefit recipient. This circumstance is referred to in the rabbinic literature as the *sh'vach be'en* case.[16]

In the *sh'vach be'en* case, A bases his claim on the presence of his property in B's domain. Making use of A's property gratis consequently amounts to unjust enrichment, notwithstanding the absence of the initiating condition. In contrast, when the benefit consists merely of a marketable service, the compensation claim is entirely based on the circumstances surrounding the *capture* of the benefit. Here, since the benefit was captured neither through the initiative of the benefit recipient nor through the initiative of his livestock, the compensation claim is not honored.[17]

Compensation Responsibility in the Quasi-Contract Case. The compensation obligation proceeding from the quasi-contract is limited to the sum we are reasonably certain the benefit recipient would have incurred to secure the said benefit had it not been provided for him in an unsolicited fashion. To illustrate, suppose the proprietor in the quasi-contracted planter case, alluded to above, opts to retain A's saplings. B's compensation obligation to A here is limited to the sum we are reasonably certain he would pay to have his field planted. This estimate takes into account both the use the field is best suited for as well as the particular circumstances of the proprietor. Should the highest use of the land be orchard cultivation, the planter would, other things being equal, receive the competitive wages of a planter for his work. If the field is, however, best suited for crops, the officious planter is entitled only to either his expenses or the market value of his benefit, whichever sum is smaller.[18] But suppose we are reasonably certain that in the absence of A's planting B would have done the job *himself* rather than hire a professional planter? This certainly would be established, for example, in the event that the proprietor (B) is a sharecropper. Here, B's responsibility, according to R. Abraham b. David of Posquières (1125–1198), is limited to no more than the value of his spared effort.[19]

The Quid Pro Quo Condition. An unsolicited benefit is not regarded in Jewish law as unjust enrichment, according to R. Shabbetai b. Meir (1621–1662), unless the benefactor transmits the gain in a manner that communicates on his part a quid pro quo intent. Hence, should A feed B's animal with C's grain, B incurs no liability to C, the owner of the grain, because C communicates no intent to receive compensation for services rendered.[20]

The Immediacy Condition. Compensation responsibility in the quasi-contract case is required in Jewish law, according to R. Moshe

Feinstein (b. 1895), only when the benefit involved is concrete and *immediate*. Should the external benefit consist merely of an increase in the market value of the benefit recipient's asset, the compensation claim is not recognized. Since the benefit is realized only when the asset is sold, it cannot be categorized as immediate in nature.[21]

The Talmudic Fencing Case

Squarely addressing itself to the external benefit problem is the talmudic fencing case. Here, A's self-motivated fencing activity generates an external benefit to B. The text of the talmudic fencing case follows:

> If a man [A] has fields surrounding those of another [B] on three sides and fences the first, second, and third, the other [B] is not bound [to share the expenses]. R. Yose said, "If he [A or B] takes it upon himself the fourth, the whole cost [his share] devolves upon him [B].[22]

Various interpretations of the above case have been advanced by the talmudic commentaries. Four of these interpretations will be presented here. Each involves applications of the general principles of quasi-contract law discussed above. The accompanying diagram is offered to facilitate the discussion.

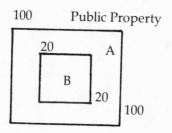

Two explanations of the above case are quoted by R. Solomon b. Isaac (1040–1105). Both understand the fencing activity to refer to the inner fences separating A's fields from B's.

1. Under the assumption that the motivational force behind A's fencing activity is a desire to protect his fields from B's visual trespass, one opinion quoted by R. Solomon b. Isaac understands the fences to be four cubits in height, the minimum height necessary to secure this

advantage. Insofar as private activities are not customarily performed in fields, A's fencing activities are regarded as atypical. Had A petitioned the courts, prior to undertaking his project, to force B to share in the expense of his fences, his claim would have been denied. Credence would be given to B's protest that the project did not offer the prospect of generating any tangible benefit for him since he was not planning to conduct any private activities in his field. Consequently, should A postpone voicing his grievance with B until after he completes his project, the former's claim would *a fortiori* be denied. Liability devolves upon B to share in the expense of the fences only when we are certain that he shares A's atypical predilection for privacy in his field. Such a predilection is communicated when B himself undertakes the construction of the fourth fence.

Another qualifying circumstance occurs when A's field surrounds B's field on only three sides and A fences in B's field on all four sides. Insofar as the fencing in of the nonadjoining side effectively cuts B's field off from the area beyond the nonadjoining side's fence, B's silence while A goes about fencing in the nonadjoining side signals his implicit approval of A's project. B's lack of protest communicates that he shares A's desire to protect his field from visual trespass.

2. Under the assumption that A's fields are not already fenced in from the public domain, another opinion quoted by R. Solomon b. Isaac understands the benefit B realizes when all four inner fences are completed to consist of the prevention of crop damage occasioned by foot trespass. Liability devolves upon B to share in the expense of the fences, according to this view, even when A constructs all four fences. Nonetheless, since protection against crop damage occasioned by trespass is adequately secured with a fence of a height of ten handbreadths, B's responsibility in the matter is limited to half the expense of the first ten handbreadths of the fences.[23]

3. Maimonides' (1135–1204) version of the fencing case deals with a constellation of ruins rather than a spatial pattern of fields. Maimonides' text of the fencing case follows:

> If one [B] has a ruin among the ruins that belong to another [A] and the latter decides to fence it on the first, second, and third sides so that the ruin of the former is fenced in on three sides, the owner of that ruin [B] is not bound to pay any of the expense because the other [A] has not benefited him—his ruin still being open to the public thoroughfare as it was before. But if the other [A] fences in the fourth side so that the ruin [B's] is now surrounded by walls on all four sides, its owner is compelled to bear his share in the cost of all the other walls, and he pays half the expense that the other

[A] has incurred for the four sides up to a height of four cubits, provided that the ground the walls stand on belongs to both. However, if the wall belongs to the one who built it [A], and he built it on his own territory [A's], it seems to me that we impose on the owner of the ruin [B] only a small payment, as the judges see fit, because he cannot use these walls. Thus also if the owner of the ruin [B] fences in the fourth side, he thereby reveals his satisfaction, and he must pay half the expense of the other three sides if the walls belong to both of them. The same rule applies to all similar cases.[24]

Disputing Maimonides' view, R. Abraham b. David of Posquières fails to see why B's liability should be reduced when A builds his walls entirely on his own territory. Quite to the contrary, argues R. Abraham b. David, B's advantage increases significantly when A builds his walls entirely on his own property, as B's area does not diminish in size on account of the space the walls occupy.[25]

Nachmanides (1194–1270), also disputing Maimonides' view, posits that should A build his walls on property belonging partly to B, the latter would escape financial obligation entirely. Credence would be given to B's claim that A's walls impose upon him a detriment in the form of precluding alternative uses of the part of his property the walls occupy. With A's walls conferring on B a net disadvantage, B escapes liability entirely.[26]

Expounding upon Maimonides' joint-territory requirement, the Spanish explicator R. Vidal Yom Tov of Tolosa (14th cent.) suggests that B incurs responsibility to share in the expense of A's walls only when the latter built his walls in a manner that allows him to acquire automatic part title in them at the time they were built. In Jewish law the transfer of property requires a symbolic act *(kinyan)*. One such recognized symbolic act is *kinyan chatzar*. Here, B deposits his property in A's domain and the latter acquires legal title to it by virtue of the fact that the property rests in his domain. Hence, when A builds his walls on territory belonging at least partly to B, the latter acquires automatic part title to A's walls by means of *kinyan chatzar*. In contrast, when A builds his walls on territory belonging entirely to himself, his building activity does not automatically and simultaneously confer B with part title to his walls.[27]

Commentators have found R. Vidal Yom Tov's position very enigmatic. B's benefit of having his ruins secured from trespass is in no way diminished when A builds his walls on territory entirely his own. Why then should the fact that the former does not acquire automatic part title to the walls reduce his assessment in the matter?

Equity appears to demand that in the absence of B's acquiring automatic title to the walls through A's building activities, the court should coerce B to perform the necessary symbolic act to acquire a half-interest in the walls once they are completed.

R. Vidal Yom Tov's point is understood by R. Moshe Feinstein to express the notion that B's responsibility to share in the expense of the walls follows only when A clearly communicates through his actions a quid pro quo intent. Such an intent is clearly communicated by A when he constructs his walls in a manner that automatically confers B with a partnership interest in them. When A, however, builds his walls entirely on his own property, his intent to benefit B in return for compensation is not at all evident. With A's intentions in the latter instance interpreted as purely self-serving, any benefit his walling activity generates to B is incidental to his intent. B, therefore, cannot be made to acquire a half-interest in the wall. Nonetheless, since B derives a certain and undeniable benefit from A's walls, he may not make use of this advantage gratis. Accordingly, he is assessed by the judges to compensate A on a day-to-day basis for the value of his benefit. Absolving B in the matter entirely would be regarded as unjust enrichment on his part since A's walling expense was necessitated entirely by the presence of B's ruin amidst his own ruins.[28]

Noting that the initiating condition, discussed above, is not satisfied in the fencing case, R. Aaron Kotler (1892–1962) explains Maimonides' joint-territory requirement on the basis of the tangible-property principle. Since B's capture of the benefits involved cannot be traced to his own initiative or to the initiative of his livestock, he cannot be made to share in the expense of A's fences unless the latter built them on territory belonging at least partly to him. In the latter instance, the benefit provided consists of tangible property deposited in B's domain, and hence the latter bears responsibility to share in half the expense of the walls, notwithstanding that the initiating condition is not met.[29]

4. In contrast to the opinions discussed thus far, Tosafot and Nachmanides understand A's fencing activities to refer to the outer fences described in our diagram, i.e., to those fences that partition A's fields from the public domain. Though A's motive in undertaking his project is one of self-interest, i.e., to secure his fields from foot trespass, completion of the four fences generates, incidentally, the same benefit to B. Consequently, upon completing the fourth wall, A may exercise a quasi-contract claim on B to share in the expense of all four fences.[30]

Since A built his fences entirely on his own property, B, according to R. Aryeh Loeb b. Joseph ha-Kohen (1745–1813), does not acquire a part title to the walls. A may demolish them at any time without consulting with B. Nonetheless, B's assessment in the matter amounts to the value of his actual benefit.[31]

Requiring B to share in the expense of the outer fences amounts to an apparent rejection of the initiating-condition requirement. Nachmanides' opposition to the above principle does not, however, follow. Completion of the four outer fences generates a *continuous-*benefit stream to B in the form of trespass prevention. With B's *capture* of the trespass-prevention benefit continuous and not confined to the *moment* the outer-fence project is completed, compensation responsibility follows, notwithstanding that the benefit involved does not consist of tangible property deposited in his domain.[32]

B's responsibility to share in the expense of the *outer* four fences is, however, limited to the value the benefit represents to him. This assertion is bolstered by the following considerations:

1. Given that a fence of the height of ten handbreadths is sufficient to secure a field from foot trespass, B bears no responsibility to share in the expense of the fences above this height. Moreover, B shares in the expense of the fences only in the proportion his field stands in relation to the total area of the adjacent fields. To illustrate, suppose the fields together have a combined area of 10,000 cubic feet, while B's inner field has an area of 400 cubic feet. B's area is thus one twenty-fifth of the entire area. Since the outer perimeter is equal to 400 feet, B's share in the expense amounts to one twenty-fifth of the cost of the first ten handbreadths of the outer perimeter.[33]
2. Why A's quasi-contract claim is not honored until he completes all four walls requires explanation. Given that the marginal cost of securing property from foot trespass is reduced as the amount of fencing already in it increases, any amount of outer fencing enhances the value of B's fields. Why then is A's quasi-contract claim denied until he completes the entire outer perimeter? Addressing himself to this question, R. Moshe Feinstein posits that the quasi-contract claim is recognized only when the benefit involved is *immediate* in nature. Consequently, though A's fencing activity enhances the sale value of B's field, credence is given to the latter's claim that he has no present plans to sell his field nor any intention of incurring the marginal cost necessary to secure his field from foot trespass. With A's partially completed project not generating an *immediate* benefit to B, the former's quasi-contract claim is not honored.[34]

3. Commenting on the inner-fencing case, Nachmanides rules that B's share in the expense of the fourth fence determines his share in the expense of the other three fences. Accordingly, if the first three fences were made of stone and the fourth fence was made of sticks, half of the cost of the first ten handbreadths of the stick fence represents B's responsibility in all four fences.[35] This ruling presumably applies to the outer-fencing case as well.

External Benefits in Economic Theory and Jewish Law

For economic theory, the main concern in the external benefit case is the elimination of the "free rider" motive. Reasonable certainty that the external benefit represents for the benefit recipient a preferred item in his expenditure pattern provides sufficient grounds to require him to compensate his benefactor. Generally coincidental with the economic approach, compensation responsibility for the external benefit recipient in Jewish law extends only to the presumed value the benefit generates for him. What proceeds, however, from Jewish law's initiating and loss conditions is a narrower conceptualization of unjust enrichment than the corresponding formula in economic theory. The applicability of these restrictive conditions is not very widespread, since three exceptions were noted in relation to the initiating condition, and the loss condition is dropped in relation to a public levy. From the standpoint of resource allocation efficiency, Jewish law's approach to the external benefit problem converges closely with the economic approach to this issue.

· 7

Value Determination and the Ethics of Business Pricing Policies

Introduction

The central thesis of the free enterprise approach is that the market system is essentially a *self-regulating* mechanism. Competitive forces can be relied upon to drive prices down to their lowest possible level and act as an automatic quality check on the products and services the economic system produces. Left to its own devices the market system will allocate resources much more efficiently than would occur under government regulation, design, or fiat. Minimal intervention by the government in the workings of the free enterprise economy, therefore, will allow society to maximize its social welfare.

Jewish law, as will be demonstrated below, rejects the self-regulating market model as the operational blueprint for the Torah-directed society. The discussion that follows focuses on the regulations Jewish law imposes on the process of value determination and the ethical prescriptions it offers regarding business pricing policies.

Economic Framework for Analyzing Price Regulation in Jewish Law

Modern economic analysis teaches that market price or value is determined by the interaction of *aggregate* supply and demand forces. The role an individual seller plays in determining market price depends entirely on the market structure he finds himself operating in. At one polar extreme stands the market structure of monopoly. Here, the firm and the industry are one and the same. Assuming the seller is a profit-maximizer, he will select the price-output combination that would best promote this goal. The monopolist is, thus, a price-seeker and plays a role in *determining* value.

At the other end of the continuum stands the market structure of perfect competition. Here, a large number of firms offer a homogeneous product for sale under conditions of perfect knowledge, freedom of entry, and resource mobility. The individual firm in this market structure produces an insignificant portion of the total market supply and perceives market price as a datum. Price is determined by the aggregate forces of supply and demand, outside the influence of the individual firm. The firm faces here a horizontal demand curve, meaning that it can sell all it can produce at the prevailing norm and would lose all its patronage to competitors if it chose to sell above market price.

Standing in an intermediate position in this range of market structures is the type of marketplace that typically prevailed in the medieval period. Economists would call it a modified form of monopolistic competition. Here, many sellers offer similar but not identical products for sale under conditions of imperfect knowledge and other bottleneck factors. The product differentiation characteristic of each market signifies that each seller faces a downward-sloping demand curve. Competitive price here would not gravitate toward a single value, as it does under perfect competition, but would rather be described as a range of values. Elasticity of demand would determine, in the final analysis, the extent of this competitive price range.

What follows from the above discussion of value theory is a convenient classification of ethical prescriptions for the marketplace into two separate categories: (1) normative rules designed to influence the *determination* of value itself; and (2) normative rules governing pricing conduct once value has already been established by the impersonal forces of supply and demand.

Subsumed under the first category is the formulation of guidelines for: (1) profit and interest controls; (2) interferences with the aggregate forces of supply and demand; (3) the ethics of profiteering as a result of a *change* in market price; and (4) the latitude the individual seller enjoys in setting a price for his own product in the absence of a competitive norm.

Relevant moral questions subsumed under the second category include: (1) the formulation of a taxonomy of grounds for invalidating or otherwise modifying transactions concluded at prices which diverge from the market norm; (2) the ethics of selling below market price; and (3) the ethics of engaging in price discrimination on the basis of the terms of payment.

Use of our framework will limit our discussion in this chapter to moral issues relating directly or very closely to pricing at either of the two relevant stages. The latitude of individual sellers in setting price (element 4 of the first category) and the ethics of selling below market price (element 2 of the second category) will not be discussed here since separate chapters are devoted to these issues. Ethical problems in market conduct not relating to price will be dealt with in the next chapter.

Normative Rules Relating
to the Determination of Value

The criterion adopted by Jewish law in determining the legitimacy of interfering with the natural process of market determination of value is evidently promotion of social welfare and the preservation of religious practices.

Promotion of social welfare, as discussed below, requires the community to safeguard the economic interests of both producers and consumers. Should the vagaries of supply and demand relegate either of these groups into a position of economic deprivation, remedial intervention should be undertaken.

Profit Regulation in the Necessity Sector
Judaism's concern for the subsistence needs of the masses[1] finds expression in the rabbinical ordinance requiring each Jewish community to enforce a profit-rate limitation of one sixth for vendors dealing in commodities essential to human life (*chayei nefesh*).[2]

Which commodities are to be regarded as essential and hence subject to regulation was disputed among the talmudic codifiers. R. Vidal Yom Tov of Tolosa, 14th-century Spanish expounder of Maimonides' teachings, posited that only foodstuffs are to be regarded as essential to life and hence subject to regulation. Ingredients essential for the *preparation* of food (*machsherei okhel nefesh*) are not subject to profit regulation.[3] A diametrically opposite view was advanced by R. Joseph Caro (1488–1575). Only products not essential even in the preparation of foodstuffs are not subject to regulation. Commodities used in the preparation of foodstuffs are considered foodstuffs and subject to profit control.[4] Finally, a third taxonomy was advanced by R. Joshua b. Alexander ha-Kohen Falk of Lemberg (1555–1614). While vendors of foodstuffs are subject to a one-sixth profit-rate limitation, the allowable profit margin is widened up to 100 percent for sellers of products used in the preparation of foodstuffs. Ingredients not used in the preparation of foodstuffs need not be regulated at all.[5]

Standing at the basis of the rabbinical enactment against profiteering in essential commodities, according to R. Falk, is the biblical injunction, "that thy brother may live with thee" (Leviticus 25:36).[6] The verse apparently intimates that the seller of essential commodities must sacrifice some part of the potential profits he could realize by means of voluntary exchange so as to lessen the deprivation effects the sale price would generate to the buyer.

Extension of the one-sixth profit-rate constraint to both necessities other than food and a basis for rent control appear to follow from R. Falk's comment.

The cost elements that enter into the base against which the allowable profit margin applies include all the explicit expenses the vendor incurs in the process of selling his product. Besides his cost price, these outlays might consist of storage and portage costs.[7] Should the sale of the product require the vendor to provide his labor services on a continuous basis (e.g., a retailer), the cost base, according to R. Menachem b. Solomon (1249–1316) and R. Asher b. Jechiel (1270–1343), expands to include an allowance for his toil and trouble as well.[8] No return for implicit wages appears in the cost base, however, when the sale of the product does not require the vendor to provide his labor services on a continuous basis (e.g., a wholesaler).[9]

Including a return for labor services in the cost base effectively allows the vendor to earn the allowable one-sixth profit rate on both his invested capital and his labor services.

To enforce the one-sixth profit-rate constraint, the Jewish court must appoint commissioners to supervise the pricing policies of the relevant firms.[10] Violators are subject to flagellation[11] and are compelled to sell at the market price.[12] Nonetheless, should the Necessity Sector generally defiantly ignore the profit-constraint rule, the individual seller, willing to submit to the authority of the Jewish court, is not ethically bound to the regulation.[13] Given the insignificant portion of the total market demand the submissive seller serves, directing him to conform with the profit-rate rule generates little impact on consumer welfare. The economic interests of the submissive seller are therefore given primacy by allowing him to follow the general trade practice.[14]

The Economics of Price-Wage Controls. Subjecting industries dealing in necessities to a profit constraint is reminiscent of modern price-wage controls. Such controls are widely regarded by economists as inefficient because they deprive the price mechanism of both its rationing and allocational roles.

In the short run, when production is fixed, price serves the function of rationing the available supply to those who are most eager to buy it. Superseding the market price with a legal price could very well create a disequilibrium between supply and demand forces. Should supply exceed demand at the legal price, producers would be deprived of the opportunity to deplete their inventory by cutting price. More complex is the reverse situation, where demand exceeds supply at the legal price. Here, queuing, the issuance of rationing coupons, or some other bureaucratic device would have to be resorted to in order to allocate the available supply among the demanders.

In the long run, when the assumption of fixity of supply may be relaxed, price signals to producers the desirability of adjusting their output levels. Rising output prices indicate the desirability of expanding output, while declining output prices signal the appropriateness of contracting production. Hence the price mechanism, in the long run, performs the function of allocating resources to their highest market uses. Freezing relative prices within the framework of a dynamic economy, characterized by rising incomes and shifting demand patterns, may well generate a misallocative effect.

The Profit-Rate Constraint: An Efficiency Analysis. Imposing a profit constraint on industries dealing in necessities, as Jewish law prescribes, does not, in all likelihood, subject society to the economic inefficiencies described above. Within the framework of a profit constraint, output prices may vary in response to market forces. Nothing prevents entrepreneurs in the *chayei nefesh* sector from rewarding resource-owners in accordance with their opportunity costs. What the profit constraint amounts to, in our view, is nothing more than a restriction on the amount of "economic rent" suppliers in the regulated sector may earn. This assertion is bolstered by the following considerations:

1. The initial market transaction of the regulated sector, according to R. Simeon b. Samuel of Joinville (12th–13th cent.), is generally not subject to the mandatory one-sixth profit-rate contraint. This point of law emerges from R. Simeon's analysis of the following talmudic passage in *Baba Bathra* 91a:

> Our Rabbis taught: It is not permitted to make a profit in eggs twice. [As to the meaning of "twice"] Mari b. Mari said: Rav [d. 247] and Samuel [d. 254] are in dispute. One says: Two for one [100 percent profit margin], and the other says: [selling] by a dealer to a dealer.

Commenting on the opinion that limits the profit rate in the egg industry to less than 100 percent, Tosafot ask why the egg industry is set apart from other industries dealing in necessities, wherein the profit constraint is one sixth. Addressing himself to this dilemma, R. Simeon posits that the initial market transaction in the regulated sector is usually not subject to any mandatory profit limitation. The egg industry, however, provides an exception to the rule. Egg farmers must limit their markup to less than 100 percent.[15] Given that the price of the initial market transaction of the regulated industry reflects the relative scarcity of the product in its final phase, the cost base of the producers in this sector would adjust to changing market conditions. Hence the pricing mechanism, within the framework of the profit constraint, is not deprived of its allocational role.

2. Venders in the regulated industry are not restrained from selling their wares at the *current* market price, notwithstanding any additional windfall above the one-sixth profit constraint they may realize thereby.[16] Accordingly, suppose a dealer buys wheat at harvest-time at $15 a bushel. Now, three months later, the price of wheat rises to $25 a bushel. The dealer may sell his wheat at the current market price of $25 a bushel, notwithstanding the 50 percent markup he realizes thereby.

3. The one-sixth profit constraint mandated on the Necessity Sector by rabbinical ordinance may be superseded by the community's legislative authority to fix prices. Since price-fixing is not a function mandated on the Jewish community, price-fixing acquires legitimacy only when arrived at by means of the majority-decision rule.

The authority of communal price legislation to supersede the one-sixth profit constraint for the Necessity Sector follows from Maimonides' treatment of this subject matter:

> The residents of a city may agree among themselves to fix a price on any article they desire, even on meat and bread, and to stipulate that they will inflict such-and-such penalty upon him that violates the agreement.[17]

Price-fixing legislation in the Necessity Sector obviously may come into conflict with the one-sixth profit constraint prescribed for this sector. Maimonides' failure to qualify communal legislative authority in this regard clearly indicates that, in his view, communal price-fixing authority is absolute and may, if necessary, supersede the one-sixth profit constraint rabbinically mandated for the Necessity Sector.

The economic rent rationale of the one-sixth profit constraint proceeds from our interpretation of Maimonides' position. It would appear reasonable to assume that when the constraint was originally enacted, the one-sixth figure was seen to strike a delicate balance between the subsistence needs of the masses and the necessary economic incentive to insure an adequate supply of staple commodities. Should the community find, sometime in the future, that the one-sixth profit constraint is not high enough to insure an adequate supply of staples, or conversely, allows producers to enjoy exorbitant profits, it may use its price-fixing powers to correct the situation. Price-fixing represents for the community its means of both improving the efficiency of the marketplace and implementing what it regards as equity in the distribution of income.

The Prohibition Against Interest Payments

Providing an example of a drastic form of intervention in the process of value creation is Jewish law's prohibition against interest payments in loan transactions.

Violation of the pentateuchal interdict against interest,[18] called *ribbit ketzuzah*, obtains when the interest stipulation is made either at the time the debt was created[19] or when the loan fell due as a condition for extending its maturity.[20]

What is interdicted is not only the stipulating and receiving of *ribbit*, but agreeing to pay it as well. Hence, both the creditor and the debtor violate the *ribbit ketzuzah* interdict by making an interest-bearing debt agreement. So stringent is the *ribbit ketzuzah* interdict that all accessories to the illicit loan agreement, including the witnesses, scribe, and guarantor, transgress the prohibition.[21]

The *ribbit* interdict cannot be circumvented under the guise of a reciprocal gift arrangement. Accordingly, A may not, for example, condition his $100 gift to B with the proviso that B, in turn, confer him at some future date a gift in the amount of $120.[22]

Since the *ribbit ketzuzah* payment is regarded as a form of robbery, it is subject to judicial recovery.[23] The lender's responsibility to return the illicit payment is, however, released when the debtor issues a waiver of his recovery right. Nonetheless, an advance declaration by the debtor to treat the *ribbit* payment as a gift transfer does not allow the lender to accept the payment, for it *remains illicit* despite the debtor's declaration.[24]

A written *ribbit* contract which clearly differentiates the principal and interest elements of the debt, though tainted, remains collectable in respect to the principal.[25] With the principal and interest elements of the debt clearly separated, the witnesses presumably reasoned that no harm would proceed from their testimony because the Jewish court would not enforce the *ribbit* element of the contract. The complicity of the witnesses in the *ribbit* crime, hence, does not disqualify their testimony, with the result that the principal remains collectable.[26]

A variant of the above case occurs when the *ribbit* contract does not differentiate the principal and interest elements of the debt, consolidating them into a single amount. Given the possibility that the Jewish court would order collection of the consolidated sum, the complicity of the witnesses in the *ribbit* crime here disqualifies their testimony and renders the contract void.[27] Nonetheless, should it be evident to the court that the witnesses were unaware of the *ribbit* element in the debt instrument, the creditor may rectify the document so that he may use it to collect his principal. Correction of the document requires him to insert a clause in the contract which releases the debtor from obligation to pay the interest charges. Once the consolidated *ribbit* contract has been produced in court, however, it may not be modified by the insertion of a release clause. Here, the legal character of the loan changes from a written to an oral loan agreement. Now, unless the debtor either comes forward and admits his obligation in respect to the principal or witnesses testify that such an admission was made to them, the creditor will have no recourse to even recover his principal.[28]

Rabbinical Extensions of Ribbit Law. By rabbinical enactment, the *ribbit* interdict is considerably expanded and extended. Highlighting the severity of *avak ribbit*, the rabbinical extensions of the *ribbit* interdict, is the restriction placed on the personal relationship between the lender (A) and the debtor (B).

While the debt remains outstanding, A may not derive benefit from B without the latter's express consent, even in respect to benefits he could have expected had he not extended the loan.[29] If A were to derive the benefits without express consent, his conduct would reflect an attitude that B must accommodate him because of his debtor relationship to him.[30] B's express consent allows A to secure the advantage, provided it would be available to him had he not extended the loan.[31] Nonetheless, deriving a benefit from B in a publicly visible manner, according to R. Jacob b. Asher et alia, is objectionable under all circumstances, despite B's express consent.[32] Anticipating A's greeting by greeting him first is objectionable when it was not B's custom to do so before A extended him the loan.[33] Similarly, while the debt is outstanding, the creditor may not request his debtor to do him favors.[34]

Commodity loans payable in kind violate the *avak ribbit* interdict.[35] What is objectionable here is the possibility that the market value of the commodities involved in the loan may increase at the maturity date. Repayment in kind at that time would involve a disguised interest premium.[36]

Reciprocal work agreements involving *different* service obligations for the parties involved are prohibited because the work of one may be more valuable than the work of the other. Prohibited for the same reason are reciprocal work agreements of the same type of work involving time periods when the value of the service is different.[37]

Avak ribbit violations in connection with credit sales, discount sales, leasing, and hiring agreements will be discussed later in this chapter.

Certain forms of partnership agreements are prohibited on the basis of the *avak ribbit* interdict. This point, along with the implications of *ribbit* law for resource allocation efficiency, will be discussed in Chapter 10.

From a legalistic standpoint, *avak ribbit* differs from *ribbit ketzuzah* in several important respects.

Unlike *ribbit ketzuzah*, *avak ribbit* is not subject to retrieval by means of judicial intervention.[38] Nonetheless, the lender has a moral obligation to return the illicit payment.[39] In certain offenses involving *avak ribbit*, however, the creditor is not even saddled with this moral obligation. These instances occur when the debtor either presents the creditor with an unsolicited gift at the time he repays the loan or sends him a gift as an inducement to extend him a loan.[40]

Out of concern for the subsistence needs of orphans, managers of their estates may invest their capital in transactions involving *avak ribbit*.[41] On similar grounds, the *avak ribbit* interdict is suspended for managers of funds devoted to charity, Torah education, and synagogue needs.[42]

Price and Wage Controls and Selling at the Market Norm
Though the Jewish community is not mandated to enforce profit-rate limitations on its industries other than the Necessity Sector, price and wage controls fall within its legitimate legislative authority.[43] Such legislation becomes effective law, according to R. Moses b. Joseph Trani of Safed (1500–1580), by means of a simple majority of those eligible to vote. R. Trani posits that the simple majority rule applies even according to the authorities who require unanimity when the legislative matter at hand would benefit some segments of the community at the expense of others. Price and wage legislation involves the determination of *relative* gains and not the generation of absolute losses and gains.[44] Jewish law thus allows the community's notion of equity in the distribution of income to determine the disposition of gains from productive activity.

In the absence of a *legal* price established by communal legislation, selling at the *market* norm, as discussed earlier, presents no moral issue in Jewish law.

The Prohibition Against Hoarding

Judaism's concern for the subsistence needs of the masses also finds expression in the talmudic ordinance against hoarding.

Prescriptions against hoarding take the form of disallowing market purchases of essential commodities in excess of normal consumption needs. Producers, though, may normally withhold any part of their crop from market sale. Nevertheless, during a period of famine, producers are subject to a quota in regard to the amount of produce they may store. The quota allows the producer to store no more than one year's supply of foodstuffs for himself and his family.[45]

Intervention in the Marketplace to Preserve Religious Practice

Another basis for intervention in Jewish law is the preservation of religious practice. The classical example of intervention of this sort is recorded in the Mishnah, *Keritut* 1:7. Noting the exorbitant price of birds of the type needed for the fulfillment of the sacrificial requirements of women who had given birth, R. Simeon b. Gamliel the Elder (d. 70 C.E.) set out to remedy the situation. Motivated by a grave concern that the exorbitant price of birds would lead to a wholesale neglect of the sacrificial obligation, this Sage boldly changed the law governing the sacrificial requirement of women who had given birth.[46] To this end he proclaimed that a woman who had five definite births need bring only one sacrifice. Formerly, each birth had required a separate sacrifice. The effect of the proclamation was quite dramatic. With the demand for sacrificial birds dropping off markedly, their price gravitated to a reasonable level.

To insure a plentiful supply of essential products in Eretz Israel, the Sages required producers to sell their products directly to consumers.[47] Middlemen were not entitled to a markup unless they worked to process the product they purchased.[48]

With the same objective in mind, the talmudic Sages prohibited the exporting or transferring of essential produce from Eretz Israel. Included in the interdict was the prohibition against exporting from one province to another province within the geographic boundaries of Eretz Israel.[49]

Insofar as the above laws apply only to Eretz Israel and not to Jewish settlements elsewhere,[50] the basis of this intervention was apparently to promote the settlement of Eretz Israel.[51] R. Tamari, in his analysis of the law restricting the markup practices of middlemen, also takes the above position.[52]

The Welfare of the Business Sector

The welfare of the business sector was also a vital concern of the talmudic Sages. Appreciation of the fact that the viability of the community's economic life hinges heavily upon the prosperity of the business sector finds expression in the talmudic dictum that public prayers are offered, even on the Sabbath, when commodity prices drop dangerously low.[53]

In a similar vein, it is reported in *Ta'anit* 20b that it was the custom of R. Huna to send his representative to the marketplace every Friday toward evening to buy up the unsold portion of the perishable vegetables purveyed by the local gardeners. He subsequently would "dump" the excess supply into the river. R. Huna's motivation in subsidizing the gardeners, the Talmud relates, was to insure that they would continue to supply the town with vegetables in the future. Unless they could earn reasonable profits for their efforts, they could not be expected to continue their enterprise.

Invoking the economic incentive argument as a justification for subsidizing the producer leads, in our view, to the proposition that a subsidy of this sort is in order only when its objective is to prevent the producer's earnings from falling below his opportunity cost. Here, in the absence of the subsidy, the producer would turn his efforts elsewhere. Should his current earnings, however, contain elements of economic rent, denying him the subsidy would not generate the above distorting effect, as his present enterprise would still represent his best market alternative.

Normative Rules Governing Pricing Policy Once Value Has Been Determined

Ona'ah (Price Fraud)

The ethics of the price terms of transactions concluded within the framework of a competitive norm are governed in Jewish law by the laws of *ona'ah*. These regulations provide a taxonomy of grounds for invalidating or otherwise modifying transactions concluded at a price that diverges from the prevailing norm.

Though constituting a separate interdict, an *ona'ah* offense is regarded in Jewish law as a violation of property rights and is classified as a form of theft.[54]

Three degrees of *ona'ah* have been identified by the Sages.

First-degree *ona'ah* occurs when the discrepancy between the sale price and the market price is more than one sixth. Here, grounds exist for invalidating the original sale.[55] Nullification rights in the above case, according to Maimonides (1135–1204) and R. Joseph Caro (1488–1575), rest exclusively with the complainant. Should the latter express a desire to uphold the transaction, despite the discrimination involved, the offender must accept this and may not, in turn, invalidate the sale. Selecting this option does not, however, avail the plaintiff of any claim for the restoration of the *ona'ah* involved. The plaintiff may either void the transaction or accept it as it was originally concluded.[56]

Another opinion in the above matter is expressed by the Spanish talmudic explicator, R. Jonah b. Abraham Gerondi (ca. 1200–1263). In his view, as long as the plaintiff does not uphold the transaction, the offender, too, is given the prerogative of voiding it. The offender's rights in this matter proceed from the magnitude of the price discrimination involved. Since the concluded price diverged more than one sixth from the market norm, the offender may insist that the original transaction be treated as an agreement consummated in error (*mikkach ta-ut*). Once the transaction is, however, upheld by the plaintiff, the offender loses his right to void the sale. Denying the offender *full* nullification rights here follows from the fact that the offender enjoys no such rights when his offense consists of the less severe crime of contracting for a sale price involving less than first-degree *ona'ah*. Conferring *full* nullification rights on him when his offense is graver seems counter to all canons of equity.[57]

Second-degree *ona'ah* occurs when the sale price differs from the market price by exactly one sixth. Here, the transaction remains binding. Neither of the parties involved may subsequently void the transaction on account of the price discrimination. The plaintiff, however, is entitled to full restitution of the *ona'ah* involved.[58]

Finally, third-degree *ona'ah* occurs when the sale price differs from the market price by less than one sixth. Here, the transaction not only remains binding, but in addition, the complainant has no legal claim to the price differential.[59]

The laws of *ona'ah* apply only when the price divergence involved falls within the margin of error.

Individuals freely entering into market transactions are presumed, by Jewish law, to have an *approximate* notion of the value of the article involved. Hence, price agreements which diverge enormously from the prevailing norm are not regarded as having occurred as a result of ignorance of market conditions on the part of the participants. Divergent price agreements are, quite to the contrary, interpreted as representing a tacit understanding between buyer and seller to treat the price differential as a voluntary gift transfer. Credence is given to the complainant's *ona'ah* claim only when the discrepancy between the sale price and the prevailing norm falls within the margin of error. Here, the three categories of *ona'ah* become applicable.[60]

It should be noted that when the presumption of imperfect knowledge is made, all victims of *ona'ah* are placed on an equal footing. No distinction is made in Jewish law between the casual market participant and the shrewd dealer. When victims of *ona'ah* are entitled to restitution or nullification rights, these apply even when the complainant turns out to be a shrewd businessman. Business acumen does not generate a legal presumption of awareness of the market norm at the moment the sale was consummated. Conversely, no special consideration or additional rights are conferred on the novice or infrequent market participant when he is victimized by *ona'ah*. [61]

The plaintiff is given a limited amount of time to register his *ona'ah* complaint. When the buyer is defrauded, the lapse of sufficient time to allow him the opportunity to show his purchase to an expert assessor forfeits for him any legal recourse against *ona'ah*. [62] This time span, as the foremost medieval talmudic commentator, R. Solomon b. Isaac (1040–1105), points out, provides the complainant with sufficient time to ascertain whether or not his purchase involved *ona'ah*. Silence beyond this interval is, therefore, taken as an implicit waiver of his legal claims against *ona'ah*. [63]

Silence beyond the legal limit on the part of the buyer is not, however, construed as an implicit waiver when the article is purchased on credit. Here, the buyer may defend his prolonged silence on the ground that he had not yet made payment and thus was not particular to investigate whether the purchase involved *ona'ah*. Nonetheless, once the credit buyer uses his article of purchase, his extended rights against *ona'ah* are no longer recognized. [64]

In contrast, when the seller is defrauded, he may exercise his legal claim against the buyer until time elapses sufficient for him to ascertain the market price of the good he sold. Should the article involved not be generally available in the marketplace, the seller's *ona'ah* claim extends until we are certain he witnessed a market sale of an article of the same type involved in the moot transaction. [65]

Circumstances in Which Ona'ah Does Not Apply
Not all market transactions are subject to the law of *ona'ah*. There are several circumstances under which the laws of *ona'ah* are either suspended or modified.

Contracting Out of the Law of Ona'ah. Transactions calling for either the seller or the buyer to waive his claims against *ona'ah* are legally valid, despite their effect of contracting out of the laws of *ona'ah*. Escape clauses against *ona'ah* claims derive their validity from the general ruling that contracting out of the laws of the Torah in monetary matters binds the parties to the terms of their agreements. [66] Waiving his right in the matter does not forfeit for the injured party his claims against *ona'ah* unless his waiver was offered in full knowledge of the price variance involved in the transaction. When the waiver was, however, offered as a *hypothetical gesture*, the injured party retains his claims against *ona'ah*. This follows from the presumption that a hypothetical waiver is tendered out of a sense of security that no *ona'ah* was involved in the transaction. Had the plaintiff been aware of the price differential, he would not have agreed to the stipulation or made such a gesture himself. Hence, his subsequent claims against *ona'ah* remain intact.[67]

Selling on Trust. When a vendor sells his wares on trust *(nosei be'emunah)*, he is not subsequently liable to *ona'ah* claims.[68] Selling on trust, according to Maimonides, requires the vendor to divulge to his prospective buyer his cost price and his proposed profit margin. Should the buyer agree to these terms and consummate the transaction with a *kinyan*, a subsequent finding that the cost price involved *ona'ah* does not allow the plaintiff to modify the original transaction in any manner. Agreeing to allow the vendor a specified profit margin demonstrates on the part of the buyer a lack of concern with the objective value of the commodity. Since realization of the agreed-upon profit rate required the sale to be concluded at the stipulated price, subsequent claims against *ona'ah* are denied.[69]

Selling on trust disallows subsequent *ona'ah* claims only when it is *discovered later* that the cost price involved *ona'ah*. Should the vendor be aware that his cost price involved *ona'ah*, he is obligated to disclose this information to the prospective buyer. Failure to do so is regarded as deceptive conduct on his part. Hence, in the event it can be established that the vendor was *aware* that his cost price involved *ona'ah*, selling on trust subsequently does not exempt him from *ona'ah* regulation.[70]

Barter Transactions. Barter transactions *(chalifin)* are generally not subject to *ona'ah* regulation.[71]

R. Jechiel Michael Epstein of Belorussia (1829–1908) rationalizes the above exemption by pointing out that money transactions differ in essence from barter transactions. When money is the medium of exchange, the clear intent of the parties to the transaction is to exchange equal objective values. Given this intent, the prevailing norm serves admirably to determine whether or not this objective was realized. Barter transactions, on the other hand, are predicated on the existence of a double coincidence of wants. With neither of the articles involved in the exchange constituting a commonly accepted medium of exchange, the intent of each party is clearly to acquire something of greater subjective value to himself than what he has to offer in exchange. The laws of *ona'ah*, therefore, do not apply to barter exchanges.

Should an appraisal of the articles involved in the barter be made before or immediately after the exchange is effected, the transaction is subject to *ona'ah* regulation. With the exchange involving appraisal, each party signals an intent to exchange his own object for another of equal *objective* value.

Barter transactions involving produce *(peirot)* are always subject to *ona'ah* regulation. Setting apart produce exchanges from other barter transactions follows from a consideration of the legal definition of a barter transaction in Jewish law. For an exchange to be legally classified as a barter transaction, it must allow A to automatically acquire B's object as soon as B acquires possession of A's object by means of executing the symbolic act *(kinyan)* of drawing A's object to himself *(meshikhah)*. When A fails to acquire B's object in this automatic fashion, but instead is also required to perform a *kinyan meshikhah*, the exchange is classified as a sales transaction and not as a barter agreement. A barter exchange involving produce becomes effective by means of this automatic mechanism only when it is accompanied by an appraisal. In the absence of appraisal, barter exchanges involving produce become effective only when both parties involved perform a *kinyan meshikhah*. Given these facts, a barter exchange of produce is always categorized as a *sales* transaction and hence is subject to *ona'ah* regulation.[72]

Selling Through an Agent. When a transaction is contracted through an agent and the agent is victimized by *ona'ah*, the principal is conferred nullification rights even when the amount of *ona'ah* involved is merely third-degree. Nullification rights for the principal here proceed from the fact that the legitimacy of an agreement concluded through an agent derives from the presumption that power of attorney *(shelichut)* was in effect when the transaction was consummated. Given the financial loss an *ona'ah* agreement imposes on the principal, the latter may protest that his agent had no authority to enter into such an agreement on his behalf. Legitimacy is given to this protest as it must be presumed that an agent is commissioned to benefit his principal and not to impair his cause *(letekunai shelechtikh vilo liavtei)*. With abuse of authority on the part of his agent forming the basis of the principal's nullification rights, the latter may exercise this right even when the degree of *ona'ah* transacted on his behalf was merely third-degree.[73]

Householder Exemption. When a householder sells his articles of personal use, he is not liable to *ona'ah* claims.[74] Some authorities extend his immunity even to first-degree *ona'ah* claims,[75] while others limit his exemption to second-degree *ona'ah* claims.[76]

The privileged status of the householder here proceeds from the presumption that anyone dealing with him realizes that he would not dispose of his personal utensils unless he could sell them above market price.[77] The Sages extended their exemption to the householder on an unqualified basis *(lo pelug)*. Hence, even if the householder was known to be pressed for cash at the time he sold his household articles, he qualifies, nonetheless, for the *ona'ah* exemption. Alternatively, selling one's own household articles is regarded as a degradation. Hence, even when pressed for cash, the householder, as a means of saving face, would hold out for more than the market price.[78]

Given the above rationalization of the householder's favored treatment against *ona'ah* claims, R. Asher b. Jechiel (1250–1327) limits the exemption to instances where the buyer was aware that he was transacting with a householder. When the buyer can establish that he was unaware that the seller was a householder, the presumption that the former waives his claims against *ona'ah* is patently invalid.[79]

The above exemption, according to R. Joshua ha-Kohen Falk (1555–1614), is limited to instances where the householder himself conducts the sale of his articles. Should the householder entrust the sale of his articles to a broker, the householder would be liable to *ona'ah* claims. Disposing of his articles through a dealer demonstrates on the part of the householder a despairing attitude regarding his prospects of obtaining more than the market price for them.[80] Disputing this view, R. David b. Samuel ha-Levi (1587–1667) posits that as long as the buyer was aware that he was dealing with the householder's agent, he should presume that the agent was instructed to sell only above market price. Hence, the *ona'ah* exemption of the householder remains intact in this case as well.[81]

Real Estate Transactions. Real estate transactions are not subject to the full scope of *ona'ah* regulations. This exclusion proceeds from exegetical interpretation of the biblical source of *ona'ah*.

> And if thou sell a sale unto thy neighbor or acquirest aught of thy neighbor's hand [Leviticus 25:14]—something that is acquired [by being passed] from hand to hand [is subject to *ona'ah* regulation], thus excluding land, which is not movable.[82]

Insofar as the biblical interdict against *ona'ah* is mentioned explicitly in connection with real estate transactions, the exemption cited above, according to R. Moses b. Nachman (1194–1270), must be taken to refer exclusively to the restitution procedure normally provided for in *ona'ah* cases. Hence, real estate transactions are subject to the prohibition against *ona'ah*, though not to its prescribed restitution procedure.[83]

The extent of the real estate exemption is a matter of dispute. R. Isaac b. Jacob Alfasi of Algeria (1013–1103) and Maimonides view it as unqualified and unlimited. Regardless of the price discrepancy, the *ona'ah* claim of the plaintiff is discarded.[84] Ruling in accordance with this school of thought is R. Shabbetai b. Meir ha-Kohen (1621–1662).[85]

Representing a more restrictive view of the real estate exemption is R. Jacob Tam of Ramerupt (ca. 1100–1171). R. Asher b. Jechiel and R. Jacob b. Asher interpret his view as extending the exemption up to the point where the discrepancy between the transaction price and the prevailing norm is less than 100 percent. When the divergence reaches 100 percent, the plaintiff is conferred with nullification rights.[86] R. Shabbetai b. Meir ha-Kohen, however, understands R. Tam to invoke nullification rights only when the discrepancy is in excess of 100 percent.[87]

Articles Legally Assimilated to Real Estate. Articles legally assimilated to real estate are also free from *ona'ah* regulation. Hence, slave transactions are not subject to the laws of *ona'ah*.[88] Since Jewish law regards a worker in a sense "sold" to his employer for the duration of his contract, the labor market in general is not subject to *ona'ah* regulation. Hence, wage agreements departing from the prevailing norm are not subject to modification on account of *ona'ah*.[89]

Maimonides et alia, however, limit the above exemption to the wage agreement of a day-laborer *(poel)*. The wage contract of a piece-worker *(kabbelan)* does fall within the scope of *ona'ah* regulation.[90] With the *poel ona'ah* exemption rooted in the assimilation of labor contracts with real estate, the limitations attached to the real estate *ona'ah* exemption, discussed above, presumably apply with equal force to wage agreements as well.

Exemption of Financial Assets. Financial assets are not subject to *ona'ah* regulation. This exemption follows from exegetical interpretation of the term "sale" that appears in reference to the biblical source of the *ona'ah* prohibition cited above. The term "sale" is taken to imply that which is intrinsically sold and intrinsically bought, excluding financial assets which are not intrinsically sold or bought and exist only as evidence.[91]

The Basis of the Ona'ah Claim

The basis of the *ona'ah* claim requires explanation. Given both the assumption of rationality and the voluntary nature of the agreement, would the complainant have freely entered into the original transaction unless he felt certain he was receiving in exchange equivalent *subjective* value? What then is the basis of his subsequent *ona'ah* claim? Strategic to the resolution of the above dilemma is the legal presumption of what the buyer and seller intend to accomplish with their transaction. Under the supposition that the basic intent of the parties to a transaction is to exchange value of *equal objective* or market worth, the legitimacy of the *ona'ah* claim is readily apparent. Given the above presumption of intent, any discrepancy between the transaction price and the market norm signifies that the original objective was not realized. Had the plaintiff been aware of the full range of market alternatives available to him at the time he consummated his *ona'ah* transaction, he would have either withdrawn from the transaction altogether or insisted upon a modification of the price terms of the agreement. The plaintiff clearly incurred an opportunity cost as a result of his *ona'ah* transaction.

The opportunity-cost basis of the *ona'ah* claim finds explicit expression in R. Jechiel Michael Epstein's analysis of the barter exemption, discussed above.

Further support of the above thesis is found in R. Asher b. Jechiel's analysis of third-degree *ona'ah*.

Noting the absence of any provision for legal redress in third-degree *ona'ah* cases, R. Asher speculates whether it might be permissible, in the first instance, to contract into third-degree *ona'ah*. Pivotal to the resolution of this question, in R. Asher's view, is the definition of market price. Is market price to be understood as a single value, or is it to be defined as the range of deviations of less than one sixth from the price of this moot transaction? Adopting the former view leads to the conclusion that knowledge of the market norm prohibits either party from contracting into a price agreement that diverges even slightly from it. The absence of legal redress for third-degree *ona'ah* would then be explained by the presumption that when the degree of *ona'ah* involved is of such a relatively small amount, the plaintiff waives his claim to restitution. The presumption follows from our inability to fix the value of the article sold. While some experts would insist that *ona'ah* took place, others would just as vehemently deny it. With the experts divided as to whether *ona'ah* occurred, and if it did by how much, we may safely presume that the victim of this possible price discrimination waives his right to restitution.[92]

Adopting the latter view, however, leads to the conclusion that third-degree *ona'ah* is not price fraud at all. Denying legal restitution here follows from the fact that the concluded price, though at variance with the prevailing norm, falls, nevertheless, within the legal price range. Why price should be defined as a range of values rather than by a single value is defended by R. Asher on the grounds that even when buyer and seller are fully aware of the prevailing norm, each would, to his own disadvantage, occasionally contract into a price agreement at variance with this norm. The vendor, for instance, would offer to sell his wares below the prevailing market price when his merchandise represents to him unwanted inventory, or when he has an urgent need to raise cash. Similarly, the buyer, finding a product to his keen liking, would, on occasion, offer to pay for it a price above the market norm. Given these facts, market price should not be defined as a single value, but rather as a range of deviations around this value.

Though offering no definitive resolution of the above dilemma, R. Asher urged the following guideline for third-degree *ona'ah* cases: Cognizant of the prevailing norm, an individual should not contract into a price agreement that departs even slightly from this value. Should an individual fall victim to third-degree *ona'ah*, on the other hand, he should accept his loss graciously and express no complaint.[93]

Implicit in R. Asher's analysis of third-degree *ona'ah* is the realization that the competitive norm in a heterogeneous product market does not gravitate toward a single value. With each seller facing a downward-sloping demand curve, the competitive norm can only be described as a *range* of prices. This insight provides R. Asher with his first approach in explaining the absence of legal redress in third-degree *ona'ah* cases. With a similar but by no means identical product available in the marketplace for a price less than one sixth of the moot transaction, we may safely presume that the plaintiff waives his legal claims against the offender. Quality differences and other features that differentiate the products being compared make it debatable whether the moot transaction represents in reality an inferior value. What follows as a corollary is that the basis of the *ona'ah* claim, when the price differential involved is one sixth or more, is the certainty that the complainant incurred an opportunity cost as a result of his transaction. Here, division among experts as to whether the moot transaction represented an inferior value would not occur. Consequently, the *ona'ah* claim is honored.

Jewish law apparently adopts R. Asher's first approach to third-degree *ona'ah*, as evidenced by the prohibition against contracting, in the first instance, into third-degree *ona'ah*.[94] What follows by logical extension is the opportunity-cost basis of the *ona'ah* claim.

Viewing the *ona'ah* claim as an opportunity-cost claim leads directly to the proposition that when the product market involved is homogeneous in nature, the complainant is entitled to restitution of the price differential even when the degree of *ona'ah* is only third-degree.

Extrapolating from R. Asher's discussion of third-degree *ona'ah*, R. Jechiel Michael Epstein reached the same conclusion.[95]

Another proposition proceeding from the opportunity-cost hypothesis is that the *ona'ah* claim should be honored even when the per unit price of the product involved is not well defined. An example of such a situation is provided by R. Moses Isserles' (1525–1572) analysis of *ona'ah* claims in the wool and milk markets. Here, it was apparently the custom of vendors to charge their customers different prices in accordance with the size of their purchases. Nonetheless, the per unit price *range* could be determined in each of these markets. With the per unit price range determinable, the legitimacy of the *ona'ah* claim, according to R. Moses Isserles, could be evaluated.[96]

Proceeding as a corollary from the opportunity-cost hypothesis is the notion that the complainant's plea is honored only when we may reasonably presume that he was ignorant of the alternative market opportunities open to him at the time he entered into the *ona'ah* transaction.

Though the *ona'ah* claim is rooted in the presumption of imperfect knowledge on the part of the complainant, certainty that he was aware of the market norm at the time he entered into the *ona'ah* transaction does not *automatically* invalidate his subsequent *ona'ah* claim. This is evidenced from the ruling of R. Eliezer b. Joel ha-Levi,[97] on the interpretation of R. Jacob Lorberbaum (1760–1832) et alia, that a victim of second-degree *ona'ah* retains restitution rights against the offender even when it can be established that he was aware of the market norm at the time the sale was finalized. Here, far from constituting an implicit waiver of his rights, the plaintiff's failure to register any complaint when he negotiated the sale could very well manifest on his part an artful design against the offender. Viewing his options, the complainant could indeed have concluded that his optimum stratagem required him to *delay* his protest until after the sale was finalized. Demanding that the transaction be concluded at the market norm might provoke the offender to break off negotiations altogether. Bargaining with him, on the other hand, to reduce the price differential might prove successful, but would at the same time reduce the degree of *ona'ah* involved from second to third degree. With no restitution rights provided for the plaintiff in third-degree *ona'ah* cases, pursuit of this course of action would effectively disallow him to recover the differential. His most attractive course, therefore, would be to allow the sale to be concluded with second-degree *ona'ah*. Once it was finalized, he would then assert his restitution rights.

A variation of the above case occurs when the concluded sale involves first-degree *ona'ah*. In this instance, certainty that the plaintiff was aware of the prevailing norm at the time he entered into the sale invalidates his subsequent claims against the offender. Insofar as first-degree *ona'ah* cases do not generate restitution rights for the complainant, his silence at the time he entered into the sale cannot be construed as a ploy to recover the price differential involved. The plaintiff's failure to protest is, therefore, taken as an implicit waiver of his claims against *ona'ah*. [98]

Subjective Value and the Ona'ah Claim

Nascent in R. Asher's analysis of his second approach to third-degree *ona'ah* is an anticipation of the modern economic concept of consumer surplus. This notion is concerned with the relationship between market price and subjective value. Market price is determined by the interplay of *aggregate* supply and demand forces, but the *subjective* esteem an individual demander attaches to the said product may or may not coincide with this norm. When the consumer's subjective evaluation of the product falls below this norm, he obviously rejects the product. When his subjective evaluation of the product either coincides with or exceeds the market price, the consumer will buy the product. In the latter instance, he will enjoy a windfall as well. The difference between the maximum price the consumer would willingly pay to obtain the product, rather than do without it, and the actual transaction price provides a measure of this windfall or consumer surplus. Does a given market price generate at least some amount of consumer surplus to the great majority of those patronizing the product at that price? Economic theory answers in the affirmative. The prevailing norm represents the market's evaluation of the *last* unit of the product demanded. Given the assumption of diminishing marginal utility, this evaluation will afford consumer surplus to the great majority of the actual patrons of the product.

With the market price of the commodity affording some consumer surplus to a vast number of its patrons, the legitimacy of presuming that the vendee realized subjective equivalence in his transaction when the degree of *ona'ah* involved was less than one sixth becomes evident.

Symmetrically, the prevailing norm may or may not allow the individual producer to recover his costs. Since market price under competitive conditions gravitates toward the marginal cost of producing the last unit demanded, the prevailing norm will allow the more efficient producers in the industry to more than recover their costs. This fact gives credence to the presumption that the producer would, at times, sell unwanted inventory below market price in order to recover his outlays *faster* than his normal selling activities would permit him to do. Hence, the vendor's *ona'ah* claim is denied when the price differential involved is less than one sixth.

Subjective value, according to the Spanish decisor R. Yom Tov Ishbili (1270–1342), plays a role in assessing first-and second-degree *ona'ah* claims. This is evidenced from his ruling that the plaintiff's subsequent *ona'ah* claim would be denied should he declare at the time he entered into the *ona'ah* transaction that the article was worth to him the entire sum the seller demands.[99]

Price Discrimination Based on the Terms of Payment

Credit Sales. Charging above market price for a credit purchase represents a form of price discrimination prohibited by Jewish law. Insofar as the price differential involved reflects a compensation the seller realizes for accepting a delay in payment due him, the transaction violates *avak ribbit* law.[100]

The above prohibition was relaxed somewhat by the early talmudic codifiers when the competitive norm for the subject article is not clearly defined. Here, the seller may engage in modest price discrimination as long as he does not explicitly tell the buyer of his policy of charging more for credit purchases than when payment is immediately made. With the degree of price discrimination small, the premium the seller realizes for credit purchases could be easily attributed to factors other than a desire on his part to be compensated for the delay in payment. The nature of the seller's pricing policy becomes obvious, however, when he charges a significant premium for credit purchases. The latter practice is therefore prohibited, notwithstanding the absence of a clearly defined norm for the article involved.[101]

Technological advances in transportation and communications have considerably widened the marketplace today. Hardly any price, as a result, is free from the possibility of sudden change on account of the vicissitudes of aggregate supply and demand factors. Noting this phenomenon, Dayan Basri posits that all prices today, with the exception of those under government control, are inherently unstable and should be regarded at any moment in time as not being well defined.[102]

Charging a premium for credit purchases is prohibited, according to R. Mordechai b. Hillel ha-Kohen, under certain conditions even when the credit transaction was concluded at the current market norm. This occurs when the vendor initiates an offer to sell his product *below* the current market norm for an immediate payment. Once such an offer is made, the parties may not proceed to conclude the transaction on credit terms at the current market norm. Nevertheless, in the event the buyer accepted the seller's original offer and the transaction became legally binding on both parties, the parties may alter the terms of the sale from cash to credit at the current market norm.[103]

Discount Sales. Discount sales which call for payment for the merchandise before its delivery violate *avak ribbit* law.[104] Since, by rabbinical enactment, *kesef* (money) does not effect transfer for movable property, payment does not confer the buyer (B) with legal title to the merchandise. B's payment is therefore essentially a loan extended to the seller (A), which is paid back on the delivery date with merchandise having a higher market value than B's transfer.[105]

The prepayment-discount scheme is, however, legitimized when the article of transfer is not a standardized product.[106] An appearance of *ribbit* is not evident here as A may theoretically opt to deliver an article commensurate in value to B's payment on the agreed-upon date.[107] To be sure, legitimacy is not given to the above business practice unless two additional conditions are met: the discount must be small,[108] and in addition, A may not expressly tell B that the discount is accorded on account of the prepayment feature of their deal.[109]

With the appearance of *ribbit* remaining intact in the standardized-product case, legitimacy is not given to the discount-prepayment scheme until yet a third condition is met. In addition to the small discount and the non-express linkage conditions, mentioned above, equivalent merchandise must be in A's possession at the time of the sale. Satisfaction of this condition is met even if the merchandise is not readily accessible to A at the time of the sale.[110]

Why satisfaction of the third condition helps remove the *ribbit* interdict in the standardized-product case is explained by R. Isaac b. Sheshet Perfet (1326–1408) as stemming from the fact that *kesef* effects transfer of movables by dint of pentateuchal law. Since A has equivalent merchandise in his possession at the time of the sale, B's payment effects for him legal title to the extent that his transfer is not regarded as a loan to A.[111]

Illustrating a discount-prepayment scheme of the nonpermissible type, according to R. Jacob Blau (contemporary), is the publisher's practice of selling magazine subscriptions on the basis of an advertisement offering a discount from the cover price if a certain number of issues are paid for in advance. Expressly linking the discount to advance payment apparently violates *avak ribbit* law. Moreover, since future issues are nonexistent at the time the discount contract is entered into, the *discount itself* is objectionable because magazine subscriptions are akin to the standardized-product case. Linking the discount offer to the *commitment* to purchase the magazine, rather than to the *advance* payment for the future issues, removes, according to R. Blau, the *avak ribbit* interdict.[112]

R. Blau's suggested change in the wording of the advertisement for magazine subscriptions would be more in line with the main motivational purpose of the discount offer. What the discount offer represents is not an inducement to make advance use of future sales revenues, but rather a ploy to increase advertising revenue. The advertisers' interest in the magazine relates very much to its circulation figures. With the discount offer aimed at increasing circulation, its ultimate purpose is to increase advertising revenues and hence the profit of the publisher.

Price Discrimination in Leasing Agreements. The renter of real estate may engage in explicit price discrimination in the form of charging a higher rental when payment is made at the expiration date of the lease than when it is made at the beginning of the leasing period. Since rent is legally due only at the expiration date of the lease, the true rental value of the property is determined by the rent attached to it when payment is made at the termination of the leasing period. The lower rental charged when the rent is paid at the beginning of the leasing period amounts to nothing more than a discount extended to the lessee for early payment of his rent.[113]

Nonetheless, once a beginning-period leasing arrangement is consummated by means of *kinyan*, it may not be changed to terms calling for a higher rental to be paid at the end of the leasing period.[114]

Price Discrimination in Labor Agreements. Wage agreements may stipulate a dual wage rate for the worker, calling for a relatively higher wage rate if the payment is made at the end of the wage period than if it is made at some earlier time. Since wages are not legally due until the end of the wage period, the *term-date* wage rate determines the true value of the worker's labor services for the relevant period. The lower wage rate called for if the worker is paid before the end of the wage period, therefore, amounts to nothing more than a discount offer accorded the employer for paying wages before they are due.[115]

Legitimacy is given to the dual-wage scheme, according to R. Solomon Adret (1235–1319), only when the plan does not call for the worker to receive his wages before he begins his assigned work. This follows from the fact that labor contracts, entered into by means of verbal consent alone, do not become legally consummated until the worker begins his assigned work. Wage payments made before the worker actually begins the stipulated work, therefore, take on the appearance of a loan, with repayment in the form of labor services rendered. If the labor services rendered are valued at a higher price than the wage advance, the labor contract violates the *avak ribbit* interdict.[116]

Proceeding from the legal principle that wages are due at the end of the wage period is the interdict against labor agreements calling for the worker to receive a premium in wages in the event the employer is delinquent in paying him on time. Since wages are due on the last day of the wage period, the premium offered in the event of delinquency amounts to an *avak ribbit* payment to the worker for tolerating the delay in receiving his wages.[117]

A mutually arrived at agreement between a worker and an employer calling for a premium wage in the event of delinquency in payment violates *avak ribbit* law even if the agreement was not made at the outset of the labor contract. Accordingly, should the worker, upon demanding his wage at the end of the wage period, acquiesce to the employer's offer to pay him a premium wage at some later time, the agreement violates *avak ribbit* law. Since an employer's holding wages in arrears violates the wage-delay interdict (*halanat sakhar*),[118] the worker's acquiescence to the delay in payment amounts to an agreement on his part to treat the balance due him as a loan. The higher wage called for at the later date, therefore, amounts to a premium for tolerating *delay* in payment and consequently violates *avak ribbit* law.[119]

A variant of the above case occurs when the employer is in default of the wages due the worker, and the worker, in consequence, exerts an opportunity-cost claim for the income he could have realized from the wages had he been paid on time. The legitimacy of the worker's claim here is disputed among talmudic decisors. While R. Eliezer of Toul (d. before 1234) et alia validated the compensation claim,[120] R. Isaac b. Moses of Vienna (late 13th cent.) et alia regarded the payment as constituting *avak ribbit*.[121]

Supporting R. Eliezer's view, R. Joel Sirkes (1561–1640) offers the following rationale of why meeting the worker's compensation demand does not violate *avak ribbit* law: Since the wages are held in arrears against the worker's wishes, the worker cannot be said to have allowed the balance due him to take on the character of a loan for the duration of the delinquency period. With the loan character absent here, the extra payment the worker seeks can in no way be characterized as a premium for tolerating delay in the payment of his wages.[122]

Noting the indirect link between the worker's opportunity-cost loss and the action of the employer, R. Judah Rosanes (1657–1727) posits that while meeting the worker's compensation demand does not violate *avak ribbit* law, the employer is under no legal obligation to honor the demand. Responsibility for meeting the worker's extra compensation demand proceeds as a definite matter only when the employer invested at a profit the wages due the worker and the worker expressed an investment intent at the time he demanded his wages.[123]

In the context of the current inflationary spiral, holding wages in arrears generates for the worker not only an opportunity cost but a definite loss in the form of reduced purchasing power. Noting this phenomenon, R. Nachum Rakover posits that imposing a penalty on the employer for delinquency in payment of wages is entirely appropriate.[124] In a similar vein, R. Jacob Blau (contemporary) concludes from his survey of Rabbinic literature that the majority view would find no objection to the employer accommodating the worker for holding his wages in arrears.[125]

· 8
Regulation of Market Conduct

Introduction

Within the framework of the free enterprise approach, the competitive process is relied upon not only to drive prices down to their lowest possible level, but to act as an automatic check against fraud and unethical conduct on the part of the market participants. Since the preference of the marketplace is for integrity and for quality products and services, market participants failing to meet these standards will in the long run be ferreted out.

The growing complexity of the products of the modern industrial economy has not dampened the faith of many proponents of free enterprise in the efficiency of the marketplace as a self-regulating mechanism against fraud. While individuals may not be capable of judging the quality of complex products, specialists capable of such assessment, to be sure, exist. The success of these specialists, such as department stores and other middlemen, hinges heavily upon the reputation of reliability they build up among their customers.

Decidedly opposed to the free enterprise attitude is the current consumerism movement. This movement has all but transformed the operational philosophy of the marketplace from one of caveat emptor ("let the buyer beware") to one of seller responsibility and accountability. Legislative acts and judicial rulings have imposed higher standards on the seller in the areas of disclosure, product safety, warranties, and truth in packaging and advertising. In addition, judicial rulings have voided business contracts on the grounds of unconscionability and unequal bargaining power between the parties involved.

The attitude of Jewish law toward the issue of consumer protection, as will be demonstrated below, is very much consonant with the current consumerism movement. Ethical prescriptions regulating consumer conduct, as will be seen, also find expression in Jewish law. After these issues are investigated, we will turn to the ethics of competitive tactics not specifically relating to pricing policy or contract law. Market conduct prescriptions relating to the seller-buyer relationship dealt with in this chapter include: (1) regulation of weights and measures; (2) disclosure obligations of the seller; (3) market conduct causing mental anguish; (4) ill-suited advice; and (5) undeserved good will.

Competitive tactics examined include: (1) the ethics of snatching away another's anticipated gain; and (2) the ethics of disparaging a competitor's product.

Regulation of Weights
and Measures

Specifications regarding the design of commercial weights and measures are prescribed in Jewish law.[1] Illustrating the weights and measures code are the detailed rules governing the construction of scales used to weigh heavy metals. In talmudic times, these scales were typically suspended from a ceiling. To allow the beam of the apparatus sufficient space to move without knocking against the ceiling and impeding the movement of the scales, the hollow handle in which the tongue of the balance rests must be removed three handbreadths from the ceiling. Similarly, the scales must be positioned three handbreadths above ground level to prevent them from knocking against the ground. The beam's length must be four handbreadths, and that of the two ropes four handbreadths each. If the length of these parts were less, the scales would move only with difficulty and small variations in weight would, hence, not be detected.

Specifications for the design of other scales varied according to the weight of the articles for which they were used.[2]

To avoid confusion and error, fine gradations between commercial weights and measures are prohibited. In the dry measure category, this rule translated in talmudic times into the prohibition of the use of the two-*kab* measure as it could easily be confused with the quarter-*se'ah* measure, which was equal to one and one-half *kab*.[3]

The vendor is admonished to use his weights and measures in an honest fashion. Keeping his weights in salt, for instance, is prohibited,[4] as salt reduces the weight.[5] Similarly, the vendor may not fill a liquid measure in a manner that creates foam,[6] as the buyer receives thereby less than a full measure of liquid.[7]

To maintain their accuracy, weights and measures must be cleaned periodically. The required frequency of the cleaning varies with the intensity of use of the weights and measures.[8]

Out of fear that defective weights and measures would be used and cause false weighing and measuring,[9] the *mere possession* of faulty weights and measures is prohibited, even if held outside the marketplace.[10] The defective weight or measure may, however, be kept for noncommercial use when the official certification seal which is required for commercial use is not affixed on it. Here, there is no concern that the faulty weight or measure will be used for commercial purposes and cause false weighing and measuring.[11]

To enforce the regulations regarding the manufacture and use of weights and measures, market inspectors are to be appointed by the Jewish court.[12] Violators may be subject to flagellation and fines, at the court's discretion.[13]

The Seller's Disclosure Obligations

The vendor, in Jewish law, is obligated to divulge to his prospective buyer any defects in his product.[14] Disclosure responsibility extends even to a flaw whose presence does not depreciate the article sufficiently to allow the vendee a price-fraud claim.[15]

Disclosure of defects must be made in an open and forthright manner and not in a manner that deludes the vendee into discrediting the seller's declaration.[16]

Disclosure of the nonforthright variety, according to Maimonides (1135–1204), occurs when, for instance, a vendor (A) of an animal enumerates to his prospective buyer (B) a number of flaws in his beast, which, if present, would be readily apparent to him, e.g., lameness. Along with these defects, A admits to the presence of some specific hidden faults in his beast as well. Now, in the event the readily apparent flaws were in actuality not present in the animal, subsequent discovery of the hidden flaw may allow B to void the original transaction. Credence is given to B's claim that he did not take seriously A's disclosure of the hidden flaw. With the readily visible flaws mentioned by A obviously nonexistent, B is presumably deluded into discrediting the existence of the real defect as well. B's claim of delusive disclosure is, however, not accepted when *one* of the readily visible flaws A mentioned was actually present in the beast. Here, B should have taken seriously A's disclosure of the hidden flaw.[17]

A variant of the latter case, according to R. Jacob b. Asher (1270–1343) and R. Joseph Caro (1488–1575), allows B to void the sale on the basis of the delusive disclosure. This occurs when A takes pains to point out *only one* of the number of readily visible flaws he mentions. His failure to do likewise in regard to the other plainly visible flaws he mentions presumably leads B to discredit his disclosure of the hidden flaw. Subsequent discovery of the hidden defect may therefore allow B to void the original sale.[18]

Discovery of a flaw not properly disclosed at the time of the sale may allow the buyer to void the original transaction. This occurs when the defect involved is objectionable to the extent that most people would return the flawed article to the seller.[19] No statute of limitations is attached to the plaintiff's recision right.[20] Use of the article by him after discovery of the defect is, however, generally[21] taken as an implicit waiver of his recision right.[22] The remedy of demanding a price adjustment on the basis of the defect, it should be noted, is not enjoyed by the complainant here. The latter's options consist of either demanding a refund or accepting the transaction as originally concluded.[23]

In the standardized-product case, the seller may insist on exchanging the defective product for a flawless model. Should the market price of the defective product have gone down, however, the plaintiff retains his recision right.[24]

Should the defect discovered be only slight, so that it may not be said that most people would have returned the flawed article to the seller, the complainant enjoys no recision right unless the seller explicitly claimed at the time of the sale that the defect he found was not present in the article. In the absence of such an explicit claim on the part of the seller, the plaintiff is denied the right to void the original sale on the basis of the slight defect he later finds.[25]

General Disclaimer Clauses

General disclaimer clauses in sale contracts do not have the effect of nullifying the buyer's recision rights should his purchase prove defective. Since the disclaimer clause is silent about the *particular* defects the seller is not responsible for, credence is given to the buyer's claim that he did not take the disclaimer seriously, presuming that in reality the product was not defective at all. The complainant's acquiescence to the disclaimer clause is, therefore, not taken as an implicit waiver of his remedy against product defect. For the disclaimer clause to be effective in freeing the seller of responsibility in relation to product defects, it must be specific in nature. The specificity requirement is met when the disclaimer clause either (1) details the defects the seller is not responsible for, or (2) sets a limit to the depreciation in value from the sale price the buyer must absorb on account of discovery of defects in the product.[26]

Market Behavior Causing Mental Anguish

Admonishment against dealing deceitfully in business transactions appears twice in the Pentateuch. The first mention of the interdict occurs in Leviticus 25:14: "And if thou sell aught unto thy companion, or buy aught of thy neighbor's hand, ye shall not be extortionate to one another." Reiteration of the warning occurs shortly afterward in verse 17: "Ye shall not therefore be extortionate one to another; but thou shalt fear thy God for I am the Eternal your God." Rather than being taken as a repetition of the warning against fraud in monetary matters, verse 17 is exegetically interpreted in *Baba Metzia* 58b to prohibit causing someone mental anguish.[27] Referred to in the rabbinic literature as *ona'at devarim*, this prohibition extends to a variety of contexts.[28]

Ona'at devarim in a commercial setting is illustrated when an individual prices an article while having no intention to buy it.[29] What is objectionable here, according to R. Menachem b. Solomon of Perpignan (1249–1316), is that pricing an article creates an anticipation on the part of the seller that he will make a sale. This anticipation is dashed when the inquirer decides not to pursue the matter further.[30] While the prospective buyer need not concern himself with the disappointment a vendor may experience should his price inquiry not consummate into a purchase by him, pricing an article he has *no intention* of buying causes the vendor *needless distress* and is hence prohibited.[31]

Comparative Shopping and Ona'at Devarim

Morally objectionable on the basis of the *ona'at devarim* interdict, in our view, are several forms of comparative shopping tactics employed by consumers. Modern retail outlets serving the consumer-durable market essentially fall into either of two categories. One set of stores offer an elaborate showroom displaying a variety of models along with expert salesmen who demonstrate their proper use and maintenance. Another set of stores are typically small and offer only a limited number of models with no expert salesmen at hand. These establishments do, however, provide their customers with catalogues which display color photographs of the models not available in the store along with instructions regarding the proper use and maintenance of the product. Due to the savings effected by maintaining a skeletal sales force, a limited range of samples, and so forth, the catalogue stores, in some instances, can manage to undersell the showroom outlets. Pricing an article, such as a piece of furniture, at the showroom establishment, and taking advantage of its display service, and then ordering the same item at the catalogue store is, in our view, morally objectionable. Since the consumer has *no* intention of purchasing the item at the showroom store, the disappointment the salesman experiences when the inquiry does not consummate into a purchase amounts to a violation of the *ona'at devarim* interdict.

A variant of the above case occurs when the householder prices a consumer durable in outlet A with the intent of making the purchase there only if, after investigating competing outlets, A's offer represents for him his best alternative. Is the householder under an obligation to explicitly disclose his comparative-shopping intent at the outset? A relevant consideration here, in our view, is the *widespread* nature of the comparative-shopping technique in the consumer-durable market. Householders are unwilling to make expenditures amounting to a sizable percentage of their income without at least some investigation of market alternatives. The frequency of the use of the comparative-shopping technique in the consumer-durable market perhaps frees the householder of any *explicit* obligation to disclose his comparative-shopping intent. If the comparative-shopping inquiry is *sincere* for the consumer-durable market, seller disappointment resulting when the inquiry does not consummate in a purchase need not concern the householder. Nonetheless, returning to a particular outlet for another examination of the product without an explicit disclosure of a comparative-shopping intent, in our view, goes beyond the bounds of propriety and violates the *ona'at devarim* interdict.

Recognition of the comparative-shopping and browsing phenomena has led some stores to issue "just browsing" buttons to their clientele. Such buttons serve a double purpose. Wearing the button affords the browser freedom of movement in the store without being subjected to any sales pressure. At the same time, identification of the browsers allows the salesmen to concentrate their energies and time on the serious customers. Issuance of such buttons *may* amount to an implicit policy on the part of the firm to refuse service to the comparative shopper. Within that context, it appears, in our view, morally incumbent upon the comparative shopper not to avail himself of the services of the store's sales personnel without explicitly disclosing his intent.

Bait and Switch

The *ona'at devarim* interdict, according to R. Judah b. Samuel He-

Chasid of Regensburg (ca. 1150–1217), disallows the vendor to conduct his business by soliciting a bid for his article from a potential customer. Rather, the vendor must quote to the interested party the price he demands for his article. The former method is objectionable on the grounds that it may cause the buyer needless disappointment in the event his bid is rejected.[32]

What follows, in our view, from the above application of the *ona'at devarim* interdict is the moral objection to the "bait and switch" technique. In its basic form, this selling tactic involves the following: To induce customers to throng to his location, A advertises an attractive item he does *not* have at a bargain price. When customers arrive they are told that the advertised item is unavailable and are shown different merchandise. Notwithstanding that use of the tactic may eventuate in the satisfaction of the customer, nothing removes the fact that the latter was filled with a sense of disappointment and annoyance *at the moment* he was advised that the item was not available. Since the offer was insincere in the first place, this business tactic also violates the "good faith" imperative in Jewish law.[33]

A variant of the above case occurs when the vendor is in possession of the advertised item but only in limited supply. Suppose the offer of the attractive item is made for a specific period of time, and crude estimates of the demand for the product at the attractive price indicate that the supply of the advertised item will be exhausted considerably before the expiration date of the offer. Given the totally unrealistic duration of the offer, the advertisement remains insincere and violates for the advertiser the *ona'at devarim* interdict. Attaching a warning to the advertisement that supplies are limited and are available on a "first-come first-served" basis may, however, be sufficient to satisfy the "good faith" imperative and free the advertiser from the *ona'at devarim* interdict. In the final analysis, whether the above caveat does in fact make the advertisement morally acceptable depends, in our view, on the interpretation the majority of people attach to the advertisement. Consumer surveys could prove very helpful here.

Offering Ill-Suited Advice

Exegetical interpretation of the biblical exhortation, ". . . thou shalt not put a stumbling-block before the blind . . ." (Leviticus 19:14), establishes the prohibition of offering ill-suited advice.[34] Violation of the interdict, according to Maimonides, occurs only in the event the counseled party suffers loss or injury in consequence of following the recommended action.[35]

Halakhot Gedolot, however, identifies the interdict as consisting of the *mere offering* of the ill-suited advice, even if the counseled party does not suffer adverse effects in consequence.[36]

Included in the *ona'at devarim* interdict, according to R. Solomon b. Isaac of Troyes (1040–1105), is the prohibition against offering ill-suited advice.[37] Since such action is already prohibited on the basis of the "stumbling-block" interdict, R. Solomon's inclusion of this conduct within the scope of *ona'at devarim* is perplexing.

Under the assumption that the "stumbling-block" interdict is violated only when the counseled party erroneously *believes* that the ill-suited advice may serve his interests, R. Solomon's intention becomes quite clear. What R. Solomon refers to in associating the offering of ill-suited advice with the *ona'at devarim* interdict is the circumstance where the counseled party is *fully aware* that the advice tendered will not serve his interests. Though such advice cannot be regarded as a "stumbling-block," the adviser violates the *ona'at devarim* interdict. The violation follows from the mental anguish the counseled party experiences on realizing that his welfare has been treated so frivolously by his adviser.

The spectrum of circumstances covered by the prohibition of offering ill-suited advice has important implications for the everyday operation of business activities. Except in instances where his expertise and discretion are explicitly relied upon, the seller should not steer his customer into a particular price range, product line, or style without being conversant with the customer's particular circumstances and needs. The temptation to unload a slow-moving item on a naive customer must be overcome in light of infringement of the prohibition of offering ill-suited advice.

Undeserved Good Will

Good will in the form of a reputation for fine customer service, low prices, or a high-quality product represents an important factor accounting for business success and expansion. Generating good will on the basis of deception and illusion violates Jewish business ethics. Such conduct is a form of deceitful misrepresentation and is interdicted under the rubric of *genevat da'at*. *Genevat da'at*, according to R. Yom Tov Ishbili of Seville (ca. 1250–1330), is a form of theft.[38] R. Jonah b. Abraham Gerondi (ca. 1200–1263), however, regards the conduct as a form of falseness.[39]

An illustration of generating undeserved good will, discussed in the Talmud, involves the sale of meat originating from an organically defective animal to a non-Jew. Duping the customer into believing he is getting a bargain by misrepresenting the meat as originating from a healthy animal constitutes *genevat da'at*. While price fraud may not be involved, as the non-Jew is charged a fair price for what he actually receives,[40] the transaction is, nonetheless, prohibited on account of the undeserved sense of obligation the customer is left with for the storekeeper. This sense of appreciation is, of course, undeserved, since the bargain is imaginary.[41]

A variant of the above case occurs when the storekeeper offers the misrepresented meat as a gift to his non-Jewish friend. Authorities are in dispute as to whether this practice is objectionable.[42]

Violation of the *genevat da'at* interdict, according to R. Joseph D. Epstein (contemporary), does not stand pending until the duped party actually performs an undeserved favor for the offender, but rather is transgressed immediately by dint of the "stolen feeling" of indebtedness the offender secures by means of his ploy. Nonactualization of the unwarranted state of appreciation into a concrete benefit for the offender does not free the latter from violation of the *genevat da'at* interdict.[43]

While misleading someone by word or action is prohibited, an individual is not obligated to correct an erroneous impression when it is the result of self-deception. The following episode, recorded in *Chullin* 94b, illustrates this point:

> Mar Zutra the son of R. Nachman was once going from Sikara to Machuza, while Rava and R. Safra were going to Sikara; and they met on the way. Believing that they had come to meet him he said, "Why did the Rabbis take this trouble to come so far [to meet me]?" R. Safra replied, "We did not know that the master was coming; had we known of it we should have put ourselves out more than this." Rava said to him, "Why did you tell him this? you have now upset him." He replied, "But we would be deceiving him otherwise." "No. He would be deceiving himself."

Talmudic decisors regard Rava's reaction as appropriate. Since Mar Zutra had no basis for presuming that his fortuitous meeting with his colleagues constituted a welcoming party, Mar Zutra was guilty of self-deception. Consequently, the group was not under obligation to correct the erroneous impression.[44]

The implications of the above discussion for modern business practices are extensive. A seller's offer to discount an item for his customer below the manufacturer's suggested retail price is a violation of the *genevat da'at* interdict. Since this suggested price is so inflated that no retail store can hope to remain competitive by charging it, the offer of a discount creates a false impression of bargain and consequently generates unwarranted good will.

Reporting financial statements in a manner that creates a false impression of earnings provides another example of a violation of the *genevat da'at* interdict.

Snatching Away Another's Anticipated Gain

Snatching away another's anticipated gain is generally morally objectionable in Jewish law.[45] Interfering with a sales transaction provides a case in point. Once negotiations between buyer and seller advance to the stage just prior to *kinyan*, a third party, according to R. Meir b. Baruch of Rothenburg (ca. 1215–1298), may not step in and offer to purchase the product at hand. The position of the buyer at this point is metaphorically compared to that of a poor person moving about a stack, anxiously waiting for its removal in anticipation of picking up a forgotten sheaf *(ani hamehapekh bechararah)*. Interference at this point brands the offender a wicked person *(rasha)*. Moreover, for the purpose of extricating the interloper from the above stigma, the Jewish court, according to R. Samuel b. Moses de Medina of Salonika (1506–1589), will enjoin him from making the purchase.[47] Nonetheless, in the event the interloper succeeded in making his interference purchase, Jewish law does not go so far as to void the purchase in order to allow the prior party realization of his anticipated acquisition.[48]

Widening the scope of the interference interdict in sales transactions, R. Joshua ha-Kohen Falk (1555–1614) posits that the prohibition applies even before negotiations between A and B advance to the stage just prior to *kinyan*. As long as the parties have not broken off their negotiations and the possibility that the bargaining process will produce a sale remains, a third party may not step in and offer to buy the article.[49]

Noting (1) that R. Falk did not advance the above view as a definite opinion, (2) that the supposition is not repeated in his commentary on the *Shulchan Arukh*, and (3) that the opinion is not taken up by the latter codifiers R. Mordechai b. Abraham Jaffe (ca. 1535–1612) and R. Shneur Zalman of Lyady, a Tel Aviv rabbinical tribunal ruled that the Jewish court would not stigmatize an interloper in a sales transaction as a *rasha* unless the interference took place just prior to the stage of *kinyan*.[50]

The interloper, according to R. Elijah b. Chayyim of Constantinople (ca. 1530–1610), must defer to the prior party even if he was unaware of the latter's efforts to secure the article at the time he began negotiating with the seller.[51] Ruling in a similar manner is the contemporary decisor R. Moshe Feinstein.[52]

The interference interdict, according to R. Jacob Tam of Ramerupt (ca. 1100–1171), extends to the labor market as well.[53] A specific application, discussed in the codes, deals with the rights of an incumbent religious teacher against the encroachment of a competitor. Religious teacher B, according to R. Isaac b. Samuel of Dampierre (d. ca. 1185), may not hire himself out to the employer of a competitor while the competitor (A) is still in the home of the employer (C).[54]

R. Solomon Luria of Ostrog (1510–1574) understands R. Isaac's dictum to refer to the case where the incumbent A was not hired for any specific term. Here, since A exerted efforts to establish an employment tie with C, B may not *initiate* negotiations to hire himself out to replace A. Should A have been hired for a specific term, however, it would not be morally objectionable for B to initiate negotiations to hire himself out to replace A at the termination of A's contract.[55]

A more stringent interpretation of R. Isaac's dictum is advanced by the Polish decisor R. Binyamin Aharon Slonick (ca. 1550–1619). In his view B violates the interference interdict even in the term contract case. Since A anticipates *renewal* of his contract, B's initiatives to replace him amount to snatching away A's anticipated gain.

A variation of the above case occurs when B's initiative succeeds in his replacing A before the latter's term of contract expires. Here, the Jewish court, according to R. Slonick, will void B's contract and force C to allow A to return to his job.[56]

Following R. Slonick's line, in our view, is an earlier ruling by R. Joseph b. Solomon Colon (ca. 1420–1480). This Italian halakhist found it morally objectionable, on the basis of the interference interdict, for A to exert efforts to secure an exclusive government license for a particular commercial venture effective when B's license for the same expires. Since business licenses are routinely renegotiated and renewed, A's interference amounts to an encroachment upon B's anticipated gain.[57]

Restriction of competition in the labor market on the basis of the interference interdict, according to R. Moshe Feinstein, applies only when the interloper cannot secure employment elsewhere. When this is not the case, interference prior to the stage of *kinyan* is not objectionable. This liberalization follows from R. Jacob Tam's ruling that the interference interdict is suspended in connection with the acquisition of ownerless property.[58] Interference is prohibited only when the offender could have easily obtained the object at hand elsewhere. With this obviously not the case in regard to the acquisition of ownerless property, interference prior to the point when legal possession takes place is not prohibited.[59]

Competition among employers for the services of religious teachers, according to R. Isaac, is subject to less restriction in Jewish law. Provided religious teacher A's agreement with his employer has not yet been consummated by means of *kinyan*,[60] C may hire him away to teach his child. The permissibility of the tactic rests on the deference given to C's judgment that his child stands to benefit more from A's pedagogical skill than from any other teacher available.[61]

What follows from R. Isaac's opinion, in our view, is the permissibility for C to negotiate with religious teacher A while the latter is still in B's employ to work for him when his contract with B expires.

The liberty R. Isaac extends to the employer in his hiring practices, according to R. Jechiel Michael Epstein, applies only when the gain the interloper seeks is not monetary but purely religious in nature. Should the gain sought not be purely religious, hiring away a worker when the latter has already reached verbal agreement with his employer is prohibited.[62]

Bargain Sales and the Interference Interdict

While the interference interdict is generally suspended in connection with the acquisition of ownerless property, interference with the consummation of a "bargain" sale is prohibited. Accordingly, once buyer A and seller B come to an agreement regarding price, C may not step in and offer to buy the article, despite the bargain involved which is not available elsewhere.[63]

Ownerless Property and the Interference Interdict

Another exception to the suspension of the interference interdict in connection with the acquisition of ownerless property occurs in the fisherman-preserve case recorded in *Baba Bathra* 21b. Casting his bait in a fish's hiding place entitles the fisherman to a limited territorial preserve. Anticipation of gain, according to R. Solomon b. Isaac, is what stands at the basis of the territorial-preserve right. Casting his bait in the fish's hiding place assures the fisherman that he will be able to lure fish into his net. Since his catch is thereby assured, another fisherman may not spread his net at the same spot, because doing so would deprive the first fisherman of an *anticipated* gain.[64]

A different rationale for the preserve rights of the fisherman is advanced by R. Moses b. Nachman of Gerona (1194–1270). What the second fisherman is prohibited from doing is to spread his net in close proximity to the net of the first fisherman, for such action could result in directly depriving the former of what is rightfully his. Fish already captured in the first fisherman's net could, at times, spring out into the second fisherman's net. Any fish caught by the interloper are, therefore, regarded as outrightly stolen and are the entitlement of the first fisherman.[65]

The stringency of the treatment of the interloper here presents a difficulty to Tosafot (12–14th cent. school of French and German talmudic commentators). Since the contested prize, the fish, is ownerless property, why are the interloper's efforts to snatch away the first fisherman's anticipated gain regarded as a form of robbery? Three theories are advanced by Tosafot as a means of resolving the above difficulty:

1. The interference interdict is suspended in connection with the acquisition of ownerless property only when the windfall cannot be secured elsewhere by the interloper. This is not the case here, as the interloper can easily cast his bait in another spot, at a safe distance from the first fisherman.
2. The interdict is not suspended here because the *action* of the first fisherman, i.e., the casting of bait, is what is responsible for *attracting* the fish and making the gain possible.
3. Since the contested gain is the source of livelihood of the first fisherman, interloping action is prohibited, despite the ownerless nature of the property involved.[66]

It should be noted that the fisherman case is not recorded in the codes of R. Isaac Alfasi, Maimonides, R. Jacob b. Asher, and R. Joseph Caro. This peculiarity has led some authorities to posit that interloping action here is not morally objectionable.[67] Nonetheless, many latter-day talmudic decisors treat interloping action in the fisherman case as robbery and subject it to restraint.[68]

Another instance where interloping action is prohibited in connection with the acquisition of ownerless property is recorded in *Gittin* 59b. The case deals with the law of forgotten sheaves (*shikcha*), i.e., the portion of the crop that is the entitlement of the poor. Restrictions were placed on the competition among the poor for *shikcha*. Accordingly, should poor man A climb to the top of an olive tree and manage to cut down some *shikcha* olives (without first taking hold of them in his hands),[69] the fallen fruit is regarded as A's exclusive preserve. Should another poor man (B) anticipate A in performing the necessary *kinyan* to acquire possession of the fruit, this act is regarded as robbery by rabbinical decree (*gezel midivreihem*). Nonetheless, Jewish law does not go so far as to force B to hand over the *shikcha* olives to A.[70]

Why interloping action is here morally objectionable is explained by R. Binyamin Aharon Slonick as stemming from the heightened level of anticipation of acquisition that A experiences as a result of his feat of removing the *shikcha* olives from their original place at the top of the tree. Snatching away A's anticipated gain at this point is, therefore, morally objectionable despite the kinship of this circumstance to the ownerless-property case. Interloping action here is, however, not regarded as outright theft as the anticipated gain is not a normal source of livelihood for A. Though presently indigent and hence qualified to collect charity in the form of forgotten sheaves, A presumably abhors his status and looks forward to the day he will become gainfully employed and no longer eligible to collect forgotten gleanings.[71]

Disparagement of a Competitor's Product

Impugning the integrity of a competitor on the quality of his product, as will be demonstrated below, presents a moral issue in Jewish law even when no misrepresentation of fact is made and the motives of the disparager are sincere.

Falsely maligning a competitor incurs for the offender violation of the biblical interdicts against slander[72] and falsehood.[73]

More complicated is the moral issue of whether A may warn customers of competitor B's unethical conduct for the purpose of averting financial loss for them. Since taking action to avert a neighbor's loss constitutes a positive duty,[74] is the biblical interdict against spreading scandalous but true information about someone (*leshon hara*) suspended here? Addressing himself to this question in general terms, the Russian Sage R. Yisroel Meir ha-Kohen (1838–1933) rules that disclosing disparaging but true remarks about a merchant is permitted only when certain very stringent conditions are met. Some of these conditions are absolutely essential, while others are either required only *ab initio* or are suspended under certain circumstances. Conditions falling into the first category include the following:

1. Impetuous action must be avoided. Before taking action the informer must be certain that the merchant's conduct constitutes unethical behavior. Should the merchant's behavior be subject to favorable interpretation, he must be given the benefit of doubt.
2. The informer must be careful not to exaggerate the extent of the merchant's unethical conduct.
3. The informer must be reasonably certain that his warning will be heeded. Should this not be the case, the discrediting information

should not be reported, for the disclosure could easily lead to a train of events wherein the victim who discarded the advice confronts the discredited seller and expresses regret for having dealt with him and not having heeded the warning of the informer. Mentioning the informer's name to the dishonest merchant constitutes a violation of the talebearing interdict on the part of the victim, a transgression indirectly brought about by the warning issued by the informer.

4. If it is likely that the merchant's reaction to the disparaging comment would be so severe that he would face penalties disproportionate to what is due him by dint of Jewish law, the disclosure should not be made.

5. Should the scandalous conduct not be known to the informer at first hand, R. Yisroel Meir ha-Kohen is unresolved as to whether the disclosure may be made. In any event, the informer may not here present his report as fact, but may merely disclose what he has heard and advise the concerned party to exercise caution on the basis of the information. Should the informer fear that despite his qualifications his report would be treated by the concerned party as undisputed fact, he may not issue the warning, for the merchant in consequence would be treated more harshly than warranted, a violation of condition (4).

6. Should the moral character of the informer be no better than the character of the man he intends to impugn, the disclosure should not be made. Relatedly, disparaging reports should not be made to people of immoral character. Feeling no sense of outrage at the misconduct, they will neither work constructively to force the offender to make amends nor take action to prevent future harm. Hence, no useful purpose is served by the disclosure.

The second category of conditions includes the following:

1. Presentation of the disparaging report may not be made when other means of preventing the potential harm are available. Nonetheless, in the case of a habitual offender, the disclosure may be made, notwithstanding the availability of other means of preventing the potential harm. Permissibility of this course of action follows from the deterrent advantage secured when habitual wrongdoers are subject to contempt and detraction.

2. Before making his disclosure, the informer should first reproach the offender and try to persuade him to make amends. Should the informer, however, feel that his reproach would be ineffec-

tive, he may issue his warning without first reproaching the offender.

3. Though obligated to make his damaging disclosure even when his motives are selfish and ulterior, the informer should force himself, as much as possible, to act with purity of motive so as to avoid possible infringement of the biblical interdict against talebearing.[75] In the absence of purity of motive, it is very difficult to avoid distortion and exaggeration of the misconduct and to avoid miscalculation regarding the ramifications of the disclosure.[76]

What proceeds from the above is that much judgmental analysis and extrapolation are necessary in weighing the appropriateness of disclosing someone's misconduct. Crucial to the moral issue at hand is whether a competitor has the capacity to exercise the requisite objectivity to assume the role of an informer. Relatedly, R. Yisroel Meir ha-Kohen rules that inquiries regarding the reputation of a craftsman should not be solicited from a rival as the report will in all probability be interspersed with slander, distortions, and exaggerations.[77]

Another aspect of the disparagement tactic concerns the ethics of the comparative-merit stratagem. Here, out of fear that the customer will engage in comparative shopping before making his purchase, seller A is eager to demonstrate the superiority of his product. He does this by pointing out that competitive models do not contain certain attractive features present in his product. While careful not to create an impression that his competitors are in any way dishonest, seller A claims that his product represents a better value. To illustrate, suppose A points out that his higher-priced vacuum cleaner features extra detachable parts not available in rival models. Insofar as the attractive features of A's product are projected more prominently by means of the comparison, this tactic, in our view, violates Jewish business ethics. While A has the legitimate right to point out to everyone the fine qualities of his product, magnifying these qualities by comparing his product with what his rivals have to offer amounts to elevating himself at his neighbor's expense. The utter contempt in which the talmudic Sages held this particular behavioral trait finds expression in the dictum of R. Yose b. Chanina (second half of the 3rd cent.): "Anyone who elevates himself at the expense of his friend has no share in the world to come" (Jerusalem Talmud, *Chagiga* II:1).

· 9

The Role of Government in the Free Enterprise Economy

Introduction

Defining the proper scope and role of governmental activity is one of the major social issues confronting the free enterprise economy. Lying at the heart of this issue is the extent to which the public sector should be allowed to alter the mix of products and the pattern of income distribution the economy would produce if left to its own devices. The relative size of the public sector consequently determines the degree of economic freedom the society enjoys as well as its level of private consumption.

Approaches to the above issue, referred to in the economic literature as the social balance problem, divide basically into two schools of thought. One approach would decide the issue of intersectoral resource allocation on the basis of economic efficiency; the rival approach would decide this issue by invoking a particular ideology, philosophy, or set of moral principles.

This chapter will compare the economic efficiency and Jewish law approaches to the issue of social balance.

Social Balance and Economic Efficiency

Expressing a strong preference for economic freedom and individual, private decision-making, the economic-efficiency approach to the question of social balance would allow the public sector to interfere with the marketplace only when such intervention would produce a clear-cut gain in social welfare. Such an indisputable gain occurs when the operations of the public sector would, at the very least, enhance the welfare of one person, while not reducing the well-being of anyone else. Though apparently prohibitively restrictive, the above criterion, referred to in the economic literature as the Pareto Optimality condition, permits the public sector an extensive role in the free enterprise–oriented economy. A taxonomy of these cases follows.

The Pure Public Good Case

Sellers of economic goods usually enjoy the ability to directly exclude nonpayers from the consumption of their good. Direct exclusion of nonpayers is, however, impossible when the benefits the said good generate are indivisible. The nature of the dilemma confronting the seller in the above instance is illustrated by the classical lighthouse case. Once the lighthouse is in operation, its benefits will be enjoyed by *all* ships in the vicinity, regardless of their willingness to pay the fee demanded by the owners of the lighthouse. The market mechanism will prove incapable of excluding nonpayers. Given the presumed strength of the free rider motive, the economic incentive to produce the lighthouse is very weak in the first place. The absence of the profit motive renders the marketplace incapable of producing a good for which an effective demand exists. Paradoxically, shipowners, the free rider motive aside, would be willing to spend part of their resources to secure the benefit of a lighthouse, yet the market mechanism is incapable of satisfying this want. Satisfaction of the effective demand for a lighthouse requires, therefore, public sector intervention in the form of taxing shipowners and using the tax yield to construct the desired facility. Intervention here clearly enhances the welfare of shipowners since it results in the production of a desired good, a good the marketplace proved incapable of producing.

Elements of nonexclusion also characterize such familiar public sector services as national defense, police, and fire protection. The transfer of these traditional public sector functions to the private sector would undoubtedly reduce their efficiency. Given the strength of the free rider motive, entrepreneurs would find it difficult to realize profits in the provision of these services. Adequate protection of subscribers to these services would require the private contractors to provide their services to nonsubscribers as well. National defense provides a case in point. Private contractors offering to protect domestic citizens from foreign invasion would, for all intents and purposes, have to provide their service to subscribers and nonsubscribers on an equal basis. Elimination of the free rider motive, therefore, requires the public sector to use its coercive power of taxation to secure the necessary funds .o satisfy these wants.

Conservation

Another function the economic-efficiency criterion would assign the public sector is to act as a proxy for future generations. Left to its own devices, the marketplace, with its short time horizon, would not conserve national resources for economically rational long-term usage. To discourage reckless exploitation of land and water resources, the public sector must use its powers to effect intertemporal resource-allocation efficiency. This goal can be accomplished by means of artificially raising the cost of extracting natural resources in the current period. Imposing a severance tax on economic units that extract natural resources represents one means of accomplishing this end.

Income Redistribution

Public assistance programs, long thought to find their justification solely on equity grounds, have recently been given an efficiency-based rationale. Arguing that man is basically altruistic and desires to spend part of his resources to reduce poverty and misery, Rodgers and Hochman posit that the marketplace, left to its own devices, would, from a social standpoint, underallocate resources toward philanthropy. The underallocation follows from the presumption that individuals derive equal satisfaction from the reduction of poverty whether it occurs by means of their own initiative or by means of the initiative of others. Given the strength of the free rider motive, optimal social provision of philanthropic activity requires the public sector to use its taxing power to transfer income from the rich to the poor.[1] The validity of the above argument hinges on the legitimacy of its premise that man is basically altruistic. Rejecting this premise, Mishan finds no efficiency basis for public assistance programs.[2]

Modification of the Rodgers-Hochman premise can, in our view, salvage the efficiency-based argument for public assistance programs. Supposing man is basically selfish rather than altruistic does not automatically preclude attributing to him a philanthropic motive. Scheler's development of the concept of ressentiment, as discussed below, explains why individuals, acting out of a motive of self-interest, would want to devote part of their resources to reduce poverty and misery.

Democracy is by nature contentious because men constantly covet what other men have. Not all societies invite invidious comparisons. The peasant did not compare his lot with the lord's; he had his allotted place in the scheme of things and accepted it fatalistically. Democracy, with its normative commitment to equality, provides a yardstick for measuring discrepancies in status, wealth, and power. When one is barred from modifying these discrepancies, the result is often *ressentiment*, i.e., envy, anger, and hatred toward those at the top.

Ressentiment is the chief psychological fuel of disruption and conflict, and the problem for society is how to reduce it.[3]

In justifying public assistance programs as a means of eliminating or reducing *ressentiment*, we will assume the following:

1. Individuals who are economically successful in a democratic society realize that their success breeds envy, or *ressentiment*, on the part of those who are economically unsuccessful, especially among those born into unfavorable social circumstances.
2. The successful individuals desire reduction of *ressentiment*.
3. The successful individuals derive equal satisfaction from the elimination or reduction of this sentiment whether it occurs by means of their own initiative or by means of the initiative of others.

Under the above conditions, the free market system would prove an inefficient mechanism for effecting a substantial reduction in *ressentiment*. Although all successful individuals would have a vested interest in eliminating this sentiment, a vast underexpenditure toward the alleviation of *ressentiment* would take place, as individuals would rely on the initiative of others.

Since the "free rider" motive is strongly operative in this particular case, government intervention in the form of public assistance programs is in order.

Other functions the economic-efficiency criterion assigns the public sector include contract law, regulation of monopoly, and interference in the marketplace in the external benefit and cost case.[4] These areas of intervention are dealt with in separate chapters.

Social Balance and Jewish Law

Jewish law's approach to the question of social balance can be found by an investigation of its treatment of the communal legislative process.

The Jewish community, as a collective, is regarded by Jewish law as having the legislative status of a court of law or a king.[5] Communal enactments, properly legislated, are therefore binding on all members of the community, including minors, and even on those not yet born.[6]

The procedural rules prescribed for legislative enactments are not uniform, but vary according to the type of legislation being considered. In some instances, as outlined below, minority sponsorship of a piece of legislation is sufficient to confer upon it legal sanction making it binding upon all, including the protesting majority.

The constellation of legislative acts that acquire legal sanction even when supported by only a minority of the community constitute the functions Judaism mandates for the public sector.

Legislation not mandated on the public sector requires majority support in order to become effective law. Within the framework of this decision rule, all voters, according to R. Meir of Rothenburg (1215–1293), are weighted equally. A legislative proposal, hence, becomes effective by means of a simple majority vote.[7] R. Asher b. Jechiel (1250–1327),[8] on the interpretation of R. Joshua ha-Kohen Falk (1555–1614), however, advances a different view of the majority decision rule. In his formulation a "double majority" is required. This consists of both a majority of those eligible to vote and in addition a majority based on a system of weighting the votes of each member according to his projected assessment in defraying the expenditure *(rov minyan verov binyan)*.[9]

Communal legislative authority is severely limited when it comes into conflict with Jewish religious law. Accordingly, should the proposed legislation violate religious, ritual law, its validity is not recognized, even if arrived at by means of unanimous consent.[10] Less restrictive is the constraint placed on the community in the event that the legislation conflicts with Jewish civil law. Here, while a majority is not sufficient to legitimize the legislative act, unanimous consent allows communal legislation to supersede the extant religious law on the particular matter at hand. Unanimity in a purely monetary matter legitimizes contracting out of Jewish civil law because those parties who stand to be injured provide an explicit waiver of their rights.[11]

How the above requirement of consonance between legislation and Jewish Civil law constrains communal enactments is illustrated by R. Solomon b. Abraham Adret's (1235–1310) treatment of the following point in tax law. The case involved the validity of a communal practice of taxing a resident on the basis of his ownership of assets located in a different town. R. Adret ruled that the practice violated tion that the expenditure in reality represents a preferred item in the virtue of biblical law. Nonetheless, should the members of the community unanimously adopt such a provision into their tax law, the ordinance becomes binding upon themselves as well as upon newcomers.[12]

Communal legislation is further linked to religious law by the requirement that all communal enactments must be approved by the locally recognized religious authority and communal leader *(adam chashuv)*.[13] Should an individual blessed with these attributes not be present locally, communal legislation is fully valid without any outside approval.[14]

Functions Jewish Law Mandates on the Public Sector

Jewish law places in the realm of the Jewish community's public sector the following functions: (1) security measures, (2) water supply projects, (3) public road repairs, (4) a variety of communal projects of a religious character, (5) contract law, (6) profit regulation of industries dealing in necessities, (7) regulation of weights and measures, and (8) intervention in the external benefit and external cost case. The latter four areas of intervention are not taken up in this chapter as they are treated elsewhere in this book.

The Security Tax Levy

Townspeople may compel each other to financially participate in the building of a wall, folding doors, and a cross-bar. The circumstances under which a coercive security tax levy is legitimized is a matter of tannaic dispute.[15] R. Shimon b. Gamaliel (1st cent. C.E.) limits the coercive levy to a town bordering hostile territory, while the Sages mandate the security tax for every town without exception. Every town requires external-security measures. Though the town may face no immediate danger, it is by no means immune from attack by roving bands sometime in the future.[16]

An Efficiency Rationale. Working within the parameters of halakhic principles, we will attempt to demonstrate that the position of the Sages, the view adopted by talmudic codifiers,[17] and R. Shimon b. Gamaliel's dissenting opinion can be rationalized on the basis of an economic-efficiency argument.

Let us first turn to the case of a town bordering enemy territory. All that is necessary here to halakhically rationalize coercive participation in a minority-sponsored external-security measure is the presumption that the expenditure in reality represents a preferred item in the current budget of the great majority of the townspeople and opposition to it merely reflects an underlying free rider motive.

The "free rider" phenomenon finds explicit expression in Jewish law in connection with laws dealing with zoning codes. In this regard, the Mishnah (*Baba Bathra* II:8) relates that to preserve the aesthetic quality of a town, trees must be kept at a distance of at least twenty-five cubits from its limits. Violation of this zoning ordinance subjects the tree-owner to the penalty of having his tree cut down, with compensation for his loss not recognized. Deference to the amenity rights of the townspeople requires the tree-owner to cut down his tree even if its presence antedates the existence of the town. Nonetheless, in the latter instance, the community is required to indemnify the owner for his loss after removal of the tree is effected.

Defending the procedure in the latter instance of first requiring the removal of the tree and only then allowing the owner to exact his compensation claim on the community, the Talmud asserts that reversing the procedure would effectively allow the tree to remain in place indefinitely since "a pot with two cooks is neither hot nor cold."[18] Elaborating on the intent of this analogy, R. Solomon b. Isaac (1040–1105) comments that given man's proclivity to avoid or delay payment as much as possible, each member of the community would refuse to inaugurate the collection with his share of the indemnity payment. With the collection process subject to snags, removal of the tree would not be accomplished unless the compensation obligation devolved upon the community only after the tree had already been removed.[19]

The relevance of the "free rider" motive for the problem of public taxation policy is explicitly found in the writings of R. Meir of Rothenburg. In a responsum dealing with the concept of unjust enrichment, R. Meir draws a distinction between a private and a communal expenditure. Hence, should A's private expenditure generate an external benefit to B, B bears no compensation responsibility to A; i.e., B's captured benefit is not regarded as unjust enrichment. Since A would, in any case, have undertaken his expenditure, and, in addition, B plays no role in making A's expenditure higher than it otherwise would be, denying the latter his captured advantage on anything less than a gratis basis would be Sodomitic (i.e., denying someone a benefit when it involves no cost to oneself). In sharp contrast, should A's expenditure consist of an outlay for a communal project, B bears compensation responsibility for his advantage. Assimilating the latter case to the former, points out R. Meir, would effectively frustrate the emergence of any communal project. Each resident of the town would rely on the initiative of his neighbors to create the communal project. Once it was completed, the nonparticipating resident would claim exemption from financial responsibility on the grounds that the sponsors' financial commitment would have taken place in any case and was not increased on account of him. Widespread maneuvering of this sort would obviously frustrate altogether the emergence of communal projects.[20]

The strength of the "free rider" motive that would arise in a town adjoining hostile forces would be particularly acute. Given the danger the town faces, individual residents could reasonably anticipate that the security needs of the town would be attended to without their aid, by means of the cooperative efforts of everyone else. This line of reasoning leads to the conclusion that it is irrational, from the individual standpoint, to support the security tax levy. To the extent

that such stratagems are universalized, the security measures necessary to protect the townspeople from the external danger would not
obtain. Coercive public sector intervention represents the only *efficient*
and *equitable* means of actuating the effective demand for security
measures. Coercive participation here is, therefore, entirely consistent
with individual choice.

Should the town face no immediate danger, the presumption that
expenditures for security measures represent a preferred item in the
current budgets of the townspeople is no longer valid. Here, R.
Shimon b. Gamaliel would not legitimize a security tax levy until the
majority of the townspeople agree to it.

Why the Sages call for coercive participation in a minority-
sponsored security tax levy even when the town faces no immediate
danger can, in our view, be explained by the presumption that
security-related expenditures represent a preferred item in the *intertemporal* demand pattern of the community. Though no immediate
danger faces it, an unsecured town serves an open invitation to
roving thieves to plunder it.[21] Extrapolating into the future, actual
crime experience would assuredly persuade the townspeople of the
necessity of adopting external-security measures. Ironically, even at
that juncture, effective communal action would be frustrated because
of the emergence of the "free rider" motive. The refusal of the
majority to adopt appropriate security measures in the current
period, hence, runs decidedly counter to their own *long-run* self-
interest. Given the short time horizon people adopt for themselves,
empowering the public sector to impose a minority-sponsored security tax levy on the entire community is consistent with maximizing
the long-run economic interests of the townspeople. Supposing that
security-related projects enter into the intertemporal demand pattern
of the community transforms the external-security function of the
community into the power to accelerate an effective demand for a
particular expenditure when such action serves to maximize the
community's long-term economic interest.

The efficiency-based rationale of the security tax levy is, in our
view, supported by the following considerations:

1. Included in the security tax measures are only town inhabitants who are regarded as permanent residents. The permanency
criterion is met when an inhabitant, prior to the imposition of the
levy, either (a) resided in the town for twelve months or (b) purchased a home in the town and resided in it.[22] The latter action is
taken as a clear communication of intent to remain in the town on a
permanent basis.[23] Limiting the tax base in the above manner is
quite understandable under the thesis that forced participation in the

security tax levy is justified on the presumption that the expenditure is a preferred item in the townspeople's intertemporal budgets. Insofar as the town faces no immediate danger and residents classified as nonpermanent cannot be presumed to harbor an intent to remain in the town for any extended period, no basis for including nonpermanent residents in the tax base exists.

2. Rabbinical scholars are exempt from the external-security levy. The rationale of the above exemption is discussed in the following talmudic passage:

> R. Judah the Prince [2d–3d cent. c.e.] levied the impost for the wall on the Rabbis. Said Resh Lakish [3rd cent. c.e.], The Rabbis do not require the protection [of a wall], as it is written: "If I should count them, they are more in number than the sand" [Ps. 139:18]. Who are these that are counted? Shall I say the righteous, are they more in number than the sand? . . . What the verse means, however, is I shall count the *deeds* of the righteous and they will be more in number than the sand. If then the sand, which is the lesser quantity, protects [the land] against the sea, how much more must the deeds of the righteous, which are a larger quantity, protect them? When Resh Lakish came before R. Jochanan [3rd cent. c.e.], the latter said to him: Why did you not derive the lesson from the verse: "I am a wall, and my breasts are like towers" [Cant. 8:10]—where "I am a wall" refers to the Torah, and "my breasts are like towers" to the students of the Torah . . .[24]

Proceeding from the above amoraic[25] dialogue is that rabbinical scholars require no protection from physical harm as their security is divinely guaranteed by virture of their piety[26] and scholarship. Invoking the benefit principle as a basis for exempting rabbinical scholars from the security tax levy follows logically from the economic-efficiency rationale of this levy. More significantly, however, the efficiency rationale allows the exemption to be interpreted in terms broader than a simple immunity claim. No contention of actual immunity is here implied. Physical injury and monetary loss befall rabbinical scholars as they do the general populace. The immunity claim exegetically derived from the above verses is merely theoretical in nature. Realization of the divine guarantee of physical security attains only to the extent that rabbinical scholars are inspired with perfect belief in their immunity blessings.[27] Given their theoretical immunity from physical harm, we may not presume that the expenditure for the external-security measure represents for rabbinical scholars a preferred item in their budgets. With coercive participation in the security tax levy justified on the basis of a presumed effective demand for the project, rather than as a quid pro quo for benefits received, the exemption of the rabbinical scholar follows.

3. The prescribed formula for distributing the tax burden in defraying the expense of the town-wall project varies according to the type of danger facing the town at the time the expenditure is adopted. Several possibilities present themselves. Under stable conditions, occasional acts of theft carried out by thieves based outside the town are regarded as the main threat to an unsecured town. Since under these circumstances, it is only movable property that is likely to be victimized in the absence of a wall, the relative distribution of movable property among the townspeople is the main consideration in assessing individual tax shares. Subsidiary to this consideration, however, is proximity to the town wall.[28] Imposing a heavier burden on households located closer to the town wall, *ceteris paribus*, is defended by R. Solomon b. Isaac on the grounds that dwellings situated in the outer perimeter of the town benefit disproportionately from the construction of the town wall. This follows from the fact that in the absence of the wall, it is these households that suffer the greatest likelihood of being victimized by thieves based outside the town limits.[29]

Combining the above elements, the tax formula under stable conditions is designed to impose a heavier tax burden on the rich household farther from the wall relative to the poor household located closer to the wall.

Should the danger threatening the inhabitants of a town be assessed to be the possible destruction of their property by fire and vandalism, the tax base for the property-ownership index expands to include immovable property as well.

In the event a state of war exists at the time the town wall is being built, and there is general fear that enemy soldiers would engage in unprovoked and wanton acts of murder, the usual tax formula for financing the wall is changed to reflect this new dimension. Under these conditions, construction of the town wall affords protection to life as well as to property. Half the necessary outlay is therefore apportioned on an equal per capita basis, while the remaining half is distributed in accordance with property ownership.

Proximity to the town wall, the subsidiary component of the security tax formula, is also sensitive to the state of security existing at the time the levy is adopted. When the town is regarded as a likely target of general ransacking, this criterion becomes inoperative, as all households, regardless of their relative proximity to the town wall, are equally likely to be victimized.[30]

The variability of the prescribed tax formula in connection with the security tax levy is readily understandable under the efficiency-rationale thesis. With public sector provision of the town wall justified only as a means of eliminating the free rider motive or maximizing the long-run economic interests of the townspeople, an individual's assessment in the project should logically be proportional to his assumed effective demand for the project. Property ownership, proximity to the town wall, and the state of security prevailing at the time the town-wall project is adopted form the relevant considerations in assessing this demand.

4. The economic-efficiency rationale imparts meaning to the solution Tosafot (12th–14th cent. school of French and German talmudic commentators) offer to a problem in connection with the tax base of the security tax levy. Why, query Tosafot, is the equal per capita component of the security tax levy applicable only when the townspeople are regarded as likely targets of unprovoked acts of murder, but dropped entirely from the formula under normal conditions? Granted that the *immediate* danger the townspeople face under normal conditions consists merely of the possible loss of their property, nevertheless, loss of life may also occur since would-be victims may attempt to frustrate the designs of the aggressors. That the intentions of the thief would be met with resistance is regarded by Jewish law as a near certainty. This behavioral prediction takes the form of a presumption: "No one will restrain himself from defending his property" (*ein adam ma-amed atzmo al mamono*).

On the basis of the above presumption, Halakhah regards the ordinary thief as one pursuing his neighbor with the intent to kill him (*rodef*). Though the thief's original intent is merely to deprive property, the presumption of resistance on the part of the proprietor forces the thief to be prepared to eliminate his victim should he be discovered in the act. The proprietor or any other passerby is therefore permitted to stop the perpetrator from committing the act of theft, even to take his life if necessary. Construction of the town wall clearly affords protection to life as well as to property, regardless of the type of danger facing the town at the time. Why then is the equal per capita component of the security tax levy not uniformly applied? Tosafot propose to resolve this problem by positing that what is crucial for the purpose of determining the nature of the security tax formula is the original intent of the penetrators and not what circumstances might actually force them to do. Clearly, their original intent is merely to deprive the inhabitants of their valuables. They will not freely engage in acts of murder unless their designs are met with resistance.[31]

Tosafot's solution is readily understandable within the framework of the economic-efficiency rationale. With an individual's assessment in the security tax levy made proportional to his presumed effective demand for the expenditure, rather than proportional to the amount of benefits he may actually derive from the project, the *proximate* danger facing the town is the only relevant factor in deciding his tax share. Only the immediate danger facing the town can be said to generate now or in the future a presumptive effective demand on his part to insure against it. Given the state of tranquility the town enjoys, insuring against the threat to human life cannot be said to similarly enter into the town resident's intertemporal demand pattern. Though the security project undeniably affords protection of human life, the townspeople cannot be presumed to want to spend their resources to secure this benefit. Hence, under normal conditions, the equal per capita component of the security levy is inoperative. In contrast, when the town faces the threat of unprovoked acts of murder, the townspeople may certainly be presumed to harbor an effective demand to insure against the risk to human life. With insurance against both property loss and loss of life forming an integral part of the townspeople's basic expenditure preference, half of the necessary outlay is raised by means of an equal per capita levy, while the remaining half is raised by means of a proportional property tax.

R. Grozovsky's Rationalization of the Security Tax Levy. A different rationalization of the security tax levy apparently proceeds from R. Reuven Grozovsky's (1887–1957) analysis of the variability of this levy. In his view, the variability of the method of assessment in connection with the security tax levy can be explained by what we will call the causation principle. Operationally, this principle calls for setting tax shares proportional to degree of responsibility in creating the need for the expenditure. What creates the need for the town wall is the existence of valuables that can be carried away. Property ownership, therefore, serves admirably as a proxy for tracing individual responsibility in creating the need to install security measures. The more property an individual owns, the more responsible he is for attracting thieves to the town. When occasional acts of theft constitute the source of danger to the town, movable property is the only identifiable cause of the menace threatening the town. The property index under these circumstances includes movable property alone. Should the peril be assessed to also consist of acts of vandalism against town property, immovable property can also be identified as a contributing cause of the danger threatening the town. The property index, therefore, expands to include immovable property as well. By logical extension, the causation principle would call for a modification of the usual security tax formula when the townspeople are regarded as likely targets of unprovoked acts of murder. With the need to construct the town wall traced to the mere presence of human life as well as the availability of valuables, one half of the security tax levy is imposed on a per capita basis and the other half is levied proportional to property ownership.

The exemption rabbinical scholars enjoy in connection with the security tax levy, according to R. Grozovsky, proceeds naturally from the causation principle. Rabbinical scholars, by virtue of their piety and Torah scholarship, bear no *responsibility* for bringing calamity upon the community. They play no role in creating the need for the town wall.

Tosafot's solution of why the equal per capita component of the security tax levy is dropped from the tax formula under normal conditions is readily understandable on the basis of the causation principle. The equal per capita component of the security tax levy enters the tax formula only when the mere presence of life can be considered as an independent cause for creating a need to install town security measures. This is certainly the case when the townspeople are regarded as likely targets of unprovoked acts of murder. In contrast, when the town's valuables constitute the entire lure for penetrators, the mere presence of life cannot be regarded as an independent cause in creating the need for the town wall.

R. Grozovsky bolsters the causation rationalization of the security tax levy with the following considerations:

1. R. Menachem of Merseburg, a 15th-century German halakhic authority, calls for a heavier levy on those households whose rooftops conspicuously tower above the average rooftop of the town. The logic offered is that these households cause the town to be visible from a greater distance than it otherwise would be. The greater visibility of the town made possible by these households generates a negative externality to the community by attracting to it a larger than otherwise number of undesirable penetrators.[32] This ruling represents an explicit adoption of the causation principle as an assessment guideline in the security tax levy.

2. Equity in the distribution of a revenue demand imposed by the sovereign on the Jewish community, according to R. Mordechai b. Hillel (d. 1298), calls for the use of a proportional tax based on the volume of business transactions. An individual's assessment is based on his *total* business transactions, whether the transactions were financed by his own capital or by means of someone else's capital.[33] Expanding the tax base to include business transactions financed by

foreign capital is defended on the ground that it is the total volume of business transactions carried out in the community that determine for the sovereign the size of his revenue demand.[34] With the causation principle providing the equity benchmark for distributing the government levy, the selfsame principle, asserts R. Grozovsky, should be used in connection with the security tax levy.

3. R. Elijah ben Solomon Zalman (1720–1797) assimilates the method of distributing the tax burden in the government-levy case with the method the Talmud prescribes for lightening the cargo of a sinking ship.[35] In reference to the latter, the Talmud in *Baba Kamma* 116b states:

> Our Rabbis taught: If a boat was sailing on the sea and a gale arose threatening to sink it so that it became necessary to lighten the cargo, the apportionment [of the loss of each passenger] will have to be made according to the weight of the cargo . . .

The underlying basis for determining participation in both the government levy and the load-reduction operation is the causation principle. In the load-reduction operation, it is the weight of the cargo that is causing the ship to sink. The responsibility of individual passengers to remove the imminent danger is, therefore, fixed in proportion to the weight of their freight. Similarly, it is the volume of business transactions carried out in the town that determines the size of the sovereign's revenue demand. What follows from the above assimilation, according to R. Grozovsky, is the logic of using the causation principle as the equity benchmark in the security tax levy.[36]

The causation principle as a rationale for the security tax levy faces, in our view, several difficulties.

Expanding R. Elijah's assimilation to the security tax levy does not appear valid in view of mainstream exposition of the load-reduction case. The analysis of this case by R. Vidal Yom Tov of Tolosa (fl. 14th cent.) is typical. In his view, the freight-weight formula for the load-reduction operation is an application of the prohibition against rescuing oneself by means of another man's property. Since the gale threatens each passenger with the loss of his entire cargo, no one may maneuver so that his share in the load-reduction operation is less than proportional to his freight weight. Any other formula, such as having the load-reduction operation distributed proportional to cargo value, allows the passenger with the cargo of higher value to salvage his property with his fellow passenger's money, shifting the incidence of the damage threatening them.[37]

Proceeding as a corollary from R. Vidal Yom Tov's rationalization of the load-reduction assessment formula is the inappropriateness of assimilating this case with the security tax levy. This follows from the principle that it is only when damage has already befallen A that he is interdicted against rescuing himself by means of B's money. Here, A may not remove the damage from himself by means of shifting it to B. When the damage, however, is not yet an actuality, A may divert the approaching harm away from himself even if the effect of the maneuver is to shift the damage to B. Hence, should the rushing waters of a bursting dike threaten to flood A's property, the latter may divert the stream elsewhere as long as the waters have not yet reached his property. Once the waters have reached his property, however, he may no longer divert the stream elsewhere, for such action would constitute rescuing himself by means of another's property.[38] Since the security tax levy, as discussed above, is imposed even when the town faces no immediate danger, distributing the levy on a basis other than proportional to property ownership should not constitute unlawful shifting of the intended incidence of damage the town faces.

Supportive of the assertion that the owners of the town's valuables are not legally required to take action to prevent penetration by thieves is Jewish law's treatment of the following negative externality case involving neighboring homeowners: A complains that B's failure to repair a breach in the outer wall of his home has the effect of attracting thieves to the vicinity, causing him property damage and loss. Noting the indirect link between the defendant's action and the resultant damage, R. Joseph Caro (1488–1575), R. Shabbetai b. Meir ha-Kohen (1621–1662), and R. Jacob Lorberbaum (1760–1832) rule that the above negative externality is not actionable in Jewish law. The defendant may not be made to secure his home and is not responsible for theft damage that may occur as a result of his failure to do so.[39] Disputing this opinion, R. Meir Abulafia (1170–1244) regards such negligence as legally actionable. To remove the menace involved, the Jewish court would accordingly order the owner of the unsecured home to undertake the necessary repairs. Moreover, the owner of the unsecured home incurs liability should he fail to meet his obligations here even after proper warning and the neighbor subsequently sustains theft loss.[40] Ruling in a similar manner is R. Moshe Gaon (appointed Gaon of Sura in 825).[41]

Proceeding clearly from the former view is the principle that an individual may not be forced to repair his home so that his neighbor may be protected against the design of thieves, even if he effectively prevented this harm from his neighbor in the past. Though the second view does require removal of the negative externality, extending this sort of obligation to the instance where the defendant did not prevent the said harm from occurring in the past appears groundless.

Moreover, a different version of R. Meir Abulafia's position is presented by R. Jacob b. Asher. The latter's version of R. Abulafia's position, shared by R. Joel Sirkes (1561–1640) as well, understands the case to refer to the circumstance where A and B own adjoining courtyards. Here, to eliminate visual trespass, Jewish law requires the neighbors to share in the expense of building a partition wall. Suppose B refuses to contribute his share and as a result the wall is not built. Should A sustain theft losses subsequent to B's refusal to participate in the partition wall, the latter is held responsible according to R. Meir Abulafia. This version of R. Abulafia's position lends plausibility to the assumption that the latter would be in agreement that B may not be required to repair his home or fence so that his neighbor, A, may be protected against the designs of thieves.[42]

Further support that the causation principle cannot be used as the rationale for the security tax levy proceeds, in our view, from the following analysis of R. Vidal Yom Tov in connection with the load-reduction operation. Noting Maimonides' adoption of the talmudic dictum that the load-reduction operation in a sinking ship is to be distributed proportional to cargo weight, R. Vidal questions why he rules that if a passenger jettisoned cargo from a sinking ship, he is not only not liable but merits acclamation as he has therewith saved the passengers' lives. Consistency appears to demand that the loss of the jettisoned cargo should be distributed among the passengers proportional to the weight of their cargo. Resolving the difficulty, R. Vidal posits that in the latter instance Maimonides refers to the circumstance where the ship is sinking not because of the sudden appearance of a gale, but rather because one of the passengers brought more cargo aboard the ship than he was allotted. Since the illegal cargo is what is causing the ship to sink, the extra weight is regarded halakhically as a "pursuer" (*rodef*) and anyone aboard is permitted to jettison it, incurring no liability for the damage. The loss here must be borne completely by the passenger who violated his cargo quota. The former instance, however, speaks of the case where no one violated the quota agreement and it is a gale that is threatening to capsize the ship. Here, should one of the passengers jettison some cargo, the loss is shared by all the passengers proportional to the weight of their freight.[43] Now, it is quite clear that were it not for the cargo aboard the ship, the gale would present no danger to the passengers; nevertheless, since no one violated the quota agreement, none of the cargo is regarded as bringing on the danger the ship faces. Analogously, though it is the valuables of the townspeople that attract thieves to the community, these valuables should not be regarded halakhically as causative agents, generating to their owners an obligation to remove the danger.

Though the causation principle finds explicit advocacy in the negative externality explanation that R. Menachem advances for his ruling of heavier assessment for households whose rooftops are conspicuously higher than average, the ruling itself is entirely consistent with the economic-efficiency rationale. Conspicuous homes are subject to a higher than average probability of being victimized because they make potentially more rewarding targets for thieves than smaller homes. The presumption that conspicuous households, *ceteris paribus*, would spend more than average to insure against the risk of looting is most reasonable. R. Menachem's ruling can, therefore, be viewed as an extension of the talmudic prescription of imposing a heavier tax burden on households located closer to the town wall. Both conspicuous size and location at the outer perimeter of the town increase the probability that a household would be victimized by thieves and validate the presumption of a higher than average effective demand for security measures.

Supportive of the assertion that R. Menachem's ruling can be rationalized on grounds other than the negative externality argument advanced by its author is a comparison of the presentation of this view by R. Moses Isserles (1525–1572)[44] against its original text. Whereas the externality argument appears in the original text, R. Isserles defends the heavier assessment merely by noting that higher than average height makes the house conspicuous (*o'sei ayin*). What R. Isserles intends to impart here could simply be that conspicuousness generates for the household, *ceteris paribus*, an above-average presumptive demand for security measures.

Moreover, the context in which R. Isserles presents R. Menachem's view makes it unclear whether he adopts his position in relation to the security levy or restricts his adoption of the view solely to the government levy. In the latter instance, as discussed above, the causation principle as an equity guideline stands on firmer ground.

The Water Supply Levy
Jewish law calls for coercive participation in a well-digging project.[45] Invoking the benefit principle, the Talmud extends the tax base for this levy to include rabbinical scholars. The inclusion of rabbinical scholars, however, is only justified when the townspeople decide to execute the project by means of taxing themselves for the necessary expenditure. Should they decide to implement the project by means of donating their own labor time for the digging operation, rabbinical

scholars may not be forced to participate, as performing common labor publicly demeans the honor of the Torah.[46] When the latter method is chosen, rabbinical scholars may not even be taxed in order to hire substitutes to do the work for them.[47] On the basis of the benefit principle, orphans are also included in the tax levy. Nonetheless, in the event the digging operation fails to locate water, orphans are entitled to a refund of their contribution. Unlike the adult members of the community, orphans lack the legal capacity to waive their claim to the money the community spent futilely on their behalf.[48]

Equity Benchmark for Communal Projects. Rabbinic authorities are in dispute regarding the appropriate equity benchmark to be used to finance communal projects. R. Solomon Adret apparently adopts the ability-to-pay principle, since he proposes a proportional property tax for all communal projects involving an expenditure.[49]

The operational character of R. Solomon Adret's equity rule can be seen by an examination of the discussions in the responsa literature regarding the appropriate base for the property tax.

Included in the individual's base for the property tax are: (1) the market value of any of his assets up for sale, including land and household articles;[50] and (2) the income he earns from any business asset.[51] The tax base is reduced by the full value of his outstanding debts,[52] and downwardly adjusted should any of his income be earned under unusual conditions of risk.[53] Unpaid earnings, even if past due, are not included in the tax base.[54] Also not included in the tax base is the value of property dedicated to the needs of the poor, or to religious and educational needs.[55]

Other authorities, however, take the view that the costs of communal projects should be distributed on the basis of anticipated benefits. Advocacy of a benefit principle emerges from the analysis of the equity guideline for water-supply projects by R. Menachem ben Abraham Krochmal (1600–1661). He points out that the benefits the town derives from a well-digging project include both a water-supply system and a fire-extinguishing mechanism. While the water-supply benefit is distributed equally among the townspeople, the fire-extinguishing benefit is distributed on an equal per house basis. Half of the cost of this project is, therefore, distributed on an equal per capita basis, while the remaining half is to be apportioned on an equal per house basis.

Should a minority of the townspeople prevail upon the government authorities to provide the Jewish community with a continuous flow of water by connecting it to the reservoir by means of a system of pipes, both the tax base and the equity guideline must be altered from the previous formulation. Since the town already enjoyed water rights, the new construction must be regarded as a mere convenience rather than as a basic need. With the demand for items of convenience income elastic, we may not presume that the pipe project represents a preferred item in the budget of a member of the town unless he so indicates. Hence, only those who have communicated such an interest share in the cost. Including only the interested townspeople in the levy, the formula calls for three fourths of the expense to be apportioned on the basis of property ownership, with the remaining fourth to be levied on an equal per house basis.[56]

Emergent in R. Krochmal's analysis, in our view, is the proposition that in the event the townspeople decide by means of majority vote to undertake the project, the entire community is included in the levy. With the project classified as a luxury, however, its cost is distributed among the townspeople on the same three-fourths/one-fourth basis as in the previous example.

What proceeds from the above analysis is that application of the benefit principle calls for the imposition of an equal per capita levy when the associated project is a necessity, and for a proportional property tax when the associated project is a luxury. How is the dividing line between a necessity and a luxury determined? Reference to the local common standard of living, rather than what constitutes physiological subsistence, is, in our view, critical in the halakhic identification of a necessity. Support of this assertion follows from Maimonides' statement that members of a courtyard may force each other to financially participate in projects that are either a great necessity or generally undertaken in accordance with local custom.[57] This assimilation defines a necessity in terms of the local standard of living. As the community's per capita income rises, items previously regarded as luxuries fall into the category of necessities.

The Well-digging Project and Economic Efficiency. Why Jewish law places the well-digging project in the realm of the public sector can, in our view, be easily explained on the basis of an economic-efficiency argument. Waterworks qualify as a natural monopoly. A single well would provide sufficient water for the needs of the entire community. Moreover, given that exploration and construction outlays comprise most of the costs associated with waterworks, the industry is decidedly a decreasing-cost industry. As output increases, per unit costs decline. Given these salient features, allowing waterworks to be provided on a competitive basis perforce raises the per unit cost of production and is, therefore, against the economic interests of the community. Public sector provision of waterworks transforms the project into a regulated monopoly and, therefore, maximizes consumer welfare.

Should experts regard the public domain as the optimal location of the well, efficiency considerations would dictate public sector provision of this project. Construction of a well in the public domain would not be likely to occur on the basis of the profit motive, for Jewish law entitles the developer of such a project with neither an exclusive right to the water he locates nor an exclusive right to the water that accumulates in his structure.[58] Moreover, waterworks constructed in the public domain would legally be regarded as an "obstacle," and the developer would consequently be held liable for livestock damage occasioned by his waterworks. Indeed, to avoid such liability, the developer would have to formally turn over the cover of his structure to the Jewish court. Only such action would release the developer from his caretaker responsibility.[59] With the market mechanism not likely to produce the well in the public domain, another efficiency-based argument for public sector provision of this project obtains.

The Public Road Repair Levy

Jewish law calls for coercive participation in a public road repair levy. Invoking the benefit principle, the Talmud extends the tax base of this levy to include rabbinical scholars, albeit on the same terms as discussed above in connection with the well-digging project. On the basis of the benefit principle, orphans are also included in the levy.[60]

Why Jewish law places the public road repair project in the realm of the public sector can, in our view, be easily explained on the basis of an economic-efficiency argument. Given the essential need this project satisfies, the presumption that it forms part of the communal effective-demand pattern is reasonable. Reliance on the private sector to undertake the project would, however, subject its execution to doubt. This follows from the strong "free rider" motive associated with public road repair. Each resident would rely on his neighbors to undertake the necessary repair. Widespread attitudes of this nature obviously frustrate the emergence of the project altogether. Public sector intervention represents, therefore, the only effective means of insuring that the repair work will be done.

Communal Religious Obligations

Jewish law empowers the Jewish community to coerce its members to financially participate in a variety of projects of a religious character. These include: (1) various levies designed to create and maintain the institution of public prayer; (2) the appointment and support of a communal religious leader; (3) the establishment of religious-educational institutions for the young; (4) the establishment of charitable institutions for the poor; (5) the purchase of Scrolls of the Law,

Prophets, and Hagiographa; (6) the construction and maintenance of a ritual bathhouse.

Provisions for Public Prayer. Various levies are imposed on the Jewish community for the purpose of establishing and maintaining the institution of public prayer. These include: (1) a public prayerhouse levy;[61] (2) a tax to defray the expense of the cantor's salary;[62] and (3) personal and financial obligations arising out of the requirement for congregational worship during the High Holidays.[63]

Equity Benchmark for Financing the Public Prayer Levy. In opposition to the ability-to-pay advocacy of R. Solomon b. Abraham Adret, various talmudic decisors have advanced tax formulae rooted in the benefit principle for the public prayer institution levies.

R. Moses Sofer (1762–1839), for instance, calls for the following tax formula for the construction of the public prayerhouse: The agreed-upon outlay for the project is divided equally into three parts—one third of the expense is distributed among the townspeople proportional to their property; another third is levied proportional to the number of seats each household will hold in the prayerhouse; the remaining third is collected on an equal per household basis.[64]

A modification of R. Moses Sofer's basic formulation for the construction of the synagogue levy apparently follows from R. Hai ben Sherira Gaon's (939–1038) equity prescription for defraying the expense of the cantor's salary. Taking notice of the multi-faceted role the cantor plays in Jewish communal affairs, his formula decomposes the cantorial function into its religious, ceremonial, and entertainment elements. Communal demand patterns for these various functions are not uniform. At one end of the continuum stands the communal demand for the cantor's distinctly religious duties when he officiates at public prayer sessions. Since participation in these events is obligatory on all male members of the community, the communal demand pattern for the services of the cantor in this context can be described as income-inelastic. With every male member of the community generating a demand for the distinctive religious function of the cantor, the minimum salary necessary to engage a cantor to perform the distinctive religious function alone is allocated among the townspeople on an equal per capita basis.

R. Hai b. Sherira points out that public prayer sessions correspond to the daily communal burnt offerings in the Temple. The equal per capita levy prescribed by Jewish law for the financing of these communal sacrifices should also apply, therefore, to the financing of the component of the cantor's salary that corresponds to his distinctive religious function.

Should the cantor, by virtue of his vocal skills, command a higher than average remuneration for his role of leading the congregation in prayer, his salary differential is allocated among the townspeople on the basis of a proportional property tax. This follows from the presumption that the pattern of communal demand for the aesthetic and artistic dimensions of the cantorial function is highly income-elastic. Similarly, the patterns of communal demand for cantorial renditions at festive and mournful occasions can also be regarded as income-elastic. The differential in earnings that the cantor commands for rendering these services is likewise to be raised on the basis of a proportional property tax.[65]

Decomposing the cantorial role into its constituent parts for the purpose of calculating a tax formula reflects a strong benefit-principle philosophy in tax matters on the part of R. Hai b. Sherira. What also emerges from the above analysis, in our mind, is the view that an individual's assessment in a communal levy is not determined by the amount of benefits he actually reaps from the associated project, but rather on the basis of his presumed money demand for the project at hand. Hence, though the poor and the wealthy *enjoy* the services of the cantor in an equal manner, the presumption that the poor would not spend the same absolute sum as the rich to secure this enjoyment reduces the assessment of the poor in the matter accordingly.

The implication for the public prayerhouse levy that may be drawn from R. Hai b. Sherira's analysis is that the equal per-household component of this levy is based on one third the *minimum* sum necessary to build a public prayerhouse, rather than on one third of the actual expenditure. Similarly, a downward adjustment of the equal per-seat component of the levy would be warranted in the event the expenditure on the seats was more than the minimum amount.

Another equity approach to the problem of defraying the expense of the synagogue project proceeds from the work of the Italian talmudist R. Meir b. Isaac Katzenellenbogen (1473–1565). Noting that the synagogue project is by nature a capital project, R. Katzenellen-bogen points out that the benefit stream this project generates is not confined to the current year, but rather extends over many years. Though all members of the community can be regarded as benefiting equally from the synagogue in the current year, the poorer elements of the community cannot reasonably expect to reap the full range of intertemporal benefits inherent in the project. This follows from the assumption that what ties an individual to a particular geographic location is his property ownership there. Insofar as the poor are propertyless, the probability of their remaining in the town over the life-span of the synagogue is small. This consideration leads R.

Katzenellenbogen to propose a proportional property tax as the most equitable means of financing the synagogue project.[66]

Congregational Worship During the High Holidays. Another fiscal responsibility arising out of the communal obligation to maintain the institution of public prayer is the requirement to maintain congregational worship during the High Holidays. Since a quorum of ten is indispensable for congregational worship, should the townspeople fall short of this number, a levy is imposed to raise a sufficient sum to hire people to complete the quorum (minyan). While Halakhah requires congregational worship on a daily basis, communal legislative authority to impose a coercive levy to complete the quorum is restricted to the High Holidays.[67]

In regard to the equity considerations in distributing the burden of the minyan levy, R. Meir ha-Kohen (fl. 13th cent.) rules that half of the expense should be collected on an equal per capita basis, while the remaining half should be raised by means of a proportional property tax. The equal per capita component of the levy follows from the consideration that all male members of the community share an equal responsibility to establish a minyan in the town for the High Holidays. The proportional property component of the levy is justified on the basis of the benefit principle. The wealthy benefit disproportionately from the establishment of the minyan in the town for the High Holidays. These individuals are reluctant to leave the town even for a short period of time, as their real estate holdings and other possessions would escape their vigilance in the period of their absence. In contrast, the poor show no such strong preference to remain in the town. As far as they are concerned, they could just as easily travel to a nearby town for the High Holidays and join a minyan there.

A variant of the above case occurs when the male members of the community number exactly ten and one or several of them desire to spend the High Holidays outside the town. Insofar as their departure would effectively frustrate the occurrence of congregational worship in the town on the High Holidays, the community may coerce these parties either to remain or to shoulder the expense of hiring substitutes to replace them.

The expense of hiring substitutes, according to R. Meir ha-Kohen, is to be distributed equally among those taking leave of the town. The causation principle is here invoked. All those taking leave are equally responsible for creating the need to hire replacements. The associated expense is, therefore, allocated equally among the responsible parties.[68] R. David b. Samuel (1586–1667) and R. David Solomon Eybeschuetz (d. 1800) call, however, for the responsible parties to share equally in only one half of the expense. The remaining half would be apportioned on the basis of a proportional property tax. This view thus equates the case at hand with the prescribed method of financing the establishment of a minyan for the High Holidays. This assimilation proceeds from the assumption that the community's power to coerce its members to remain in the town for the High Holidays so as not to disrupt congregational worship on these days *derives* from its authority to mandate the creation of a minyan for the High Holidays. With the authority of the community in the former matter of a derivative nature, its method of finance should parallel the tax formula used to distribute the cost for *creating* a minyan for the High Holidays.[69]

Religious Educational Functionaries. The Jewish community is required to appoint and maintain an individual to provide it with religious instruction.[70]

Rabbinical scholars, according to R. Moses Alshekh (d. ca. 1593), are not to be included in the levy as they do not personally benefit from the services of the instructor.[71]

By dint of the ancient ordinance of R. Joshua b. Gamala (d. 69/70 C.E.), every Jewish community is required to establish and maintain religious schools for its young.[72] Should some parents desire to instruct their children themselves, they may not be forced to subsidize the expense of hiring a teacher for the other children of the townspeople. Opting to instruct their own children does not, however, free these parents from their obligation to support the religious education of orphans and children from poor homes.[73]

Coercive participation in the communal educational levy is limited, according to Tosafot and R. Asher b. Jechiel, to the instance where the pupil population in the town is at least twenty-five. Moreover, once the above minimum attains, the townspeople may not force each other to hire more than one instructor until the pupil population reaches forty. At this point, a teacher's aide must be hired to assist the instructor in his duties. This arrangement of hiring one teacher with an assistant suffices until the class size reaches fifty. At this level, the class must be divided and instructed separately.[74]

Maimonides et alia, however, maintain that coercive participation in the communal educational levy applies no matter how small the size of the town's pupil population. Another point of stringency advanced by Maimonides in religious educational law is the requirement to have a teacher's aide to assist the instructor for a class whose size is in excess of twenty-five pupils. An additional aide must be hired when the pupil population exceeds forty. This arrangement of hiring one teacher and two aides to assist him no longer suffices when the pupil population reaches fifty. At this level, the class must be divided and instructed separately.[75]

Charitable Institutions. The Jewish community is required to establish and maintain charitable institutions to provide for the needs of the poor.[76] In talmudic times this obligation was carried out by means of weekly collections for the community charity box *(kuppah),* and daily collections for the community charity plate *(tamchui).*[77] In addition, a special charity drive was conducted before the Passover season for the purpose of allowing the poor to purchase matzos for the holiday *(ma'ot chittin).*[78] Another dimension of the public subsidy to the poor consisted of a compulsory hospitality scheme, wherein the townspeople were forced to take turns providing lodging for guests.[79]

Residency Requirements for Inclusion in Public Charity Levies. Liability for contributing to the public charity levies attains only after a residency requirement is met. This requirement is not the same for the various charity levies. Twelve months is required for inclusion in the *ma'ot chittin* drive,[80] nine months for inclusion in the burial fund, and six months for the clothing levy.[81] The residency requirement for inclusion in the daily charity collections and the weekly food collections is a matter of dispute. R. Isaac Alfasi and Maimonides require thirty days for the former and three months for the latter.[82] Reversing these requirements, R. Asher b. Jechiel and R. Jacob ben Asher prescribe thirty days for inclusion in the weekly food collections and three months for inclusion in the daily charity collections.[83]

Individual assessments in these collections were based on a proportional property tax.[84] Refusal on the part of an individual to meet his assessment allows the Jewish court to subject him to physical duress and/or to seize his property as a pledge, if necessary, to exact payment.[85]

Widespread poverty forced many Jewish communities in the rishonic period (mid-11th–mid-15th cent.) to abandon most of the above elements of public philanthropy in favor of private philanthropy.[86]

Income Redistribution in Jewish Law. Public and private philanthropy perforce change the community's pattern of income distribution from what it would be if the marketplace were left to its own devices.

Judaism's notion of equity in the income-distribution pattern is revealed by an examination of the laws relating to the obligation to give charity and the eligibility requirements to receive charity. A brief treatment of these laws follows. Our discussion will be confined to a treatment of Jewish charity laws that are applicable in the Diaspora today.

The charity obligation in Jewish law consists of satisfying the needs of the poor.[87] Simultaneous requests for assistance must be treated on a priority basis.[88] Accordingly, a food request, for instance, must be dealt with before a plea for clothing, since it is more urgent.[89] Nonetheless, means permitting, even the purely psychological needs of the poor must be met. In this regard the Talmud relates that Hillel the Elder (1st cent. B.C.E.–1st cent. C.E.) provided a certain poor man with a horse to ride on and a slave to run in front of him, because this individual had been accustomed to these luxuries while he was wealthy.[90]

Assistance must be rendered with the utmost care to preserve the recipient's dignity and minimize his shame.[91]

To adequately meet demands for public assistance, charity wardens are required, if necessary, to borrow money in the name of charity. These debts are discharged as new revenues accumulate into the public charity chest, even without consulting the donors.[92]

Satisfying a supplicant's needs *fully* is mainly a collective rather than an individual responsibility. Confronted with an assistance request, an individual is not himself required to shoulder the entire burden of financing the need. The entire community must share this responsibility. Nonetheless, in the event of refusal or absence of cooperation, the individual, means permitting, is required to shoulder *alone* the burden of financing the need.[93]

The obligation to satisfy fully the needs of the poor is subject to a means constraint. Three characteristics of charity-giving have been identified by the Sages: donating 20 percent of one's income to charity reflects a magnanimous nature; contributing 10 percent is a middling virtue; devoting less than 10 percent of one's income to charity reflects a penurious nature.[94] Out of fear that overgenerosity in giving charity could make the donor himself vulnerable to poverty, the Sages enacted an interdict against donating more than 20 percent of one's income to charity.[95] This interdict has been variously interpreted. Some authorities understand it as a restriction on the proportion of his income that an individual may devote to a charity fund in the *absence* of requests for assistance. Should an individual be confronted, however, with pleas for assistance, no maximum restriction on the amount of his aid is prescribed. Other authorities suspend the interdict only in relation to bequests and to situations where the aid would avert loss of human life.[96]

The base against which the 10 percent charity obligation applies is arrived at by deducting from gross receipts business expenses, business losses,[97] and income taxes paid to various governments.[98]

We now turn to the eligibility requirements Jewish law prescribes for receiving charity. Wealth level and liquidity position are of critical importance in Judaism's definition of poverty. Halakhically, a house-hold is classified as poor when its capital is insufficient to support it for an entire year. In talmudic times, this criterion translated into defining poverty as failure to attain a net worth of two hundred *zuz*. When net worth consisted of capital invested in business transactions, the above sum was reduced to fifty *zuz* on the assumption that an active capital of such size would generate subsistence for a year.[99]

Claims for assistance on the basis of an inadequate cash flow are usually denied when net worth exceeds the poverty line. Under these conditions, the household is expected to liquidate its real estate and other asset holdings to increase its cash flow to an adequate level. Several exceptions to this general rule should, however, be noted. An individual is not expected to sell his home or any other essential household article to attain a liquidity level consistent with a subsistence standard of living. Under these conditions, the household qualifies for private, though not public, assistance even though its net worth is above the poverty line.[100] In addition, Jewish law recognizes the fact that the market value of farmland is given to seasonal fluctuation.[101] Close to harvest-time, during the summer months, its value is relatively high. Immediately after the harvest, during the autumn, its market value is relatively low. Should the household's liquidity squeeze occur during the depressed autumn market, it qualifies for public assistance until it can manage to sell its land for at least one half of its harvest-time value.[102]

Should the household's liquidity squeeze compromise its bargaining position to such an extent that it cannot manage to sell its holdings at the prevailing market price, the household qualifies for public assistance until it can sell its holdings at the prevailing market price.[103]

When real estate values are, however, generally depressed, a family, regardless of the size of the capital loss it would sustain by liquidating its real estate holdings, does not qualify for public assistance as long as its net worth remains above the poverty line.[104]

Jewish law's definition of poverty also takes into account the location of an individual's assets. In order for an asset to be included in net worth, it must be accessible to its proprietor. Hence, a traveler, whose assets are situated in his place of permanent residence, qualifies for public assistance when his funds run out. When he returns home he need not return any charity he received while on his travels.[105]

Charity in its noblest form, according to Jewish teachings, consists of aiding a faltering individual from falling into the throes of poverty. The position of such a person must be stabilized, with his dignity preserved, by either conferring him with a gift, extending him a loan, entering into a partnership with him, or creating a job for him.[106]

Taking action to prevent an individual from falling to the poverty level translates, in our view, into the obligation of the public sector to pursue policies that would create a favorable economic environment, thereby minimizing unemployment and poverty.

Modern economic analysis tells us that a free enterprise–oriented economy cannot attain a high per capita income and a high level of employment unless its public sector assumes a very large scope and role. This follows from the Keynesian insight that it is the level of aggregate demand that determines the equilibrium level of income. Equilibrium obtains when the level of spending equals the value of the goods and services produced. Should the aggregate level of demand fall short of this value, suppliers would find it rational to contract output in the next decision period. An examination of the constituent elements of the aggregate demand schedule, i.e., consumption, investment, and government spending, demonstrates that avoidance of secular stagnation requires government spending to assume a high level.

Cross-sectional studies have consistently shown consumption spending to be a declining function of income. The leakage of savings, therefore, can be expected to become more acute as the national income level increases. A secular decline in the growth of consumption spending, combined with a sluggish population growth rate and the piling up of the capital stock, produces an environment inimical to investment. Aggregate demand would therefore not be expected to achieve a high level unless it is artificially propped up by means of a high level of government spending.

The Ritual Bathhouse Levy. Townspeople may coerce each other to contribute toward the construction and maintenance of a ritual bathhouse (mikveh).[107] Since Halakhah requires married women to periodically immerse themselves in a mikveh before normal marital relations may be resumed, this institution has a central role in Jewish family life.[108] Men, too, by force of custom,[109] immerse themselves in a mikveh on the eve of Festivals and on the eve of the Day of Atonement.[110]

Assimilating the mikveh levy with the synagogue levy, R. Moses Feinstein (b. 1895-) calls for half the revenue need in the mikveh levy to be raised on an equal per capita basis, with the remaining half to be collected proportional to property ownership.[111]

R. Chayyim Benveniste (1603–1673) posits that the inclusion of widowers in the mikveh levy follows even according to the benefit-principle advocacy of R. Moses Alshekh. These individuals apparently derive no tangible benefits from the mikveh since they can perform the custom of ritual immersion on the eve of Festivals and the eve of the Day of Atonement by making use of the town lake. Nevertheless, should the authorities, for some reason, prohibit use of the lake on these several occasions, circumstances would force the widowers to make use of the communal ritual bathhouse. The above possibility, remote as it may seem, provides ground for assessing widowers in the communal mikveh project.[112]

Religious Project Levies and Economic Freedom

Within the framework of Judaism's conceptualization of involuntary action, coercive participation in the various religious projects outlined above can, in our view, be easily reconciled with the Pareto Optimality criterion. Coercing an individual to discharge his religious obligations is not regarded by Jewish law as duress. Maimonides' treatment of legal compulsion in connection with Jewish divorce law illustrates this position.

> If a person who may be legally compelled to divorce his wife refuses to do so, an Israelite court in any place and at any time may scourge him until he says, "I consent." He may then write a divorce bill, and it is a valid divorce bill . . . . And why is this divorce bill not null and void, seeing that it is the product of duress . . . ? Because duress applies only to him who is compelled and pressed to something which the Torah does not obligate him to do, for example, one who is lashed until he consents to sell something or give it away as a gift. On the other hand, he whose *evil inclination* induces him to violate a commandment or commit a transgression, and who is lashed until he does what he is obligated to do, or refrains from what he is forbidden to do, cannot be regarded as a victim of duress; rather, *he has brought duress upon himself by submitting to his evil intention.* Therefore, this man who refuses to divorce his wife inasmuch as he desires to be of the Israelites, to abide by all the commandments, and to keep away from transgressions—it is only his inclination that has overwhelmed him—once he is lashed until his inclination is weakened and he says "I consent," it is the same as if he had given the divorce bill voluntarily . . . [113]

Moreover, within the framework of Judaism's belief system, it appears valid to presume that even in the absence of specific direction, the Jew harbors an effective demand to create and maintain the aforementioned religious projects. This follows from the teaching of

Simeon the Just (4th cent. B.C.E.), "The world stands on three things: on Torah, Divine worship, and acts of loving-kindness."[114]

Relatedly, Maimonides, in his treatment of Jewish religious education law, states:

> If a city has made no provision for the education of the young, its inhabitants are placed under a ban, till such teachers have been engaged. And if they persistently neglect this duty, the city is excommunicated, for the world is only maintained by the breath of schoolchildren.[115]

Moreover, Judaism teaches that the quality and fullness of material well-being depend on the degree of moral elevation and piety society attains.[116]

Given the essential *material* benefits that religious education, public prayer, and charity generate to society, the presumption that support of these institutions forms part of the individual's demand pattern seems reasonable. Reliance on a system of voluntarism, however, would likely result in an underallocation of resources for these purposes.

The inadequacy of the voluntarism approach is most obvious in the public prayerhouse and ritual bathhouse projects. Here, the inability to exclude those who did not participate in the construction would, at the very least, subject these projects to inordinate delay, for townspeople would rely on each other to undertake the projects. Given man's selfish side, voluntary support of religious education and the needs of the poor could easily result in an underallocation of resources from a social standpoint. Public sector intervention to insure adequate spending and widespread participation to finance religious obligations is therefore justified.

· 10
Public Finance

Public Debt Finance in Economic Theory

Debt creation, as opposed to tax collection, is recommended by modern public finance as the appropriate method of financing capital projects. This prescription follows from both efficiency and equity considerations.

Since the free enterprise economy, left to its own devices, would not generate sufficient aggregate demand to allow full-employment GNP, government spending must be relied upon to close this gap. Insofar as income taxes would, for the most part, be spent in any case by the private sector, financing governmental activity by means of taxation does not sufficiently increase aggregate demand. For government to exert an expansionary influence on the economy, some of its activities must be financed from income that would otherwise have been saved. Financing government capital projects by means of debt creation accomplishes this end. Debt finance is hence what makes government spending effective in taking up what would otherwise be a slack in aggregate demand. While overexpansion of the public sector may prove harmful to the economy, deficit finance contributes positively to the attainment of a high per capita income and stands as a bulwark against severe recession.

Debt creation as a means of financing capital projects recommends itself over taxation from the standpoint of equity too. While taxation confines the burden of financing capital projects to the income stream of the current period, debt creation allows this burden to be spread over the length of the asset's benefit stream. Amortizing the debt over the length of the asset's life accomplishes this end.

Public Debt Finance in Jewish Law

Figuring prominantly in the role Jewish law assigns the public sector, as discussed in Chapter 9, is the responsibility to finance a variety of capital projects.

Given the social welfare aspect of the public debt, deficit finance appears, in our view, to be consistent with the Jewish State's obligation to provide for the needs of the poor. Charity, in its noblest form, according to Jewish teaching, as discussed in Chapter 9, consists of aiding a faltering individual from falling into the throes of poverty. Taking action to prevent an individual from falling to the poverty line translates, in our view, into an obligation of the public sector to pursue policies that would foster a favorable economic environment, minimizing thereby unemployment and poverty. Given the pivotal importance of the public debt in fostering economic well-being, the Jewish State's social welfare obligation would require it to finance its capital projects by means of debt creation.

Jewish law's espousal of the benefit principle of taxation leads, in our view, to the appropriateness of making use of debt creation as the means of financing capital projects.

Consideration of the intertemporal benefit stream in the synagogue project led R. Katzenellenbogen, as discussed in Chapter 9, to propose a proportional property tax as the method of financing this capital project. Relating R. Katzenellenbogen's equity guideline to modern public finance leads, in our view, to the appropriateness of financing capital projects by means of debt creation.

The Ribbit Constraint

The ability of the Jewish public sector to raise revenue by means of debt creation is apparently severely constrained by the interdict against loan transactions involving interest payments (ribbit).[1]

Insofar as ribbit law does not prohibit the Jew from paying or receiving an interest premium in his dealings with a non-Jew,[2] the Jewish public sector could feasibly borrow funds from non-Jews at an interest premium. Financing public sector needs in this manner may prove unattractive, however, as it entails incurring an *externally* held debt.

The Monopoly Concession Method

Financing public expenditures by means other than taxation engaged the interest of the early talmudic decisors. R. Isaac b. Sheshet Perfet (1326–1408), for example, suggested that the community should auction to its members the exclusive privilege of trading in particular commodities. Interested parties would pay for their monopoly concessions by means of promissory notes. To raise immediate cash, the community could then sell these notes at a discount.[3]

R. Abraham Slonick's Fiscal Plan

Pointing out the limited revenue potential of such a scheme, R. Abraham Slonick (d. ca. 1642) recommended a more sophisticated plan. The following hypothetical example provides the essential features of his fiscal plan: Suppose the debt of the community totals $900. With the objective of eliminating this debt, a wealthy member of the community (A) is prevailed upon to write to the community a promissory note of $1000 payable in six months. To raise immediate cash, the community then sells this note at a discount price of $900 to B. When A's promissory note matures, the community prevails upon another of its wealthy members (C) to produce a note payable to the community in six months in the amount of, say, $1200. C's promissory note is then sold to B in exchange for his $1000 claim. The community then returns the $1000 promissory note to A. Should B desire cash for his claim, A would be prevailed upon to produce another note of indebtedness to the community in the amount of, say, $1200, payable in six months. A's new note would then be sold by the community at a $1000 discount price to D, with the proceeds of the sale used to satisfy B's $1000 cash claim. Having retrieved A's original note of indebtedness in exchange for the $1000 payment to B, the community returns this note to A.[4]

Playing a central role in R. Slonick's fiscal scheme is the sale of notes of indebtedness at a discount. To avoid *ribbit* violation, discount sales of this variety, it should be noted, must follow certain procedures. One vitally necessary condition is buyer C's agreement to absorb the loss in the event the original debtor (A) defaults. Should the seller (B) guarantee the note against default, the transaction is legally not regarded as a sale and instead is categorized as a loan. Characterized as "near to gain and far from loss" from C's standpoint, the transaction violates the rabbinical extension of the *ribbit* interdict *(avak ribbit)*. The capital gains C realizes when he collects the debt at maturity amounts to a *ribbit* charge. Though C receives the *ribbit* payment from the original debtor (A), rather than from his own debtor (B), the debtor-creditor relationship that remains intact between A and B makes it as if A instructed B to pay the *ribbit* payment to C on his behalf.[5]

Avoidance of *ribbit* violation in debt transfers also requires that the sale be arranged by means of a proper symbolic act *(kinyan)*. The type of symbolic act required depends on whether the debt is oral or written. Transfer of ownership of an oral debt requires the original creditor (B) to instruct his debtor (A) to make payment of the debt to another party (C). Referred to as the *ma'amad sheloshtan* condition, the instruction must be made in the presence of B. In the case of a written debt, B must write either on a separate document or on the debt instrument itself that he is transferring ownership of the debt with all the liens it generates to C. The written instrument of indebtedness must then be actually handed over to C. This requirement is referred to as the *kanu miyado* condition.[6]

Noting the common business practice of effecting transfer of ownership of a written debt by means of the original creditor endorsing the reverse side of the debt instrument, Dayan Basri legitimizes this method too. This follows from Jewish law's recognition of prevailing business practice as satisfying its requirement of a symbolic act.[7]

Failure to transfer ownership of the debt by means of a proper symbolic act, according to many authorities, removes the transaction from the legal category of sale and confers upon it the status of a loan. The loan status disallows the purchaser of the note to collect from the debtor more than he paid for it.[8]

Integrating the above conditions into R. Slonick's fiscal scheme requires the community to transfer A's note of indebtedness to B by means of a proper symbolic act. In addition, the community may not guarantee A's note against default. B's failure to agree to absorb the loss in the event A defaults characterizes his subsequent capital gain as a *ribbit* payment.

R. Joshua ha-Kohen Falk's Fiscal Plan

A variant of R. Slonick's public finance scheme is advanced by R. Joshua ha-Kohen Falk. Otherwise identical with R. Slonick's plan, R. Falk's plan requires the supplier of the note of indebtedness (A) to pay in advance his share of communal taxes for the term of the note. This condition follows from the consideration that raising cash by means of selling A's note averts for the community, for the present, the necessity of taxing itself to pay off its collective debt. Should A not have paid his communal taxes in advance for the term of his note, communal sale of his note generates for A this selfsame benefit of temporary tax relief. Hence, A's provision of a note of indebtedness to the community amounts to a subterfuge on his part to borrow money at interest to pay off his share of the communal debt. Such action violates *ribbit* law. In contrast, when A has paid his communal taxes in advance for the entire term of the note, the discount sale of his note generates no benefit to him in the form of temporary tax relief. With the community not viewed as acting as A's agent in the sale of his note here, the transaction involves merely the sale of A's indebtedness to B. No violation of *ribbit* law is entailed.[9]

R. Moshe Sofer's Fiscal Plan

Another public finance plan having direct implications for the modern state is found in the work of the Hungarian decisor R. Moshe Sofer (1762–1839). In a responsum dealing with the public financing of a communal guesthouse for the poor and a cemetery wall, R. Sofer ruled that an individual who borrowed money at interest from a non-Jew in order to lend the community the necessary funds is entitled to tax relief. Providing for the needs of the poor is a responsibility devolving on all residents of the town. Analogous to a division of labor agreement among partners, assumption of the burden of financing these projects by a segment of the community entitles them to lighter tax treatment in connection with other communal levies.[10]

Extension of R. Sofer's analysis has led some modern decisors to find no *ribbit* objection against the Jewish State's directly issuing interest-bearing debt.[11]

Hetter Iska

Raising capital at a cost without violating *ribbit* law is frequently resorted to in the private sector by means of the *hetter iska* arrangement. A description of this arrangement and its applicability to public finance follows.

Though parties to an ordinary business partnership enjoy, in Jewish law, considerable latitude in drawing up the terms of their agreement, a special form of business organization, called *iska,* is subject to *ribbit* regulation. The distinctive feature of iska is that the financier plays no operational or managerial role in the business enterprise. Should the active partner, however, also furnish part of the venture's capital, the arrangement loses its *iska* character.[12]

To be free of *avak ribbit,* the rabbinical extensions of the *ribbit* interdict, the *iska* arrangement is (1) subject to a profit-loss division constraint; and (2) must provide for compensation for the labor services of the active partner.

Profit-Loss Division Constraint

An *iska* agreement calling for the financier to reap more than 50 percent of the profits but to absorb less than 50 percent of the losses is prohibited. From the standpoint of the financier such an arrangement, in talmudic terms, is "near to profit and far from loss" and hence violates *avak ribbit* law.[13]

While any *symmetrical* profit-loss division frees the *iska* arrangement from the "near to profit and far from loss" prohibition, transferring capital for *iska* purposes without any stipulation in regard to the profit-loss division confers upon the transfer a half-loan, half-deposit character. Profits and losses in the non-express case are therefore divided equally between the financier and the active partner.[13a]

Compensation for Labor Services

The compensation requirement, referred to as the *sekhar tircha* condition, follows from an examination of the legal status of the *iska* transfer. Given that responsibility for accidental loss is what differentiates the legal status of the debtor from the bailee, Jewish law confers a loan-deposit status on the *iska* arrangement. The portion of the capital transfer that the active partner assumes responsibility for takes on the character of a debt, while the remaining portion takes on the character of a deposit. Now, since the agreement calls for the active partner to invest the funds for the benefit of both himself and his financier, performing his managerial function gratis amounts to a disguised interest premium as a precondition for receiving the loan.[14]

Provided the stipulation is agreed to before the capital transfer is made, the *sekhar tircha* requirement may be satisfied with a nominal fee. Pre-*iska* term arrangement of *sekhar tircha* allows the nominal fee to suffice even when the *iska* generates an opportunity cost to the managing partner in the form of calling for him to desist from selling his own wares while merchandising the *iska*.[15]

Hetter Iska and the Efficiency of Capital Markets

Given the "near to profit and far from loss" constraint of the talmudic *iska*, this financial arrangement may prove an inefficient means of attracting capital for projects involving much risk and uncertainty. What is needed is a financial arrangement that would provide sufficient inducement to channel surplus funds to investment demand, but would not at the same time violate *ribbit* law. To meet this need, a variant of the talmudic *iska*, popularly referred to as *hetter iska*, evolved. Going through different phases of development, this financial arrangement culminated in the use of a formal text in business transactions of various sorts in the late 1500s. What the *hetter iska* involves essentially is the attachment of conditions to the talmudic *iska* for the purpose of both guaranteeing the financier's principal against loss and increasing his chances of realizing a profit from the capital transfer.

To insure his principal, the financier (A) may attach conditions to the *iska* and stipulate that if they are not met, responsibility for losses devolves entirely on the managing partner (B). Specification of the types of investment B may enter into with the *iska* and the security measures he must adopt for the *iska* income are examples of conditions A might want to attach to the *iska*. Since fulfillment of the conditions is feasible, and B may avert full responsibility for losses by adhering to them, the arrangement is not regarded, from A's standpoint, as "near to profit and far from loss."[16] What follows is the inadmissibility of setting conditions that are either impossible to fulfill or are not usually undertaken by business people. Such stipulations on the part of A constitute a subterfuge to exact *ribbit* and are therefore forbidden.[17] On similar grounds, R. Abraham Y. Karelitz disallows the financier to stipulate conditions that do not in any way relate to the *iska* arrangement. Violating the *avak ribbit* interdict on this account, for example, would be a stipulation disallowing B from eating oranges for the entire term of the *iska* agreement and calling for his assumption of full responsibility for losses should he violate this condition.[18]

Stipulations of the permissible variety, it should be noted, do not impede the managing partner's flexibility to depart from the conditions. Since his intention is to seize upon opportunities for greater profit, his departure from the stipulation is not morally objectionable as long as he faces the consequences of failure.[19]

Another clause that may be inserted in the *iska* agreement for the purpose of securing A's principal is the stipulation that B's claim for loss will be accepted only if it is corroborated by the testimony of designated witnesses (C and D).[20] Disqualifying the testimony of all witnesses except C and D is permissible, according to R. David b. Samuel ha-Levi (1586–1667), as long as these designated individuals are known to be at least slightly conversant with the *iska* affair.[21]

To increase the chances of earning a profit on the capital transfer, A may stipulate that B's claim regarding the amount of profits the *iska* realizes will be accepted only by means of his solemn oath (*shevuah chamurah*). Insofar as B can always maintain accurate records of the *iska* transactions and take the solemn oath in regard to the profits realized, the solemn oath element of the agreement does not characterize it, from the standpoint of A, as "near to profit and far from loss."[22]

Requiring corroboration of the profit claim by means of designated witnesses violates, however, *avak ribbit* law. Why the designated-witness condition is admissible in connection with the loss claim but not here is explained by an examination of the strength of A's counterclaim in each case. While A can positively attest to the amount of the *iska* transfer, he cannot with certainty dispute B's profit statement. Given the weak nature of A's counterclaim in the latter case, he may not disqualify all but a few designated witnesses from validating B's statement. Moreover, assuming the veracity of the loss statement, the overpayment occasioned by agreement to the designated-witness clause could be given to A in the form of a gift. Since the payment in its entirety amounts to no more than the principal, *ribbit* law is not violated. In contrast, any overpayment of profits to A occasioned by the designated-witness clause would violate *ribbit* law even if the differential is given as a gift, since the total payment A receives exceeds his principal. [23]

To further increase his chances of earning a profit, A may stipulate that payment of an agreed-to sum, referred to as *sekhar hitpashrut*, would relieve B of both his solemn-oath obligation and any further monetary obligation should A's share in the profits exceed this sum. Similarly, the *iska* agreement may call for A to receive a fixed sum as his share in the profits, with the proviso that B may reduce this payment by any amount by taking a solemn oath that A's share in the profits did not amount to this sum. [24] To increase the probability that A will actually realized the *sekhar hitpashrut*, the *iska* agreement may call for the attachment of all B's business profits to the *iska* venture. [25] This clause effectively precludes B from opting for the solemn oath unless A's prorated share in the profits that *all* B's ventures earned during the *iska* term fell short of the *sekhar hitpashrut* sum.

Another advantage proceeding from the garnishment clause for A is to severely restrict B's ability to plead self-evident loss and extricate himself thereby from both his profit-sharing obligation and submission to the solemn oath. [26] Self-evident loss is illustrated when the *iska* transaction involved a real estate investment and its market value declined. Now, with the profits of all B's ventures attached to the *iska* agreement at hand, a plea of self-evident loss would be admissible only if it were common knowledge that all B's business dealings during the *iska* term had failed.

Limitations of the Hetter Iska Arrangement

The legitimacy of the *hetter iska* arrangement as a financial mechanism is limited to commercial ventures. Having received capital for the purpose of *iska* (business), the recipient is obligated to invest it in a commercial venture and is prohibited from making personal use of it. [27] Misappropriating the capital for personal use, according to R. Baruch b. Samuel of Mainz (ca. 1150–1221) transforms the deposit part of the *iska* into a debt. With the *entire* capital transfer taking on now the legal character of a debt, return of anything more than the principal violates *ribbit* law.[28] Following this line of reasoning, R. Shneur Zalman of Lyady (1745–1813) posits that even if the *iska* agreement expressly allows B to make personal use of the capital transfer on a loan basis, appropriation for personal use of more than A's percentage share in the profits disallows A from collecting his agreed-to share in the profits. The original part loan–part deposit legal character of the *iska* may, however, be restored by returning the temporary loan to a third party (C). Acting on behalf of A, C repossesses the appropriated sum and returns it to B for *iska* purposes. This device does not suffice in the misappropriation case. Here, the original character of the *iska* is not restored unless the misappropriated sum is directly returned to A and recycled by him to B for *iska* purposes.[29]

Given the inapplicability of *hetter iska* in relation to transactions for consumption purposes, the segment of the capital market covered by this arrangement hinges on how broadly Jewish law defines a business transaction.

Advancing a very broad view of an investment transaction is R. Joseph Saul Nathanson of Lemberg (1810–1875). Classified as *iska*, in his view, is a capital transfer that makes it possible for the recipient to continue his normal income-generating activities. Accordingly, R. Nathanson ruled that a religious-school teacher may acquire capital by means of *hetter iska* for the purpose of paying off his debts. Without the capital transfer, the teacher would be forced to leave his job and seek a higher-paying one elsewhere. Since the transaction allows him to continue on his job it is classified as *iska*, with the consequence that it may call for dividends for the financier.

Also qualifying as *iska*, in R. Nathanson's view, is the acquisition of capital by an individual for the purpose of debt reduction to avert the forced sale of his home. Receiving dividends here is legitimized because the profit for the recipient of the transfer consists of both the avoidance of a capital loss and the circumstance that it is unnecessary for him to rent an apartment.[30]

Disputing the above view, R. Meir Arik (ca. 1925) conceptualizes *iska* profit as earnings realized either form the investment of the original capital or from a capital or merchandise the recipient substitutes for it. Profits in the form of avoidance of liquidation or loss would not, in his view, legitimize the receipt of dividends on the part of the financier.[31]

Despite the narrow application of *hetter iska* proceeding from the view of R. Arik et alia, this arrangement can easily accommodate the *businessman* desiring to acquire capital for personal needs. Toward this end, the *iska* arrangement would be designed in the following manner: A transfers capital to B for general *iska* purposes, but gives him permission to make immediate use of the funds for personal finance. To legitimize the payment of dividends to A, B transfers to A part ownership of merchandise in his possession, equivalent in value to the original capital transfer. This merchandise substitutes for the original sum and assumes its legal character. Should B not have in his possession substitutable merchandise at the time the *iska* was entered into, he obligates himself to acquire merchandise during the *iska* term and sell it at a profit for the benefit of himself and A.[32]

Hetter Iska and Public Finance

The *hetter iska* arrangement has, in our view, much applicability for Jewish public sector finance. Since government spending financed by means of debt creation allows the economy to achieve a much higher level of income than would otherwise be possible, public debt would appear to fall into R. Nathanson's conceptualization of *iska*. While R. Arik's narrower formulation of *iska* leads to the inadmissibility of *hetter iska* for general public debt creation, the substitution clause, discussed above, allows the *hetter iska* mechanism to accommodate public finance needs. Accordingly, the *hetter iska* could call for the public sector to substitute some amount of its assets for the capital transfer. With the profits of the *iska* consisting of the appreciation in market value of these assets during the *iska* term,[33] legitimacy would be given to a *sekhar hitpashrut* arrangement.

R. Shimon Greenfeld (d. 1930) finds legitimacy in the Jewish public sector issuing interest-bearing debt without recourse to the *hetter iska* mechanism. Debt status obtains in Jewish law only when the loan transaction generates for the creditor a *personal lien* on the debtor. Should the debt be collectable only from specific designated assets of the debtor, the transaction is not legally characterized as debt and hence is not subject to *ribbit* regulation. Now, since government debt does not generate for the bondholders a personal lien on any individual, and for that matter not even a privilege to collect their debt from specific assets, public debt is not subject to *ribbit* regulation. Similarly, since the corporate form of business organization generates liability for the share-owners only to the extent of the value of their investment, corporate borrowers would not be subject to the *ribbit* constraint.[34]

Objecting to his line of reasoning, R. Mordechai Yaakov Breisch cites rishonic opinion that the limited-liability feature frees a transaction from *ribbit* regulation only when its intrinsic structure involves *avak ribbit*. Should the transaction involve violation of the pentateuchal interdict against *ribbit*, it remains prohibited despite the limited-liability status of the debtor. Moreover, limited liability may be invoked as an extenuating factor only when the debt is made collectable from the future, uncertain income of a designated asset.[35]

Public Debt in the Modern State

Public debt in the modern state can be financed by selling bonds to either the general public, the commercial banking system, or the central bank. While the former methods, as the foregoing discussion indicated, may entail questions of *ribbit* violation, selling bonds to the central bank, in our view, does not. Here, the debt is financed by means of creating new money. Mechanically, the central bank buys public sector debt and pays for it by increasing the public sector's account by the appropriate amount. Now, the public sector can write checks against its expanded account. Though more sophisticated, this scheme is much akin to financing a deficit by means of printing up new fiat money. Between the two methods, the former is preferable on economic grounds because the printing costs are avoided.

Debt finance by means of expanding the money supply amounts to nothing more than the exercise on the part of the government of its seigniorage and coinage powers.

Within the context of high unemployment and idle resources, monetary expansion may provide a powerful stimulus for economic growth. In contrast, when the economy is fully employed or suffers from bottleneck factors in its key sectors, monetary expansion exerts mainly an inflationary impact. Promotion of social welfare, therefore, requires the public sector to exercise caution and restraint in the use of this method of public finance.

With the objective of minimizing inflationary pressures and at the same time not violating *ribbit* law, the government could raise at least part of its capital requirements by means of issuing a consul bond. This instrument merely obligates the government to pay the bearer a fixed dividend periodically. With the government meeting its fixed dividend responsibility by means of monetary expansion and bearing no obligation to redeem the consul, *ribbit* law would not be violated. Given that the market price of the consul would approximate the amount of capital it would take to realize a profit commensurate with the fixed dividend, the instrument could prove very productive.

The Jewish public sector, in our view, could at least partially meet its social welfare obligations by subsidizing the banking industry in return for its commitment to extend interest-free loans to the nontax-paying poor. Such a scheme would not involve *ribbit* violation because Jewish law does not prohibit A from offering B an inducement to lend money to C.[36] Legitimacy is given to the above procedure even when A offers his inducement to B at C's behest.[37] Now, since the recipients of the interest-free bank loans are nontaxpayers, the subsidy the bank receives from the government is in no part provided by these debtors.

Glossary of Economic and Legal Terms

AGGREGATE DEMAND. Total spending for consumption, investment, and government goods and services. It increases as the national income increases.

AMORTIZATION. Payments which reduce the principal amount of a debt.

CARTEL. An agreement, often in writing, among manufacturers, dealers, etc., to restrict output or prices or to divide territories.

CETERIS PARIBUS. Latin for "other things being equal." The usual assumption in economic theory under which only one phenomenon is permitted to vary at a time to facilitate tracing the effects of the variation.

CONSUL. Abbreviation for "consolidated annuities." Funded government securities or stock which the government need not repay until it wishes. An investor in consuls can, however, sell them at prices reflecting the yield on securities of comparable security.

DISEQUILIBRIUM PRICE. A price which is inherently unstable. At the disequilibrium price, supply exceeds demand or demand exceeds supply.

DIVISION OF LABOR. The separating of an overall task into separate tasks so that each individual involved performs only a small part of the overall task. Division of labor usually results in increased efficiency.

DOWNWARD SLOPING DEMAND. An inverse relationship between market price and quantity demanded. Given the stability of the non-price factors influencing demand, the higher the hypothetical market price of the subject good, the lower will be the quantity demanded, and the lower the price, the higher the quantity demanded. Most economic goods conform to the law of downward sloping demand.

ECONOMIC RENT. The difference between the current earnings of a resource and what that resource could earn in its next alternative use.

ECONOMIES OF SCALE. The reduction in unit cost as one producer makes larger quantities of a product. Such reduction results from a decreasing marginal cost due to increasing specialization, use of capital equipment, and the benefit of quantity purchasing.

ELASTIC DEMAND. Market demand that is relatively responsive to changes in the price of the subject product. How the firm's total revenue changes in consequence of either an increase or a decrease in its pricing of the subject product provides a measure of this responsiveness. If a cut in price increases the number of units demanded so much that the firm's total

173

revenue increases, or if an increase in price reduces the number of units demanded so much that the firm's total revenue decreases, the demand is characterized as "price-elastic."

EQUILIBRIUM LEVEL OF INCOME. The income level the economy will gravitate toward provided the factors determining aggregate supply and demand conditions remain stable. In modern theory, the aggregate demand is said to determine the equilibrium level of income.

EQUILIBRIUM PRICE. The market price that clears the market. At equilibrium, the number of units suppliers want to offer is equal to the number of units demanders want to buy. Given the stability of supply and demand influences other than the price of the subject product, market price will tend toward the equilibrium price.

GROSS NATIONAL PRODUCT (GNP). The market value of all final goods and services produced in a country during the year.

HORIZONTAL MERGER. A form of combining business enterprises in which the combining members are performing the same function in the same product lines.

INCOME–INELASTIC DEMAND. Household demand for a good or service that does not change as the subject household's income changes.

INCOME REDISTRIBUTION. Change in the aggregate amount of income which is enjoyed by each of several identified blocks of income recipients.

INELASTIC DEMAND. Market demand that is relatively unresponsive to changes in the price of the subject product. If the firm's total revenue changes in the same direction as its pricing change, the demand it faces for its product is characterized as "inelastic."

INPUT. Anything that goes into the production of goods and services. Inputs consist of land, labor, capital, and entrepreneurial ability.

MARGINAL COST. The additional cost incurred by producing one more unit of a product.

MARGINAL REVENUE. The addition to total revenue which will result from selling one more unit.

MISALLOCATIVE EFFECT. The deployment of a resource in a use which yields a lower market value than is possible under alternative deployments.

OPPORTUNITY COST. The dollar amount that would be derived from the employment of a resource in its best alternative use.

PREDATORY COMPETITION. An economically unhealthy form of competition in which fairness is disregarded, usually for the purpose of driving competitors out of the market.

PRESCRIPTIVE RIGHT. Mode of acquiring title to incorporeal hereditaments by long-continued enjoyment.

PRICE–ELASTICITY. See ELASTIC DEMAND.

PRICE–INELASTICITY. See INELASTIC DEMAND.

QUASI–CONTRACT. An obligation similar in character to that of a contract, which arises not from an agreement of parties but from some relation between them, or from a voluntary act of one of them.

RATIONING. A system of distributing goods and services in which there is a maximum limit to the quantity of a good or service that a consuming unit can purchase or obtain.

RESOURCE ALLOCATION EFFICIENCY. The optimal selection of the use of a resource over alternative uses.

RESOURCE MOBILITY. The ease with which factors of production can be transferred from one avenue of employment to another.

SEIGNIORAGE. The profit the treasury of a country makes on its coinage. It is the difference between the nominal value of the coin and its cost of production.

SENIORITY. Rights which are built up for no other reason than that the person continues to be employed. Layoff procedures in unionized industries, for example, usually follow the seniority rule.

SHIFT OF THE DEMAND CURVE. An increase or decrease in the number of units of a particular product demanded at any hypothetical price charged, compared to a previous period. The shift is due to a change in the influence of factors other than the price of the subject product, such as a change in income, wealth, tastes, or the price of a complementary product.

SITE VALUE. Real estate market value attributed *solely* to the property's favorable location, as opposed to improvements undertaken by the owner.

STAGNATION THESIS. An argument developed in the 1930s that in a rich country opportunities for further profitable capital expansion will tend to decline, while the propensity to save will at least be maintained. This combination of circumstances is likely to produce a chronic tendency to underemployment of the country's resources.

TIED CONTRACT. An arrangement whereby the seller, as a condition for the sale of one product, requires the buyer to purchase a second product from him.

TORT. A private or civil wrong or injury, not involving a breach of contract.

TORTFEASOR. One who commits or is guilty of a tort.

TOTAL REVENUE. The number of units sold, multiplied by the per unit price charged.

UNJUST ENRICHMENT DOCTRINE. Doctrine that a person should not be allowed to profit or enrich himself inequitably at another's expense.

VERTICAL MERGER. A form of combining business enterprises in which the combining members are at different levels in the manufacture and distribution of a product.

Glossary of Hebrew and Aramaic Terms

ADAM CHASHUV. A distinguished person, combining in himself both halakhic expertise and recognized leadership in public affairs.

AMORA, AMORAIC. Designation of scholars who were active in the period from the completion of the Mishnah (ca. 200 C.E.) until the completion of the Babylonian and Jerusalem Talmuds (end of the fourth and fifth centuries respectively).

AVAK RIBBIT. The "dust" of interest. Violation of Jewish law's prohibition against interest by virtue of rabbinical, as opposed to pentateuchal, decree.

BARAITA. A teaching or a tradition of the Tannaim that was excluded from the Mishnah and incorporated in a later collection compiled by R. Chiyya and R. Oshaiah.

CHALIFIN. Barter.

CHAYEI NEFESH. Necessities.

DAVAR HAAVUD. Irretrievable loss.

GEMIRAT DA'AT. A firm resolve to conclude an arrangement at hand.

GENEVAT DA'AT. Conduct designed to deceive or create a false impression.

GERAMA D'GI'RI. Tortious damage caused indirectly by the tortfeasor's action.

GI'RI DE'LEI. Tortious damage caused directly by the tortfeasor's action.

HAGBAHAH. Mode of acquisition of movable objects involving the lifting of the subject article by the acquirer. The article may be raised merely by the force of the acquirer's body. Authorities differ as to whether it must be lifted one handsbreadth or three.

HALAKHAH. Jewish law.

HETTER ISKA. An elaborate form of the *iska* business partnership wherein conditions are attached with the design of protecting the financier from absorbing a loss on his principal and increasing the probability that he will realize a profit as well. These clauses are structured in such a manner that *ribbit* law is not violated.

HEZEK RE'IYAH. Injury caused by visual penetration into someone's premises.

ISKA. A form of business partnership consisting of an active partner and a financier who is a silent partner. In the absence of stipulation, half the capital transfer takes on the legal character of a loan, while the remaining half takes on the character of a pledge. The *iska* arrangement may violate *ribbit* law and is therefore subject to regulation.

KAB. Measurement of capacity equal to four *log*, or one sixth of a *se'ah*. In modern terms, 1 *log* = about 549 cubic centimeters.

KABBELAN. A pieceworker hired to perform a specific task, with no provisions regarding fixed hours.

KINYAN. Acquisiton of legal rights by means of the performance of a symbolic act.

KINYAN CHATZAR. Acquisition by means of one's courtyard. B deposits his property in A's domain, and A acquires legal title to it by virtue of the fact that the property rests in his domain.

KINYAN KESEF. Acquisition by means of the buyer transferring to the seller the agreed-to price or part payment thereof.

KINYAN SHETAR. Acquisition by means of a deed.

KINYAN SUDAR. A legal form of acquisition of objects or confirmation of agreements, executed by the handing of a scarf (or any other article) by one of the contracting parties (or one of the witnesses to the agreement) to the other contracting party as a symbol that the object itself has been transferred or the obligation assumed.

KUPPAH. Communal charity box.

MA'AMAD SHELOSHTAN. A method of transferring or assigning a debt. Mechanically, in a meeting of the creditor, debtor, and assignee (A), the creditor declares to the debtor: "There is a debt owing to me by you, give it to A." On the basis of this oral declaration, the assignee (A) acquires legal title to the debt and may collect it directly from the debtor. A pledge is transferred in the same manner.

MAKKAT MEDINAH. Unavoidable circumstances of a pandemic nature.

MAOT CHITTIN. Money for the poor to buy wheat for matzos on Passover.

ME'SHAPARAH. A judicial imprecation imposed on a buyer or seller who retracts before the transaction is legally consummated but after the purchasing price has been paid. The formula of the imprecation is: "He who punished the generation of the Flood and of the Dispersion will exact paypayment from one who does not stand by his word."

MESHIKHAH. Acqusition by means of pulling. It is employed for movables which are either too heavy to lift or can be raised only with difficulty. *Meshikhah* is valid only in premises owned by both parties or in a side street. In the case of an animal, *meshikhah* can be effected by striking or calling it so that it comes to the acquirer.

MESIRAH. Acquisition of movable property by means of grasping. Valid only for derivative acquisition, it must be done at the behest of the transferer. *Mesirah* is employed where *meshikhah* is ineffective, i.e., in a public place or in a courtyard not belonging to either party.

MIKVEH. A ritual bath containing not less than forty *se'ah* (175 liters) of water.

MINYAN. The quorum of ten male adults, aged thirteen years or over, necessary for public synagogue services and certain other religious ceremonies.

ONA'AH. Price fraud involving selling above or below the competitive norm.

ONA'AT DEVARIM. Conduct causing needless mental anguish to others.

O'NES. Unavoidable circumstances.

POEL. Day-laborer hired for a specific period of time or required to work at fixed hours.

POEL BATEIL. Idle or unemployed worker.

RASHA. Wicked person.

RIBBIT. Prohibition against interest.

RIBBIT KETZUZAH. Interest proper in an amount or at the rate agreed upon between a lender and a borrower. *Ribbit ketzuzah* violates pentateuchal law.

RISHON, RISHONIC. Designation of scholars who were active in the period from the eleventh to the middle of the fifteenth century.

RODEF. A pursuer. In Jewish law, should an individual pursue another with the manifest intent to kill him, everybody is under a duty to rescue the victim, even by killing the pursuer, if no other means are availabe to induce the would-be murderer to desist. This general rule has been extended to cover the killing of a fetus endangering the life of the mother and the killing of a rapist caught before completion of his offense.

SE'AH. Measure of capacity equal to six *kab*.

SEKHAR HITPASHRUT. Agreed-to sum of money.

SEKHAR TIRCHAH. Remuneration for toil and effort.

SHEVUAH CHAMURAH. A severe oath, i.e., an oath imposed on an individual by dint of pentateuchal, as opposed to rabbinical, law. In cases requiring the Pentateuchal oath, the deponent holds the Scroll of the Torah in his hand and swears by God. Before administering the oath, the court warns the deponent of the gravity of the oath and the inescapability of divine punishment for any false oath. In cases involving the oath administered by dint of rabbinical law, the former feature is absent and the latter is not required.

SHIKCHA. Forgotten sheaves. This portion of the crop is the entitlement of the poor.

SH'VACH BE'EN. A benefit consisting of tangible property, as opposed to a service.

SODOMITIC. Exhibiting the character trait of a citizen of Sodom, i.e., denying a neighbor a benefit or privilege which involves no cost to oneself.

TAMCHUI. Community charity plate.

TANNA, TANNAIC. Designation of scholars active in the period from the beginning of the common era up to 220 c.e. The period of the Tannaim spans six generations of scholars from Gamaliel the Elder and his contemporaries to Judah ha-Nasi (the redactor of the Mishnah).

ZUZ. A coin of the value of a denarius, six *ma'ah*, or twelve dupondia.

Notes

NOTES TO CHAPTER 2

1. Richard Posner, *Antitrust Law: An Economic Perspective* (Chicago: University of Chicago Press, 1976), pp. 12–22.

2. Ibid., pp. 39–77.

3. The text of R. Asher b. Jechiel (1250–1327) reads: "There were butchers . . ." (*Rosh, Baba Bathra* I:33).

4. See R. Moshe Feinstein (b. 1895), *Iggerot Moshe, Choshen Mishpat* 59.

5. Nachmanides (1194–1270), *Ramban, Baba Batra* 9a; R. Meir of Rothenburg (ca. 1215–1293), quoted by R. Mordechai b. Hillel (ca. 1240–1298), *Mordechai, Baba Kamma* X:176; *Rosh*, loc. cit; R. Yom Tov Ishbili (1270–1342), *Ritva, Baba Bathra* 9a; R. Jacob b. Asher (1270–1340), *Tur, Choshen Mishpat* 231:30; R. Moses Isserles (1525 or 1530–1572), *Rema, Shulchan Arukh, Choshen Mishpat* 231:28.

6. R. Solomon b. Abraham Adret (ca. 1235–1310), *Responsa Rashba* IV:185, V:125; R. Menachem b. Solomon Meiri (1249–1316), *Meiri, Baba Bathra* 8b; *Rosh*, loc. cit.; *Ritva*, loc. cit.; R. Isaac b. Sheshet Perfet (1326–1408), *Responsa RiBash* 399.

7. R. Meir b. Baruch, quoted in *Mordechai, Baba Bathra* I:481; *Responsa Rosh* VI:19, 21; R. David b. Solomon Ibn Abi Zimra (1479–1573), *RadBaz* II:65; *Rema, Sh., Ar.,* op. cit., 163:6.

8. R. Meir of Rothenburg, loc. cit.; *RadBaz*, loc. cit.

9. In the mode of acquisition called *kinyan sudar* (*kinyan* of the kerchief), the alienator draws to him an article owned by the acquirer.

10. R. Yehuda b. Samuel Rosanes (1657–1727), *Mishneh le-Melekh, Yad, Shevu'ot* VI:7; R. Chayyim Halberstam (1793–1876), *Divrei Chayyim I, Choshen Mishpat* 31; R. Solomon Leib Tabak (1832–1908), *Erekh Shai, Mekach Ve-Memkar* 205; *Teshurat Shai* I:598; R. Jechiel Michael Epstein (1829–1908), *Arukh ha-Shulchan, Choshen Mishpat* 60:II. Decisors of the view that *kinyan* can give legal force to commitments even when the obligations involved are not concrete in nature include: R. Isaac b. Sheshet, *Responsa Ribash* 281; R. Samuel b. Moses de Medina of Salonika (1506–1589), *Responsa Maharashdam* 370; R. Aharon b. Chayyim ha-Kohen, *Perach Matah Aharon, sefer* 1, *simon* 8 (pub. 1703)

11. *Erekh Shai*, loc. cit.

12. *Responsa Maharashdam, Choshen Mishpat* 274; R. Mordechai Shalom Schwadron (1835–1911), *Responsa Maharsham* II:18; R. Jekuthiel Asher Zalman Zausmir (d. 1858), *Responsa Mahariaz* 10.

13. R. Solomon Abraham Adret, *Responsa Rashba ha-Meyuchasot le-he-Ramban* 249; R. Meir Arik (d. 1925), *Imrei Yosher* I:169.

14. R. Chayyim Eliezer b. Isaac of Vienna (late 13th cent.), *Maharach Or Zaru'a* 251; *Mahariaz*, loc. cit.

15. See *Baba Metzia* 49a; R. Isaac b. Jacob Alfasi (1013–1103), *Rif*, ad loc.; see Maimonides' commentary on *Mishnah Shevi'it* X:9; *Rosh, Baba Metzia* IV:12.

16. *Baba Metzia* 49a; *Rif*, ad loc.; *Yad, Mekhirah* VII:9; *Tur*, op. cit., 204:11–12; *Rema*, op.cit., 204:11; *Ar. ha-Sh.*, op. cit., 204:8–9.

17. *Baba Bathra* 49a; *Rif*, ad loc.; *Yad*, op. cit., XIV:11 on interpretation of *Kesef Mishneh*, ad loc.; *Tur*, op. cit., 231:30; *Sh. Ar.*, op. cit., 231:28; *Ar ha-Sh.*, op. cit., 231:27–28.

18. R. Joseph Ibn MiGash (1077–1141), *Ri MiGash, Baba Bathra* 9a; R. Meir Abulafia (ca. 1170–1244), quoted in *Ritva, Baba Bathra* 9a. A minority opinion regarding the attributes of the Distinguished Person is advanced by R. Solomon Adret, *Responsa Rashba* IV:185. In his view the Distinguished Person need embody either recognized Torah scholarship or undisputed communal leadership, but not both.

19. *Ramban, Baba Bathra* 9a; *Ran, Baba Bathra* 9a; *Ritva, Baba Bathra* 9a. Why the butchers' restraint of trade agreement (*Baba Bathra* 9a) required outside approval was understood by R. Joel (12th cent., Bonn), quoted in *Mordechai, Baba Bathra* I:483, to stem from the nature of the penalty it called for, rather than the inherent disadvantage it imposed on consumers. Since the arrangement called for the violator's property to be destroyed instead of having him pay a fine to the other participants in the agreement, the arrangement required outside approval. Had the agreement merely called for the violator to pay a fine to the other members of the arrangement, no outside approval would have been needed, despite the inherent disadvantage it imposed on consumers. R. Moshe Feinstein (*Iggerot Moshe, Choshen Mishpat* 58) apparently follows this line of analysis.

20. *Yad*, loc. cit.; *Ramban*. loc. cit.; *Ramah, Baba Bathra* 9a.

21. Price and wage controls represent a legitimate communal prerogative, see *Baba Bathra* 8b; *Rif*, ad loc.; *Yad*, op. cit., XIV:9; *Tur*, op. cit., 231:30; *Sh. Ar.*, op. cit., 231:27; *Ar. ha-Sh.*, 231:27.

22. R. Levi b. Chaviv (ca. 1483–1545), *Responsa Maharalbach* 2:99.

23. R. Menachem Mendel Krochmal (1600–1661), *Tzemach Tzedek* 28.

24. R. Joseph Saul Nathanson (1810–1875), *Responsa Sho'el u-Meshiv* 3:97, part 4.

25. *Divrei Chayyim*, op. cit., I:20.

26. *Baba Bathra* 90a; *Rif*, ad loc.; *Yad*, op. cit., XIV:1; *Tur*, op. cit., 231:27; *Sh. Ar*, op. cit., 231:20; *Ar ha-Sh.*, op. cit., 231:20.

27. *Tur*, op. cit., 231:26; *Sh. Ar.*, op. cit., 231:20; *Ar ha-Sh.*, op. cit., 231:20

28. *Baba Metzia* 58b.

29. R. Hai b. Sherira, *Ketab-al Shira wa-al*, translated into Hebrew by R. Isaac al Bargeloni, *Sefer Ha-Mikkach ve-ha-Mimkar* (Venice, 1602).

30. *Rif, Baba Metzia* 58b.

31. R. Channanel (11th cent.), *Rabbenu Channanel, Baba Metzia* 58b.

32. R. Moses ha-Kohen of Lunel quoted in *Shittah M'kubbetzet, Baba Metzia* 58b.

33. R. Meir b. Isaac Eisenstadt (1670–1744), *Panim Me'irot* II:25; see R. Ezra Basri, *Dinei Mamonot*, vol. 2 (Jerusalem: Sucath David, 1976), p. 172.

34. Real estate transactions are not subject to the full scope of *ona'ah* regulation. This exclusion proceeds from exegetical interpretation of the biblical source of *ona'ah*: "And if thou sell a sale unto thy neighbor or

acquirest aught of thy neighbor's hand" (Leviticus 25:14)—something that is acquired (by being passed) from hand to hand (is subject to *ona'ah* regulation), thus excluding land, which is not movable (see *Baba Metzia* 56b). Nachmanides (commentary on Leviticus 25:14) points out that insofar as a biblical interdict against *ona'ah* is mentioned explicitly in connection with real estate transactions, the exemption above must be taken to refer exclusively to the restitution procedure normally provided for in *ona'ah* cases. Hence, real estate transactions are subject to the prohibition against *ona'ah*, though not to its prescribed restitution procedure.

What follows as a corollary from our analysis of the ethics of monopoly pricing is that the interdict is violated only when the real estate transaction involved an authentic opportunity cost; i.e., property of the same general characteristics was available in the marketplace at a price above or below the transaction price at hand. No moral issue, however, is involved regarding the price differential attributed to "site" value.

35. See R. Samual b. Meir (ca. 1080–1174), *Rashbam, Baba Bathra* 48a; *Yad*, op. cit., X:3; *Tur*, op. cit., 242:1; *Sh. Ar.*, op. cit., 242:1; *Ar. ha-Sh.* 242:1.

36. A "fair market value" duress sale, according to R. Isaac Alfasi, on the interpretation of R. Abraham b. David of Posquières (quoted in *Beit Yosef, Tur*, op. cit., 205:1, and *Rema, Sh. Ar.*, op. cit., 205:1), is valid only when the buyer makes full payment at the time the transaction is entered into. Should the duress sale have been entered into by means of a deed, the sale is invalid, despite its fair market value price.

R. Joshua ha-Kohen Falk (*Sma, Sh. Ar.*, ad loc., n. 5) interprets this view to void a "fair market value" duress sale consummated by means of *kinyan* but accompanied only by the buyer's promissory note instead of actual payment.

Disputing this interpretation of R. Isaac Alfasi's view, R. Shabbetai b. Meir ha-Kohen (*Siftei Kohen, Sh. Ar.*, ad loc., n. 2) posits that what the latter refers to is the circumstance where the "fair market value" duress sale was consummated by means of *kinyan shetar* and the purchasing price was not paid at the time of the transaction. Here, the duress element renders the transaction void.

R. Isaac Alfasi, on the interpretation of R. Joseph Caro (*Beit Yosef*, loc. cit.), and R. Asher b. Jechiel, on the interpretation of R. Joseph Caro (*Beit Yosef*, loc. cit.), validate a "fair market value" duress sale provided it was consummated by means of proper *kinyan*. The cash transfer, in this view, is not at all essential.

With authorities in dispute regarding the validity of a "fair market value" duress sale not accompanied by the necessary cash transfer, the party in physical possession of the disputed article has the advantage. See R. Ezra Basri, *Dinei Mamonot*, vol. 2, p. 70.

37. *Baba Bathra* 47b, 48a; *Yad*, loc. cit.; *Tur*, op. cit., 205:1; *Sh. Ar.*, op. cit., 205:1; *Ar. ha-Sh.*, op. cit., 205:1.

38. R. Jacob Lorberbaum (1760–1832), *N'tivot ha-Mishpat, Sh. Ar.*, loc. cit., n. 1.

39. Exodus 20:13-14, Deuteronomy 10:18.

40. *Yad, Gezelah* I:9; *Tur*, op. cit., 359:9; *Sh. Ar.*, op. cit., 359:10–12; *Ar. ha-Sh.*, op. cit., 359:8.

41. Deuteronomy 10:18.

42. *Yad*, op. cit., I:10; *Tur*, op. cit., 359:10; *Sh. Ar.*, loc. cit.; R. Eliezer b. Samuel of Metz (ca. 1115–1198, *Sefer Yereim*) is, however, of the view that the

pentateuchal injunction against "desiring a neighbor's possessions is not violated unless the "desiring culminates in the actual acquisition of the object involved."

43. *Teshurat Shai* II:4.

44. *Baba Bathra* 21b.

45. *Rif, Baba Bathra* 21b; Tosafot, *Baba Bathra* 21b; *Yad, Shekhenim* VI:18; *Rosh* II:12; *Tur.*, op. cit., 156:10; *Sh. Ar.*, op. cit., 156:5; *Ar. ha-Sh.*, op. cit., 156:6.

46. *Piskei Din shel Botei ha-Din ha-Rabbaniyim bi-Yisroel*, vol. 6, no. 3 (Jerusalem, 1965), p. 90; see R. Nachum Rakover, *Halikhut ha-Mischar* 42 (Jerusalem: Misrad ha-Mishpatim, 1976), p. 12.

47. *Rosh*, op. cit., II:12; *Tur*, op. cit., 156:11; *Sh. Ar.*, op. cit., 156:7; *Ar. ha-Sh.*, op. cit., 156:10.

48. *Beit Yosef, Tur, Sh. Ar.*, op. cit., 156:11.

49. *Ri MiGash, Baba Bathra* 21b.

50. *Ramban, Baba Bathra* 21b.

51. R. Joseph Chabib (14th cent.), *Nimmukei Yosef, Baba Bathra* 21b.

52. *Beit Yosef, Tur, Sh. Ar.*, op. cit., 156, part 3; R. Mordechai b. Hillel on interpretation of R. Abraham Chiyya di Boton.

53. *Lechem Rav* (ca. 1560–1609), *Lechem Rav.*, loc. cit., 216.

54. *Baba Bathra* 22a; *Rosh*, loc cit.; *Yad*, op. cit., VI:10; *Tur*, loc. cit.; *Sh. Ar.*, op. cit., 156:7; *Ar. ha-Sh.*, loc. cit.; R. Joel Sirkes (1561–1640, *Bach, Tur, Sh. Ar.*, loc. cit) understands *yoma dishuka* to refer to the weekly market days and not to the elaborate annual fairs. R. Jechiel Michael Epstein (loc. cit.), however, understands *yoma dishuka* to refer to the annual fairs.

55. *Beit Yosef, Tur, Sh. Ar.*, loc. cit.

56. Tosafot, *Baba Bathra* 22a and *Rosh*, loc. cit., both on the interpretation of R. Joseph Caro (*Beit Yosef*, loc. cit.).

57. R. Joshua ha-Kohen Falk, *Perishah, Tur, Sh. Ar.* op. cit., 156 n. 11; *Derishah* ad loc.; *Sma, Sh. Ar.*, op. cit., n. 20. R. Falk understands this to be the position of R. Jacob too. R. Jechiel Michael Epstein, *Ar. ha-Sh.*, loc. cit., rules in accordance with R. Falk.

58. *Baba Bathra* 22a; *Rosh*, loc. cit.; *Yad*, loc. cit.; *Tur*, loc. cit.; *Sh. Ar.*, loc. cit.; *Ar. ha-Sh.*, loc. cit.

59. *Rif, Baba Bathra* 22a; *Yad*, op. cit., *Rosh*, op. cit., II:12; *Tur*, op. cit., 156:11; *Sh. Ar.*, op. cit., 156:6; *Ar. ha-Sh.*, loc. cit.; Maimonides (*Yad*, ad loc.) and R. Joseph Caro (*Sh. Ar.*, loc. cit.) understood the phrase *It lan ashe'ra'ei*, in *Baba Bathra* 22a, to mean that the foreign merchants were conferred commercial privileges because they were *debtors* to members of the local community. R. Asher b. Jechiel (*Rosh*, ad loc.) and R. Jacob b. Asher (*Tur*, ad loc.), however, interpret the phrase as meaning that the foreign merchants attained the privileged status as a result of being creditors to members of the local community. R. Jechiel Michael Epstein (*Ar. ha-Sh.*, loc cit.) cites this exemption for both loan and debt connections.

60. *Beit Yosef, Tur, Sh. Ar.*, loc. cit.; *Rema, Sh. Ar.*, op. cit., 156:6; *Ar. ha-Sh.*, op. cit., 156:11.

61. *Baba Bathra* 22a; *Rif* ad loc.; *Yad*, op. cit., VI:9; *Tur*, op. cit., 156:12; *Sh. Ar.*, op. cit.; *Ar ha-Sh.*, op. cit., 156:9.

62. *Beit Yosef, Tur, Sh. Ar.*, loc. cit.; *Ar ha-Sh.*, op. cit., 156:11.

63. R. Eliezer b. Nathan of Mainz (ca. 1090–1170), *Ramban, Baba Bathra* 21b; *Beit Yosef*, loc. cit.; *Derisha* ad loc., note 13. For a variant view, see Tosafot, *Baba Bathra* 21b.

64. See *Nedarim* 37a.

65. R. Joseph Saul Nathanson (1810–1875), *Responsa Sho'el u-Meshiv* 4:13, part 1.

66. R. Moshe Sofer, *Responsa Chatam Sofer, Choshen Mishpat* 79.

67. Members of the protectionist school include R. Eliezer b. Joel ha-Levi of Bonn (1140–1225), quoted in *Mordechai, Baba Bathra* II:516, and in *Haggahot Maimuniyyot, Shekhenim* VI:8; R. Joseph Ibn MiGash (*Ri MiGash, Baba Bathra* 21b); R. Moshe Sofer (*Responsa Chatam Sofer, Choshen Mishpat* 38). Members of the freedom-of-entry school of thought include R. Ephraim Zalman Margolioth (1762–1828), *Beit Ephraim, Choshen Mishpat* 26; R. Mordechai Jacob Breisch (contemporary), *Chelkat Yaakov*, vol. 2, no. 65; R. Isaac Arieli (contemporary), *Enayim le-Mishpat, Baba Bathra* 21b; *Piskei Din shel Botei ha-Din Ha-Rabbaniyim bi-Yisroel*, vol. 4, p. 9, vol. 8, p. 82; see *Halikhut ha-Mischar*, op. cit., 1–27.

68. Responsum given orally by R. Abraham I. Kook in reply to a query regarding Jewish law's view of labor strikes (see *N'tiva*, Mamar Nissim, 1949).

69. R. Ben Zion Uziel, *Mishpetei Uziel*, vol. 3; *Choshen Mishpat* 41.

70. R. Moshe Feinstein, *Iggerot Moshe, Choshen Mishpat* 58.

71. R. Joseph Colon, *MaHarik*, no. 191. Though R. Joseph Caro (*Tur, Choshen Mishpat* 156, *ha-Chelek ha-Shlishi*) rejects R. Colon's view, his opinion is accepted by R. Moses Isserles (*Rema, Sh. Ar., Choshen Mishpat*, 156:7); R. Samuel b. Moses di Medina, *Responsa Maharashdam, Choshen Mishpat* 407; and R. Moses Sofer (*Responsa Chatam Sofer, Choshen Mishpat* 44).

72. R. Kasrial Fischel Tcursch, "Dinei Shevita ba-Halakha," *Shana beShana* (1963), 24–26. For further analysis of the labor strike issue in Jewish law, see R. Shillem Warhaftig, *Dinei Avodoh ba-Mishpat ha-Ivri*, vol. 2 (Jerusalem: Moreshet, 1969), pp. 974–84.

73. *Responsa Chatam Sofer, Choshen Mishpat* 79.

NOTES TO CHAPTER 3

1. Phillip Areeda and Donald F. Turner, "Predatory Pricing and Related Practices Under Section 2 of the Sherman Act," 88 *Harvard Law Review* 697 (1975).

2. Richard A. Posner, *Antitrust Law: An Economic Perspective* (Chicago: University of Chicago Press, 1976), pp. 184–96.

3. Richard A. Posner, *Economic Analysis of Law*, 2d ed. (Boston: Little, Brown, 1977), pp. 225–29.

4. R. Issac Alfasi (1012–1103), *Rif, Baba Bathra* 21b; Tosafot (12–14th cent. school of French and German talmudic commentators), *Baba Bathra* 2lb; Maimonides (1135–1204), *Yad, Shekhenim* VI:18; R. Asher b. Yechiel (1250–1327), *Rosh, Baba Bathra* II:12; R. Jacob b. Asher (1270–1343), *Tur, Choshen Mishpat* 156:10; R. Joseph Caro (1488–1575), *Shulchan Arukh, Choshen Mishpat* 156:5; R. Jechiel Michael Epstein (1829–1908), *Arukh ha-Shulchan, Choshen Mishpat* 156:6.

5. *Piskei Din shel Botei ha-Din ha-Rabbaniyim bi-Yisroel*, vol. 6, no. 3 (Jerusalem, 1965), p. 90; see Nachum Rakover, *Halikhut ha-Mischar*, no. 42 (Jersalem: Misrad ha-Mishpatim, 1976), p. 12.

6. R. Eliezer b. Joel ha-Levi of Bonn (1140–1225), quoted in R. Mordechai b. Hillel (1240–1298), *Mordechai, Baba Bathra* II:516, and in R. Meir ha-Kohen (fl. 13th cent.), *Haggahot Maimuniyyot, Shekhenim* VI:8.

7. R. Moses Isserles (1525–1572), *Responsa Rema* 10; see also *Darkhei Moshe, Tur, Choshen Mishpat* 156, n. 4.

8. R. Joseph Ibn MiGash, *Baba Bathra* 2lb.

9. R. Moses Sofer, *Responsa Chatam Sofer, Choshen Mishpat* 78.

10. *Ibid.,* 118.

11. R. Moses Feinstein, *Iggerot Moshe, Choshen Mishpat* 38.

12. *Yad, Mekhirah* XVIII:4; *Tur,* op. cit., 228:16; *Sh. Ar.,* op. cit., 228:18; *Ar. ha-Sh.,* op. cit., 228:14.

13. R. Shillem Warhaftig, *Hassagat Gevul ve-Tovat ha-Tzebur,* no. 38 (Jerusalem: Misrad haMishpatim, 1975), pp. 19–20.

14. R. Chayyim Sofer, *Machaneh Chayyim, Choshen Mishpat* II:46.

15. R. Isaac Aaron Ettinger, *MaHari ha-Levi,* vol. 2, no. 130.

16. R. Mordechai Yaakov Breisch (contemporary), *Responsa Chelkat Yaakov* II:65.

17. R. Joseph Katz (1510–1591), *She'erit Yosef* 17; R. Binyamin Aharon Slonick (ca. 1550–1619), *Masat Binyamin* 27.

18. See R. Ephraim Zalmon Margolioth (1762–1828), *Beit Ephraim, Choshen Mishpat* 26; *Chelkat Yaakov,* op. cit.; R. Isaac Arieli (contemporary), *Enayim le-Mishpat, Baba Bathra* 21b.

19. *Chelkat Yaakov,* op. cit.

20. Ibid.

21. *Responsa Rema* 10; see also *Darkhei Moshe, Tur, Choshen Mishpat* 156, n. 4.

22. *Rema, Sh. Ar.,* op. cit., 156:5.

23. *Chelkat Yaakov,* op. cit.

24. *Piskei Din Rabbaniyim,* vol. 6, p. 90; see Nachum Rakover, *Halikhut ha-Mischar,* no. 41 (Jerusalem: Misrad ha-Mishpatim, 1976), pp. 1–27.

25. *Piskei Din Rabbaniyim,* vol. 6, p. 90; see *Halikhut ha-Mischar,* op. cit., pp. 1–27.

26. *Machaneh Chayyim,* op. cit.

27. R. Solomon Leib Tabak (1832–1908), *Teshurat Shai* II:4.

NOTES TO CHAPTER 4

1. Richard Posner, *Economic Analysis of Law,* 2d ed. (Boston: Little, Brown, 1977), pp. 65–99.

2. *Baba Metzia* 74a.

3. See R. Shalom Albeck, *Dinei ha-Mamonot ba-Talmud* (Tel Aviv: Dvir, 1976), pp. 112–75; R. Shillem Warhaftig, *Dinei Chozim ba-Mishpat ha-Ivri* (Jerusalem: Harry Fischel Institute, 1974), p. 2.

4. *Baba Metzia* 94a; R. Isaac b. Jacob ha-Kohen Alfasi (1012–1103), *Rif,* ad loc.; Maimonides (1135–1204), *Yad, S'khirut* II:9; R. Asher b. Jechiel (1250–1327), *Rosh, Baba Metzia* VII:17; R. Jacob b. Asher (1270–1343), *Tur, Choshen Mishpat* 291:27; R. Joseph Caro (1488–1575), *Shulchan Arukh, Choshen Mishpat* 291:27; R. Jechiel Michael Epstein (1829–1908), *Arukh ha-Shulchan, Choshen Mishpat* 291:57.

5. *Baba Bathra* 173b; *Rif,* ad loc.; *Yad, Malveh* XXV:2; *Rosh, Baba Bathra* X:2; *Tur,* op. cit., 129:1; *Sh. Ar.,* op. cit., 129:2; *Ar. ha-Sh.,* op. cit., 129:1.

6. *Ketubbot* 102b; *Rif,* ad loc.; *Yad, Ishut* XXIII:13; *Rosh, Ketubbot* XII:3;

Tur, Even ha-Ezer 51:1; *Sh. Ar., Even ha-Ezer* 51:1; *Ar. ha-Sh. Even ha-Ezer* 51:1. See, however, *Noda bi-Yehuda, Mahadura Kamma, Choshen Mishpat* 28.

7. R. Meir b. Baruch of Rothenburg (ca. 1215–1293), quoted in *Haggahot Mordechai, Shabbat* XVII:472–73; R. David b. Solomon Ibn Zimra (1479–1573), *Responsa Radbaz* I:380. For a contrary view, see *Responsa Rosh k'lal* 12:3.

8. See *Sh. Ar., Choshen Mishpat* 195.

9. *Baba Bathra* 114a; *Rif,* ad loc.; *Yad, Mekhirah* V:10; *Rosh, Baba Bathra* VIII:5; *Tur, Choshen Mishpat* 195:12; *Sh. Ar., Choshen Mishpat* 195:6; *Ar. ha-Sh., Choshen Mishpat* 195:11.

10. See R. Joseph Caro, *Beit Yosef, Tur,* loc. cit.; R. Shabbetai b. Meir ha-Kohen (1621–1662), *Siftei Kohen, Sh. Ar.,* op. cit., 195, note 9; *Ar. ha-Sh.,* loc. cit.

11. *Baba Metzia* 47a.

12. See *Baba Metzia* 78b; *Sh. Ar.,* op. cit., 190:10; *Ar. ha-Sh.,* op. cit., 190:5–15.

13. See *Sh. Ar.,* op. cit., 191:1–2, and *Sma,* ad loc.

14. *Kiddushin* 21a; *Rif,* ad loc.; *Yad,* op. cit., I:4; *Rosh, Kiddushin* I:33; *Tur,* op. cit., 190:8; *Sh. Ar.,* op. cit., 190:7; *Ar. ha-Sh.,* op. cit., 190:25.

15. *Yad,* op. cit., III:3; *Tur,* op. cit., 198:11; *Sh. Ar.,* op. cit., 198:7; *Ar. ha-Sh.,* op. cit., 198:11.

16. *Baba Metzia* 49a and *Rashi* ad loc.

17. See *Ar. ha-Sh., Yoreh De'ah* 258:39. *She'iltot* of R. Achai, *Parshat Vayechi,* no. 36, relates the following episode in the life of the Amora R. Safra. Once, while he was reciting the *Shema,* someone offered to buy an article of his. Prohibited from interrupting his religious duty, R. Safra could not even indicate by means of facial expression his acceptance of the offer. Interpreting R. Safra's apparent indifference as dissatisfaction with his bid, the man increased his offer. Upon completing his religious duty, R. Safra agreed to sell his article to the man for his original bid. Having firmly resolved in his heart to accept the original bid, R. Safra would not accept the higher offer.

Alluding to the above incident, the Talmud in *Baba Bathra* 88a regards R. Safra's conduct as exemplifying the behavior of a "God-fearing" man. *Arukh ha-Sh.,* as it appears to us, would have to understand the *Baba Bathra* passage as pointing to R. Safra's behavior as an example of "extraordinary piety" *(middat chasidut,* i.e., a standard not demanded by the strict letter of the law).

R. Mordechai b. Hillel (1240–1298), *Kiddushin* I:495, however, equates *Rema's* charity case with the R. Safra incident. What follows is that in both instances there is a *moral obligation* to carry out the mental resolve.

18. R. Moshe Isserles (1525–1572), *Rema, Sh. Ar., Yoreh De'ah* 258:13; *Ar. ha-Sh.,* loc. cit. For a contrary view, see *Responsa Rosh* 13, quoted in *Rema,* ad loc.

19. R. Yochanan, *Baba Metzia* 49a; *Rif,* ad loc.; *Yad, Mekhirah* VII: 8–9; *Rosh, Baba Metzia* IV:12; *Tur,* op. cit., 204:11–12; *Sh. Ar.,* op. cit., 204:7–8; *Ar. ha-Sh, Choshen Mishpat* 204:8–9.

20. Ibid.

21. R. Vidal Yom Tov of Tolosa (fl. 14th cent.), *Maggid Mishneh, Yad,* loc. cit.; *Rema,* op. cit., 204:11. For a contrary view, see R. Zerachiah b. Isaac ha-Levi of Gerondi (1135–after 1186) quoted in *Tur,* loc. cit., and *Ar. ha-Sh.,* op. cit., 204:9.

22. *Rema, Sh. Ar., Yoreh De'ah* 258:13.

23. See references cited in note 19.

24. *Mordechai,* quoted in *Beit Yosef, Tur,* op. cit., 204:12.

25. R. Moses b. Nachman (1194–1270), *Ramban, Baba Metzia* 76b.

26. *Rabad* and *Rashba,* quoted in *Shittah M'kubbetzet, Baba Metzia* 76b.

27. *Baba Metzia* 76b; *Rif,* ad loc.; *Yad, Sekhirut* IX:4; *Rosh, Baba Metzia* VI:2; *Tur,* op. cit., 333:1; *Sh. Ar.,* op. cit., 333:1; *Ar. ha-Sh.,* op. cit, 333:1.

28. R. Israel Salanter, oral tradition.

29. See *Sh. Ar.,* op. cit., 198.

30. *Baba Metzia* 44a; *Rif,* ad loc.; *Yad, Mekhirah* VII:1–6; *Rosh, Baba Metzia* IV:13; *Tur,* op. cit., 204; *Sh. Ar.,* op. cit., 204; *Ar. ha-Sh.,* op. cit., 204.

31. Tosafot, *Baba Metzia* 109b; *Mordechai, Baba Metzia* IX:399; *Yad, Sekhirut* X:7; *Tur,* op. cit., 306:12; *Sh. Ar.,* op. cit., 306:8; *Ar. ha-Sh.,* op. cit., 306:16.

32. *Rashi, Baba Metzia* 109a; *Yad,* loc. cit.; *Tur,* loc. cit.; *Sh. Ar.,* loc. cit.; *Ar. ha-Sh.,* loc. cit.

33. Tosafot, *Baba Bathra* 21b.

34. R. Nissim b. Reuben Gerondi (1488–1575), *Ran, Baba Bathra* 21b; *Maggid Mishneh, Yad,* loc. cit.

35. *Rashi, Baba Metzia* 109a.

36. R. Joseph Ibn Chabib (fl. 14th cent.), *Nimmukei Yosef, Baba Bathra* 21b; R. Joshua ha-Kohen Falk (1555–1614), *Sma, Sh. Ar.,* op. cit., 306, note 20.

37. *Maggid Mishneh,* loc. cit.

38. *Rashi, Baba Bathra* 21b.

39. *Rabad,* quoted in *Shittah M'kubbetzet, Baba Metzia* 109a.

40. *Shittah M'kubbetzet, Baba Metzia* 109a and *Baba Bathra* 21b.

41. *Yad,* loc. cit., on interpretation of R. Isser Zalman Meltzer (1870–1953) in *Even ha-Ezel, Yad,* ad loc.; *Hassagot Rabad, S'khirut* X:7; R. Menachem b. Solomon (1249–1316), *Beit ha-Bechirah, Baba Metzia* 109a; *Tur,* op. cit., 306:8 quoted in *Rema, Sh. Ar.,* loc. cit. See, however, *Ar. ha-Sh.,* loc. cit., for a different view.

42. *Rabad,* quoted in *Maggid Mishneh,* loc. cit; *Ran* and *Rashba,* quoted in *Nimmukei Yosef, Baba Metzia* 109a; *Ar. ha-Sh.,* loc. cit.

43. *Mordechai, Baba Kamma* III:34. R. Moses Isserles rules in accordance with Mordechai (*Rema, Sh. Ar.,* op. cit., 421:6).

44. R. Yitzchak ha-Kohen ha-Chasid, *Ohel Yitzchak, Choshen Mishpat* 53; R. Malkhiel Tenenbaum, *Divrei Malkhi'el, Choshen Mishpat* III:151; see R. Shillem Warhaftig, *Dinei Avodah ba-Mishpat ha-Ivri,* vol. 2 (Tel Aviv: Moresheth, 1969), pp. 574–75.

45. *Responsa Maimonides,* quoted by R. David b. Solomon Ibn Abi Zimra in *Responsa RiBash,* no. 2078, part 5.

46. R. Jair Chayyim Bacharach (1638–1702), *Chavvot Ya'ir* 211.

47. *Dinei Avodah,* op. cit., p. 580.

48. *Ramban, Baba Metzia* 76b.

49. See R. Areyeh Loeb b. Joseph ha-Kohen (1745–1813), *K'tzot ha-Choshen, Sh. Ar.,* op. cit., 333, note 3; R. Jekuthiel Asher Zalman Ensil Zusmir (d. 1858), *Mahariaz* 14.

50. *Ramban, Baba Metzia* 76b.

51. *Responsa Rashi,* quoted in R. David b. Samuel ha-Levi (1586–1667), *Turei Zahav, Sh. Ar.,* op. cit., 333, note 1.

52. See *Baba Metzia* 77a.

53. *Responsa Rashba* II:260, quoted in *Beit Yosef, Tur,* op. cit., 333:5; *Responsa Radbaz,* part 2, *siman* 750. For a comprehensive discussion of the various nuances surrounding this point that have developed in the rabbinic literature, see *Dinei Avodah,* vol. 2, op. cit., pp. 610–16.

54. *Tur*, op. cit., 333:1; *Talmedei ha-Rashba* on interpretation of R. Joshua ha-Kohen Falk, *Perishah*, *Tur*, op. cit., 333:1.

55. R. Joel Sirkes (1561–1640), *Bach*, *Tur*, op. cit., 333:1.

56. R. Abraham Isaiah Karelitz (1878–1953), *Chazon Ish*, *Baba Kamma* 23:4.

57. *Siftei Kohen*, *Sh. Ar.*, op. cit., 333, note 13.

58. *K'tzot ha-Choshen*, *Sh. Ar.*, op. cit., 333, note 4.

59. *Ramban*, *Baba Metzia* 76b; *Rashba* and *Ran*, quoted in *Shittah M'kubbetzet*, *Baba Metzia* 76b.

60. The disappointed worker here, according to R. Asher b. Jechiel in *Rosh*, *Baba Metzia* VI:2, has legitimate cause for grievance. R. Joseph Chabib, *Nimmukei Yosef*, *Baba Metzia* 76b, however, does not regard the complaint as just.

61. *Tosafot*, *Baba Metzia* 76b; *Ramban* and *Rashba*, quoted in *Shittah M'kubbetzet*, *Baba Metzia* 76b; *Rosh*, *Baba Metzia* loc. cit.; *Tur*, op. cit., 333:2; *Sh. Ar.*, op. cit., 333:2; *Ar. ha-Sh.*, op. cit., 333:2.

62. *Baba Metzia* 77a; *Rif* ad loc.; *Yad*, *S'khirut* IX:4; *Rosh*, *Baba Metzia* VI:6; *Tur*, op. cit., 333:3; *Sh. Ar.*, op. cit., 333:5; *Ar. ha-Sh.*, 333:18.

63. R. Joel, quoted in *Rosh*, *Baba Metzia* VI:3; see *Rema*, *Sh. Ar.*, op. cit., 333:4.

64. *Baba Metzia* 76b; *Yad*, loc. cit.; *Tur*, op. cit., 333:1; *Sh. Ar.*, op. cit., 333:1; *Ar. ha-Sh.*, 333:4.

65. *Rosh*, loc. cit.; *Ar. ha-Sh.*, loc. cit.

66. *Rosh*, loc. cit.

67. R. Meir b. Baruch, quoted in *Mordechai*, *Baba Metzia* VI:343. R. Moses Isserles, *Rema*, *Sh. Ar.*, op. cit., 321:1, rules in accordance with R. Meir.

68. *Sma*, *Sh. Ar.*, op. cit., 321, note 6.

69. *Ar. ha-Sh.*, op. cit., 334:10.

70. R. Aharon Walkin, *Zaken Aharon* 2:143.

71. R. Mordechai Birdugo, *Nofet Tzufim*, *Choshen Mishpat*, no. 346.

72. *Tosefta*, *Baba Metzia* XI:13; R. Solomon b. Simeon Duran (ca. 1400–1467), *Responsa Rashbash* 112.

The specific case dealt with in the Tosefta concerns the power of the community to restrain a publicly employed bath attendant, barber, baker, or money changer from leaving his post, even to join his family for the festival, if substitutes are not available.

R. Yehuda Gershuni ("Ha-Shevita le'Or haHalakhah," in I. Raphael, ed., *Torah she-be'al Peh* [Jerusalem: Mosad Harav Kook, 1977], p. 86) posits that the ruling of the above Tosefta is not in accordance with mainstream Jewish law. His theory is based on the fact that the Tosefta case is not recorded in the codes. Furthermore, its basic teaching appears to be contradicted by the Abtinas incident in *Yoma* 38a. Here the Talmud relates that the house of Abtinas were expert in preparing the Temple incense but would not teach the art. Thereupon, the Sages sent for replacement incense-compounders from Alexandria. The replacements proved inadequate, however, because the smoke of their incense scattered in all directions instead of rising straight like a stick. Upon seeing that the Alexandrian replacements were not as consummate as the house of Abtinas, the Sages recalled the latter. The house of Abtinas refused to return to work, however, until the Sages agreed to double their hire.

Now, if the community may restrain a public servant from leaving his post, why didn't the Sages simply *force* the house of Abtinas to return to work without acceding to their wage demands?

R. Menachem b. Solomon Meiri (*Beit ha-Bechirah, Yoma* 38a) understands the action of the Sages in sending for replacements as imparting the message that the house of Abtinas were *formally* deposed from their position and, as punishment for refusing to teach their art, cut off from further installments of their yearly stipend drawn from the public treasury. Upon seeing that the replacements were not as expert as the house of Abtinas, the Sages desired to restore the latter to their former position.

Meiri's comment leads, in our view, to a ready reconciliation of the Tosefta case with the Abtinas incident. What the Tosefta refers to is the power of the community to restrain a public employee *under contract* from leaving his post. In contrast, a *discharged* public employee, as in the Abtinas case, may not be *forced* to return to his job.

Tosafot Yeshanim, *Yoma* 38a, and R. Joseph Caro (*Beit Yosef, Tur Orach Chayyim* 133) comment that while it is most preferable that the smoke of the incense should ascend straight like a stick, this aspect of the incense service is not indispensable, and in the event the smoke scattered in all directions, the service is, nonetheless, valid.

The above teaching leads, in our view, to another way of reconciling the Tosefta and the Abtinas incident. Since the incense service of the Alexandrian compounders was fully valid, the Sages could not force the house of Abtinas to return to their job, for the community's power in this regard is inoperative when substitutes are available.

In respect to R. Gershuni's first point, it should be noted that while the Tosefta case itself is not discussed in the codes, a *derivative* case is prominently mentioned. This case, dealt with in detail in Chapter 9, involves the financial obligations arising from the community's responsibility to maintain and not disrupt congregational worship during the High Holidays (see the comment of *Ha-Gra* on *Shulchan Arukh, Orach Chayyim* 55:21).

73. *Chazon Ish, Baba Kamma* 23:1; see, however, *Siftei Kohen, Sh. Ar.,* op. cit., 333, note 4.

74. *Rashba,* quoted in *Maggid Mishneh S'khirut IX:4,* op. cit., 333:5.

The availability of other workers at the time the labor contract was entered into is not regarded by *Ramban* (quoted in *Beit Yosef, Tur,* op. cit., 333:3) as an indispensable condition for liability. Penalty consequences, in his view, may ensue for the worker retracting at the point of *kinyan* as long as replacement workers could not be secured to complete the job.

Narrowing the difference between the two schools of thought, R. Joseph Caro posits that *Ramban* would be in agreement that penalty consequences for the worker do not ensue unless it is assessed that the employer, through the exertion of some effort, could have originally secured other workers for the job at hand.

75. *Rashi, Baba Metzia* 112a; *Beit ha-Bechirah, Baba Metzia* 112a; *Responsa R. Meir b. Baruch* 477; R. Isaac b. Moses of Vienna (late 13th cent.), *Or Zaru'a, Baba Metzia* VI:242; *Sma, Sh. Ar.,* op. cit., 333, note 16.

76. *Baba Metzia* 10a; *Rif, Baba Metzia* 77b; *Yad,* op. cit., IX:4; *Rosh Baba Metzia* VI:6; *Tur,* op. cit., 333:2; *Sh. Ar.,* op. cit., 333:3; *Ar. haSh.,* op. cit., 333:6.

77. *Rif,* loc. cit.; *Yad,* loc. cit.; *Tur,* loc. cit.; *Sh. Ar.,* op. cit., 333:4; *Ar ha-Sh.,* loc. cit.

78. *Sma, Sh. Ar.,* op. cit., 333, note 16.

79. *Baba Metzia* 75b and Tosafot, ad loc.

80. See *Mordechai, Baba Metzia* VI:343.

81. *Rema, Sh. Ar.,* op. cit., 333:5.

82. *Teshuvot Maimuniyyot, Sefer Kinyan,* no. 30. See *Dinei Avodah,* vol. 2, pp. 699–701.

83. R. Israel b. Pethachiah Isserlein (1390–1460), *Terumat ha-Deshen* 329; *Beit Yosef, Tur,* op. cit., 333:7; *Rema, Sh. Ar.,* op. cit., 333:5; see *Dinei Avodah,* vol. 2, pp. 702–3.

84. *Rashi, Baba Metzia* 76b; *Tur,* op. cit., 333:2; *Rema Sh. Ar.,* op. cit., 333:4; *Ar. ha-Sh.,* op. cit., 333:16.

85. *Baba Metzia* 76b; *Tur,* loc. cit.

86. *Tur,* loc. cit.

87. K'tzot ha-Choshen, Sh. Ar., op. cit., 333, note 8.

88. *Siftei Kohen, Sh. Ar.,* op. cit., 333, note 19.

89. *Yad,* op. cit., IX:4; *Tur,* op. cit., 333:2; *Sh. Ar.,* op. cit., 333:4 and *Sma,* note 16; *Ar. ha-Sh.,* loc. cit.

90. *Rosh, Baba Metzia* IV:9; *Mordechai, Baba Metzia* VI:346; *Responsa Rashba* II:72; *Responsa RiBash* 476; *Siftei Kohen, Sh. Ar.,* 333, note 14; *K'tzot ha-Choshen, Sh. Ar.,* op. cit., 333, note 5; *Dinei Avodah,* vol. 2, p. 674.
A minority opinion is here expressed by R. Yom Tov Ishbili. Quoting his teachers R. Ishbili (*Ritva, Baba Metzia* 75b) advances the view that retraction rights are denied the day-laborer in the event the labor agreement was originally entered into by means of *shetar* (deed) or *kinyan* rather than mere oral consent. *Ar. ha-Sh.,* op. cit., 333:8, rules in accordance with R. Ishbili.

91. *Responsa R. Meir b. Baruch* 72; *K'tzot, Sh. Ar.,* op. cit., 333, note 7.

92. *Tur,* op. cit., 333:2; *Rema, Sh. Ar.,* op. cit., 333:4; R. Joseph b. Moses Trani (1568–1639), *Responsa Maharit, Yoreh De'ah,* no. 50; *Ar. ha-Sh.,* op. cit., 333:17.

93. R. Jechiel of Paris, quoted in *Responsa MaHarit,* loc. cit.; R. Yechezkiel Katzenellenbogen, *K'nesset Yechezkiel, Orach Chayyim,* no. 8.

94. R. Ephraim Nabon (d. 1735), *Machaneh Ephraim, S'khirut Poalim, siman* 1.

95. *Baba Metzia* 75b; *Rif,* ad loc.; *Yad,* op. cit., IX:4; *Tur,* op. cit., 333:3; *Sh. Ar.,* op. cit., 333:5–7; *Ar. ha-Sh.,* op. cit., 333:18–22.

96. *Yad,* loc. cit.; *Ar. ha-Sh.,* op. cit., 333:19.

97. *Shittah M'kubbetzet, Baba Metzia* 78a; *Siftei Kohen, Sh. Ar.,* op. cit., 333 note 32. For a different view, see *Rashi, Baba Metzia* 78a.

98. *Siftei Kohen, Sh. Ar.,* op. cit., note 37; *Ar. ha-Sh.,* loc. cit.

99. *Ramban, Baba Metzia* 76b; *Shittah M'kubbetzet,* ad loc.

100. *Maggid Mishneh, Yad,* loc. cit.; *Sma, Sh. Ar.,* op. cit., 333 note 26; *Siftei Kohen,* ad loc. note 35; *Ar. ha-Sh.,* op. cit., 333:20.

101. *Rosh,* op. cit., VI:6; *Rema, Sh. Ar.,* op. cit., 333:6; *Siftei Kohen, Sh. Ar.,* op. cit., 333, note 39; *Ar. ha-Sh.,* loc. cit.

102. *Rabad,* quoted in *Rosh,* op. cit., VI:6; *Ramban, Rashba,* and *Ritva,* quoted in *Shittah M'kubbetzet, Baba Metzia* 76b; *Tur,* op. cit., 333:3.

103. *Baba Metzia* 77b; *Rif,* ad loc.; *Yad,* loc. cit.; *Rosh,* loc. cit.; *Tur,* loc. cit.; *Sh. Ar.,* op. cit., 333:5; *Ar. ha-Sh.,* op. cit., 333:18.

104. *Rosh,* loc. cit.; *Tur,* loc. cit.; *Rema, Sh. Ar.,* op. cit., 333:5; *Ar. ha-Sh.,* loc. cit.

105. *Baba Metzia* 77b.

106. *Terumat ha-Deshen, siman* 329, quoted in *Rema,* loc. cit.; *Ar. ha-Sh.,* loc. cit.

107. *Ar. ha-Sh.,* op. cit., 336:7.

108. R. Akiva Eger (1761–1837), *Novelae R. Akiva Eger, Sh. Ar.,* op. cit., 333:5.

109. R. Jacob Moses Lorberbaum (1760–1832), *N'tivot ha-Mishpat, Sh. Ar.,* op. cit., 333, note 9.

110. R. Moshe Schick (1807–1879), *Responsa Maharam, Choshen Mishpat, siman* 32; R. Shalom Mordechai b. Moses Schwadron (1835–1911), *Responsa Maharsham* II:152; *Piskei Din Rabbaniyim* VIII, *choveret* 5, pp. 129–160.

111. R. Moshe Feinstein, *Iggerot Moshe, Choshen Mishpat* 75, 76.

112. R. Meir b. Baruch, quoted in *Mordechai, Baba Metzia* VI:346.

113. Tosafot, *Kiddushin* 17a.

114. *N'tivot ha-Mishpat, Sh. Ar.,* op. cit., 333, note 6.

115. *Teshuvat Ramban,* quoted in *Sma,* op. cit., 104, note 1.

116. *Iggerot Moshe,* op. cit., 81.

117. Deuteronomy 17:20.

118. *Sifrei,* Deuteronomy 17:20; *Yad Kelei ha-Mikdash* IV:20; *Rema, Sh. Ar., Yoreh De'ah* 245:22.

119. R. Moses b. Joseph Trani, *Responsa MaBit* III:200.

120. R. Isaac b. Sheshet Perfet, *Responsa RiBash* 271.

121. *Responsa Rashba* V:283, quoted in *Beit Yosef, Tur, Orach Chayyim* 53.

122. *Responsa MaBit,* loc. cit.

123. *Yad, S'khirut* X:7.

124. *Responsa Maimonides,* quoted in *Radbaz* VI:2075; for a different version of Maimonides' position, see *Sha'arei Teshuvah, Sh. Ar., Orach Chayyim* 53, note 31.

125. *Responsa Mahari'az* 13.

126. *Responsa Beit Yitzchak, Yoreh De'ah* II:70.

127. R. Solomon Zalman Lipschitz (1765–1839), *Chemdat Shelemo, Orach Chayyim* 7; R. Isaac Elchanan Spector, *Be'er Yitzchak, Yoreh De'ah* 3; *Piskei Din Rabbaniyim* VIII.

128. R. Joseph Raphael b. Chayyim Joseph Chazzan (1741–1820), *Chikrei Lev, Orach Chayyim* 50.

129. *Ketubbot* 103b; *Tosafot M'nachot* 109b; *Yad, M'lochim* I:7.

130. *Ketubbot* 103b; Tosafot, *M'nachot* 109b; *Yad, M'lochim* I:7.

131. *Rashba,* on interpretation of R. Abraham b. Mordechai ha-Levi in his *Responsa Ginnat Veradim, Yoreh De'ah, k'lal* 3, *siman* 7.

132. *Ginnat Veradim,* loc. cit.

133. R. Simeon b. Tzemach Duran, *Responsa Tashbez* IV, *tur* 1, *siman* 7; *Responsa Chikrei Lev, Orach Chayyim* 20.

134. R. Chayyim Chezekiah Medini (1832–1904), *Sedei Chemed* VIII; *Maarekhet Chazkat beMitzvot; Chikrei Lev,* loc. cit.; R. Solomon b. Aaron Chatan, *Responsa Beit Shelomo, Orach Chayyim* 18.

134a. Jewish law does not recognize custom when it comes into conflict with *ritual* law. In connection with *civil* law, custom overrides Halakhah only when the custom involved is (1) widespread, (2) of frequent application, and (3) unequivocally clear. For a discussion of the Rabbinic literature relating to these points, see Menachem Elon, "Minhag," in Menachem Elon, ed., *The Principles of Jewish Law* (Jerusalem: Keter Publishing House, 1975), cols. 91–110.

135. See *Dinei Avodah,* vol. 1, p. 521.

136. *Responsa RiBash* 271; *Responsa MaBit* III:610; *Rema, Sh. Ar., Yoreh De'ah* 245:22.

137. R. Samuel B. Moses de Medina (1506–1589), *Responsa Maharashdam, Yoreh De'ah* 85, quoted in *Magen Avraham, Sh. Ar., Orach Chayyim* 53, note 33. See *Dinei Avodah,* vol. 1, pp. 516–17.

138. R. Joseph Saul ha-Levi Nathanson, *Responsa Sho'el u-Meshiv*, vol. 1, part 2:17.

139. *Responsa Chatam Sofer, Orach Chayyim* 12.

140. *Torat Kohanim, Parshat Be'har; Yad, Avadim* I:1.

141. R. Meir b. Baruch, quoted in *Mordechai, Baba Metzia* VI:459–60. The interdict, according to R. Abraham b. Moses di Boton (1710–after 1780), is only rabbinical, as opposed to pentateuchal, in nature (*Lechem Rav* 81).

142. *Rema, Sh. Ar.*, op. cit., 333:3.

143. R. Chayyim b. Israel Benveniste (1603–1673), *K'nesset ha-Gedolah, Choshen Mishpat* 334, *Haggahot Beit Yosef*, note 19.

144. *Siftei Kohen, Sh. Ar.*, op. cit., 333, note 16.

145. *Responsa Chatam Sofer, Orach Chayyim* 206.

146. Tosefta, *Baba Metzia* VIII:2; Talmud Jerusalem, *Demai* VIII:3; *Rif, Baba Metzia* 90b; *Yad*, op. cit., XIII:6; *Rosh, Baba Metzia* VII:3; *Tur*, op. cit., 337:19; *Sh. Ar. ha-Sh.*, op. cit., 337:19; *Sh. Ar.*, 337:25.

147. Talmud Jerusalem, *Demai*, loc. cit.; *Rif*, loc. cit.; *Yad*, loc. cit.; *Rosh*, loc. cit.; *Tur*, loc. cit.; *Sh. Ar.*, loc. cit.; *Ar. ha-Sh.*, loc. cit.

148. *Yad*, loc. cit.; *Tur*, loc. cit.; *Sh. Ar.*, loc. cit.; *Ar. ha-Sh.*, loc. cit.

149. *Mordechai, Baba Metzia* VI:343.

150. *Ar. ha-Sh.*, loc. cit.

151. *Dinei Avodah*, vol. 1, p. 331.

152. Ibid.

NOTES TO CHAPTER 5

1. For a general discussion of the misallocative effects of negative and positive externalities, see William J. Baumol, *Economic Theory and Operations Analysis*, 4th ed. (Englewood Cliffs, N.J.: Prentice-Hall, 1977), pp. 517–22; Bernard P. Herber, *Modern Public Finance*, 3d ed. (Homewood, Ill.: Richard D. Irwin, 1975), pp. 36–41.

2. Ronald H. Coase, "The Problem of Social Cost," *Journal of Law and Economics*, October 1960, pp. 1–45.

3. G. Calabresi, "Transactions Costs, Resource Allocation and Liability Rules: A Comment," *Journal of Law and Economics*, April 1968, pp. 67–74.

4. Larry E. Ruff, "The Economic Common Sense of Pollution," *Public Interest*, no. 19 (Spring 1970), pp. 69–85.

5. Coase, op. cit.

6. R. Meir Abulafia ([1170–1244] *Ramah, Baba Bathra* II:107) bases the interdict either on the verse "Thou shalt not execrate the deaf, nor put a stumbling-block before the blind . . ." (Leviticus 19:14) or on the verse ". . . thou shalt love thy fellow man as thyself" (Leviticus 19:18). R. Asher b. Jechiel ([1250–1327] *Responsa Rosh, K'lal* 108, par. 10), however, bases the prohibition on the verse "Her ways are ways of pleasantness, and all her paths are peace" (Proverbs 3:17). A variant minority view in this matter is held by R. Moses b. Joseph Trani (1500–1580). He regards the prohibition as only rabbinical in origin, since biblical law merely requires the defendant to *compensate* his victim for damage he is responsible for, but would not enjoin a harmful act with the objective of preventing damage from occurring (*Kiryat Sefer, Shekhenim* IX). See also R. Jacob Tam (1100–1171), *Sefer ha-Yashar, simon* 522.

7. *Baba Bathra* 25b, 26a.

8. Ruling of R. Judah in the name of Samuel (fl. 300), *Baba Bathra* 25b; R. Isaac b. Jacob Alfasi (1013–1103), *Rif*, ad loc.; Maimonides (1135–1204), *Yad, Shekhenim* X:5; R. Asher b. Jechiel, *Rosh, Baba Bathra* II:25; R. Jacob b. Asher (1270–ca. 1343), *Tur, Choshen Mishpat* 155:44–46; R. Joseph Caro (1488–1575), *Shulchan Arukh, Choshen Mishpat* 155:32; R. Jechiel Michael Epstein (1829–1908), *Arukh ha-Shulchan, Choshen Mishpat* 155:1.

9. *Baba Bathra* 18a; R. Solomon b. Isaac (1040–1105), *Rashi*, ad loc.; *Rif*, ad loc.; *Yad*, op. cit., IX:12; *Rosh*, op. cit., II:6; *Tur*, op. cit., 155:6; *Sh. Ar.*, op. cit., 155:2; R. David b. Samuel ha-Levi (1586–1667), *Turei Zahav, Sh. Ar.*, loc. cit.; *Ar. ha-Sh* op. cit., 155:4.

10. R. Solomon Adret (1235–1319), quoted by R. Bezalel Ashkenazi (1520–1591), *Shittah M'kubbetzet, Baba Bathra* 22a; *Tosafot, Baba Bathra* 22a; R. Aaron Kotler (1892–1962), *Mishnat Rabbi Aharon*, vol. 1, p. 68; R. Yechezkel Abramsky (1886–1976), *Chazon Yechezkel, Tosefta Baba Bathra* I:5.

11. *Baba Bathra* 20b; 21a; *Tosafot, Baba Bathra* 21a; *Sh. Ar.*, op. cit., 155:37; R. Isaac b. Sheshet (1326–1408), *Responsa RiBash*, no. 197, quoted by R. Moses Isserles (1525–1572), *Rema, Sh. Ar.*, op. cit., 155:15; *Ar. ha-Sh.* op. cit., 155:15, 30.

12. *Baba Kamma* 79b; *Rashi*, ad loc.; *Yad, Nizkei Mamon* V:1–2; *Baba Bathra* 21a; *Rif*, ad loc.; *Yad, Shekhenim* VI:12; *Sh. Ar.*, op. cit., 156:3; *Ar. ha-Sh.*, op cit., 156:3, 5.

13. *Baba Bathra* 25b. The vibration-producing enterprise does not qualify for restraint, according to the Talmud ad loc., unless the lid of a pitcher located in the neighboring house is caused to rattle by the shaking. Talmudic decisors differ as to whether the rattling must occur while the pitcher is standing on a wall, or whether it is sufficient if it occurs while the pitcher is held in one's hand. R. Solomon b. Isaac ad loc. takes the former position, while R. Isaac b. Samuel (d. 1185), quoted in Tosafot ad loc., takes the latter view. R. Solomon b. Isaac's view is adopted by the talmudic codifier R. Joshua ha-Kohen Falk (1555–1614), see *Sma, Sh. Ar.*, op. cit., 155, note 36.

14. Nachmanides (1194–1270), *Ramban, Baba Bathra, dinei d'garmi.*

15. Nachmanides (*Ramban, Baba Bathra* 18a), quoting Talmud Jerusalem II:2, extends the interdict to the establishment of these enterprises under an upper-story *residence*. Representing also the view of R. Solomon Adret (quoted in *Shittah M'kubbetzet, Baba Bathra* 18a), this ruling is adopted by R. Aryeh Loeb b. Joseph ha-Kohen (1745–1813), *K'tzot, Sh. Ar.*, op. cit., 155, note 2. R. Joseph b. Meir Ibn MiGash (1077–1141), *Ri MiGash, Baba Bathra* 18a, and R. Meir Abulafia, *Ramah, Baba Bathra* II:27, however, limit the interdict to the circumstance where the upper story is a storehouse.

16. Mishnah, *Baba Bathra* II:2; *Rif*, ad loc.; *Yad*, op. cit., IX:12; *Rosh*, op. cit., II:6; *Tur*, op. cit., 155:4; *Sh. Ar.*, op. cit., 155:2; *Ar. ha-Sh.*, op. cit., 155:3.

17. R. Abraham b. David of Posquières (1125–1198) would not entitle the plaintiff with restitution for damages sustained unless the damage proceeds directly and immediately as a result of the defendant's action. With this condition not met here, the defendant escapes liability. R. Isaac b. Abba Mari of Marseilles (1120–1190) et alia, however, extend liability to all *gi'ri de'lei* cases, whether or not the damage proceeds directly and immediately from the defendant's action. See *Tur*, op. cit., 155:49–50; *Sh. Ar.*, op. cit., 155:33; *Ramban*, op. cit, *dinei d'garmi.*

18. *Baba Bathra* 26a; *Rif*, ad loc.; *Yad*, op. cit, XI:1–2; *Rosh*, op. cit, II:27; *Tur*, op. cit., 155:50; *Sh. Ar.*, op. cit., 155:34; *Ar. ha-Sh.*, op. cit., 155:25.

19. Ibid.

20. Members of the school of thought that would enjoin even a potentially harmful *gi'ri de'lei* activity include R. Solomon Adret *(Responsa Rashba* 1:1144); R. Isaac b. Sheshet *(Responsa RiBash* 471); R. Solomon b. Isaac and R. Isaac Alfasi, both on interpretation of R. Jacob *(Tur,* op. cit., 155:47). Decisors espousing the view that a potentially harmful *gi'ri de'lei* enterprise is not legally subject to restraint include: Tosafot, *Baba Bathra* 18b; *Rosh,* op. cit., II:3; R. Zerachiah b. Isaac ha-Levi of Gerondi (1135–after 1186), *Ha-Ma'or ha-Gadel to Rif, Baba Bathra* II. This lenient view is quoted in *Rema,* op. cit., 155:19. A middle road in this matter is taken by R. Joseph b. Meir Ibn MiGash (see *Responsa RiBash,* loc. cit.). In his view a potentially harmful activity is not subject to restraint. Nonetheless, the moment the enterprise becomes *concretely* harmful, it must be withdrawn despite its non–*gi'ri de'lei* character at the time it was initiated. For a somewhat similar view, see Tosafot, *Baba Bathra* 17b.

21. *Baba Bathra* 18a; *Rif,* ad loc.; *Yad,* op. cit., IX:12; *Rosh,* op. cit., II:6; *Tur,* op. cit, 155:6; *Sh. Ar.,* op. cit., 155:2; *Ar ha-Sh.,* op. cit., 155:4.

22. *Rashi, Baba Bathra* 18a; *Turei Zahav, Sh. Ar.,* loc. cit.; *Ar. ha Sh.,* loc. cit.

23. *Baba Bathra* 59b; *Rif,* ad loc.; *Yad,* op. cit., VII:5; *Rosh,* op. cit., III:75; *Tur,* op. cit, 154:2; *Sh. Ar.,* op. cit., 154:3; *Ar. ha-Sh.,* op. cit., 154:7.

24. R. Jonah b. Abraham Gerondi (ca. 1200–1263) quoted in *Rosh,* op. cit., II:2; *Ramban,* op. cit., *Baba Bathra* 18b; *Responsa Rashba* I:1144; *Responsa RiBash,* no. 471. For a dissenting view, see *Responsa Rosh, k'lal* 99, *siman* 6.

25. R. Jacob Lorberbaum (1760–1832), *N'tivot ha-Mishpat, Sh. Ar.,* op. cit., 154, note 17; R. Akiva Eger (1761–1837), *Responsa R. Akiva Eger,* no. 151.

26. The term Rishon (pl. Rishonim) designates scholars who were active in the period from the eleventh to the middle of the fifteenth century.

27. *Rashba,* quoted in *Shittah M'kubbetzet, Baba Bathra* 22a.

28. *Rashba,* loc. cit; Tosafot, *Baba Bathra* 22a.

29. R. Aaron Kotler, *Mishnat Rabbi Aharon,* vol. I, p. 68.

30. R. Yechezkel Abramsky (1886–1976), *Chazon Yechezkel, Tosefta, Baba Bathra* I:5.

31. The length of time necessary for the defendant to establish a prescriptive right to continue on his own premises an enterprise that generates a negative externality is a matter of rishonic dispute. Maimonides *(Yad,* op. cit., XI:4) posits that as soon as the injured party becomes aware of the damage the enterprise presents for him and registers no protest, the defendant acquires a prescriptive right to continue the activity. This is also the view of Nachmanides *(Ramban, Baba Bathra* 58a). R. Solomon Adret (quoted in *Shittah M'kubbetzet, Baba Bathra* 23a), however, would not entitle the defendant with a prescriptive right to carry on his activity unless the following two conditions are met: (1) the defendant claims that the injured party gave him permission or sold him the right to conduct the enterprise generating the negative externality, and (2) the defendant must have carried out his enterprise for a period of three years without protest. The latter view is also held by R. Tam and R. Asher b. Jechiel (see *Tur,* op. cit., 154:15).

32. *Sh. Ar.,* op.cit., 155:37; *Ar. ha-Sh.,* op. cit., 155:30.

33. *Baba Bathra* 20b; Tosafot, *Baba Bathra* 21a; R. Joseph Ibn Chabib (fl. 15th cent.), *Nimmukei Yosef,* op. cit., II.

34. *Responsa RiBash,* no. 197, quoted in *Rema, Sh. Ar.,* op. cit., 155:15; *Ar. ha-Sh.,* op. cit., 156:2.

35. *Baba Bathra* 21a.

36. *Rif,* op. cit., II; *Yad,* op. cit., VI:11; *Rosh,* op. cit., II:11; *Tur,* op. cit., 156:1–2; *Sh. Ar.,* op. cit., 156:1; *Ar. ha-Sh.,* op. cit., 156:1. R. Mordechai b.

Hillel ha-Kohen (1240–1298), *Mordechai, Baba Bathra* II:514, advances the view that neighboring residents may interfere with the rental of an apartment in the courtyard to one of these professionals. The *sale* of a home to one of these individuals, however, may not be blocked. Should the professional subsequently desire to set up his enterprise in his newly acquired home, any resident of the courtyard, at that time, may, of course, obtain a restraining order to halt his activity. For an explanation of R. Mordechai's view, see R. Joshua ha-Kohen Falk, *Derishah, Tur,* ad loc., note 1.

37. *Ramah, Baba Bathra* II:54; *Yad,* op. cit., VI:12; *Rashba,* quoted in *Shittah M'kubbetzet, Baba Bathra* 20b; *Sh. Ar.,* op. cit., 156:2.

38. *Ramah, Baba Bathra* II:56.

39. *Tosafot, Baba Bathra* 21a; *Ramban, Baba Bathra* 20b; *Rashba,* quoted in *Shittah M'kubbetzet, Baba Bathra* 20b; R. Menachem b. Solomon (1249–1316), *Meiri, Baba Bathra* 20b: *Mordechai, Baba Bathra* II:512; R. Israel of Krems (fl.14th cent.), *Haggahot Asheri, Baba Bathra* II. This view is quoted in *Rema,* op. cit., 156:2, and in *Ar. haSh.,* op. cit., 156:2. R. Joshua ha-Kohen Falk *(Derishah, Tur,* op. cit., 156:3) rules in accordance with this opinion.

40. *Yad,* op. cit., VI:12; R. Jerucham b. Meshulum (ca. 1290–1350), quoted in R. Joseph Caro, *Beit Yosef, Tur,* op. cit., 156:1; *Sh. Ar.,* op. cit., 156:1; *Sh. Ar.,* op. cit., 156:2. This view is quoted in *Ar. ha-Sh.,* op. cit., 156:2.

41. *Derishah, Tur,* op. cit., 156, note 3; *N'tivot haMishpat, Sh. Ar.,* op. cit. 156, note 1.

42. *Baba Kamma* 79b, 80a; *Rif,* ad loc.; *Yad, Nizkei Mamon* V:1–2; *Rosh, Baba Kamma* VII:13; *Tur,* op. cit., 409:1–3; *Sh. Ar.,* op. cit., 409:1; *Ar. ha-Sh.,* op. cit., 409:1–2.

43. *Yad,* op. cit.

44. *Rashi, Baba Kamma* 79b.

45. *Baba Bathra* 21a; *Rif,* ad loc.; *Yad, Shekhenim* VI:12; *Rosh, Baba Bathra* II:6 *Tur,* op. cit., 156:8; *Sh. Ar.,* op. cit., 156:3; *Ar. ha-Sh.,* op. cit., 156:3.

46. *Tur,* op. cit., 156:8; *Sh. Ar.,* op. cit., 156:3; *Ar. ha-Sh.,* op. cit., 156:3. For a variant minority opinion, see *Ramban,* quoted in *Beit Yoset, Tur,* ad loc.

47. *Ar. ha-Sh.* (op. cit., 156:5) on authority of R. Mordechai b. Abraham Jaffe of Prague (ca. 1535–1612).

48. Mishnah, *Baba Bathra* II:9; *Rif,* ad loc.; *Rosh,* op. cit., II:24; *Tur,* op. cit., 155:28; *Sh. Ar.,* op. cit., 155:22; *Ar. ha-Sh.,* op. cit., 155:21.

49. Tosefta, *Baba Bathra* I:7; *Tur,* op. cit., 155:29; *Sh. Ar.,* op. cit., 155:23; *Ar. ha-Sh.,* op. cit., 155:23.

50. Mishnah, *Baba Bathra* 2:5; *Rif,* ad loc.; *Rosh,* op. cit., II:19; *Tur,* op. cit., 155:31; *Sh. Ar.,* op. cit., 155:24; *Ar. ha-Sh.* loc. cit.

51. Mishnah, *Baba Bathra* II:10; *Rif,* ad loc.; *Yad,* op. cit., X:3; *Rosh,* op. cit., II:24; *Tur,* op. cit., 155:29; *Sh.Ar.,* op. cit., 155:23; *Ar. ha-Sh.,* op. cit., 155:23.

52. *Yad,* op. cit., X:4; *Tur,* op. cit., 155:30; *Sh. Ar.,* loc. cit., *Ar. ha-Sh.,* loc. cit. For a minority variant view on this matter, see *Nimmukei Yosef, Baba Bathra* II.

53. *Rashi, Baba Bathra* 25a.

54. R. Mordechai b. Abraham Jaffe of Prague, quoted by R. Shabbetai b. Meir ha-Kohen (1621–1662), *Siftei Kohen, Sh. Ar., Yoreh De'ah* 365, note 2.

55. *Baba Bathra* 24b; *Yad,* op. cit., X:1; *Tur,* op. cit., 155:27; *Ar. ha-Sh.,* op. cit., 155:23. For a different rationalization of this ordinance, see Jerusalem Talmud, *Baba Bathra* II:7.

56. *Baba Bathra* 24b; *Rif,* ad loc.; *Yad,* loc. cit., *Rosh,* op. cit., II:24; *Tur,* loc. cit.; *Ar. ha-Sh.,* loc. cit.

57. *Ramban, Baba Bathra* 24b; *Rashba,* quoted in *Shittah M'Kubbetzet, Baba Bathra* 24b; *Tur,* loc. cit.; *Ar. ha-Sh.,* loc. cit. For a minority variant view, see *Ramah Baba Bathra* II:95; *Siftei Kohen, Sh. Ar., Choshen Mishpat* 155, note 12.

58. Mishnah, *Baba Bathra* II:7; *Rif,* ad loc.; *Yad,* loc. cit.; *Rosh,* op. cit., II:24; *Tur,* loc. cit.; *Ar. ha-Sh.* loc. cit.

59. *Rema, Sh. Ar.,* op. cit., 155:22; *Ar. ha-Sh.,* op. cit., 155:21.

60. *Baba Bathra* 24b; *Yad,* loc. cit.; *Rosh,* loc. cit.; *Tur,* loc. cit.; *Sh. Ar.,* loc. cit.; *Ar. ha-Sh* loc. cit.

61. *Meiri, Baba Bathra* 17b.

62. *Ramban, Baba Bathra* 26a. R. Aryeh Loeb b. Joseph ha-Kohen *(K'tzot, Sh. Ar.,* op. cit., 155, note 3) posits that R. Isaac b. Jacob Alfasi's view on this matter accords with *Ramban's.*

63. *Responsa Rosh, k'lal* 108, *simon* 10, quoted in *Tur,* op. cit., 155:20.

64. *Yad, Nizkei Mamon* V:1; *Ramban, Dinei d'garmi;* R. Jacob Kanivsky (contemporary), *K'hilot Yaakov, Baba Bathra, siman* 1.

65. *Rema,* op. cit., 155:22.

66. *Responsa Ri MiGash* 186; *Responsa Rashba* I:616; *Yad, Chovel u-Mazik* V:I; *Rif (Baba Kamma* VIII) and *Rosh (Baba Kamma* VIII:13) on interpretation of R. Solomon b. Jechiel Luria (1510–1594), *Yam shel Shelomo, Baba Kamma* VIII; *Tur,* op. cit., 420:21. A minority variant view is here held by R. Meir Abulafia. In his view the self-infliction of a wound violates no biblical or rabbinical interdict. R. Meir Abulafia's opinion is quoted in *Shittah M'kubbetzet, Baba Kamma* 91b, and in *Tur,* loc. cit.

67. *Rashba Baba Kamma* 91b; *Tosafot, Baba Kamma* 91b.

68. *Imrei Tzvi, Baba Kamma* 91b (pub. 1887).

69. Though Halakhah recognizes the legislative authority of the community (see *Baba Bathra* 7a), communal enactments may not contract out of the law of the Torah in matters of ritual prohibition. See *Responsa Rashba* 3:411; R. Shimon b. Tzemach Duran (1361–1444), *Tashbez* 2:132 and 239.

70. See *Berakhot* 32b; R. Ezekiel b. Judah Landau (1713–1793), *Noda bi-Yehuda, Yoreh De'ah, siman* 10.

NOTES TO CHAPTER 6

1. Ronnie J. Davis, "The Social and Economic Externalities of Education," in *Economic Factors Affecting the Financing of Education,* ed. Roe L. Johns (Gainesville, Fla.: National Education Finance Project, 1970), 1, pp. 59–81.

2. For a general discussion of the misallocative effects of negative and positive externalities, see William J. Baumol, *Economic Theory and Operations Analysis,* 4th ed. (Englewood Cliffs, N.J.: Prentice-Hall, 1977), pp. 517–22; Bernard P. Herber, *Modern Public Finance,* 3d ed. (Homewood, Ill.: Richard D. Irwin, 1975), pp. 36–41.

3. *Baba Metzia* 101b; Maimonides (1135–1204), *Yad, Gezelah* X:5, on the interpretation of R. Joseph Chabib (fl. 15th Cent.); R. Meir Abulafia (1170–1244), quoted by R. Jacob b. Asher (1270–ca. 1343) in *Tur, Choshen Mishpat* 375:1; R. Asher b. Jechiel (1250–1327), *Baba Metzia* VIII:22; R. Joseph Caro (1488–1575), *Beit Yosef, Tur, Choshen Mishpat* 375:1. For a variant opinion, see R. Solomon Adret (1235–1319), *Rashba, Baba Metzia* 101b; Nachmanides (1194–1270), *Ramban, Baba Metzia* 101b; Maimonides, *Yad, Gezelah* X:5, on interpretation of R. Yom Tov Vidal (14th cent.) in *Maggid Mishneh,* ad loc.

4. *Maggid Mishneh, Yad Shekhenim* III:3; *Beit Yosef, Tur,* op. cit., 155:13.

5. R. Jacob Moses Lorberbaum, *N'tivot ha-Mishpat, Shulchan Arukh, Choshen Mishpat* 375, note 2.

6. R. Abraham I. Karelitz, *Chazon Ish, Baba Bathra*, chap. 2.

7. *Baba Kamma* 21a; *Yad, Gezelah* III:9; *Rosh, Baba Kamma* II:6; *Tur*, op. cit., 363:6; R. Joseph Caro, *Shulchan Arukh, Choshen Mishpat* 363:6; R. Jechiel Michael Epstein (1829–1908), *Arukh ha-Shulchan, Choshen Mishpat* 363:15.

8. R. Meir Simcha ha-Kohen of Dvinsk, *Or Same'ach, Yad, Gezelah* III:9.

9. The term Rishon (pl. Rishonim) designates scholars who were active in the period from the eleventh to the middle of the fifteenth century.

10. R. Ephraim Nabon, *Machaneh Ephraim, Gezelah*, chap. 13.

11. R. Joseph b. Meir Ibn MiGash (1077–1141), *Ri MiGash, Baba Bathra* 5a.

12. R. Meir b. Baruch of Rothenburg, *Responsa Maharam*, no. 39.

13. Tosafot, *Baba Kamma* 101a; *Rosh, Baba Kamma* IX:17.

14. *Yad, Gezelah* III:9; *Rosh, Baba Kamma* II:6; *Tur*, op. cit., 363:6; *Sh Ar.*, op. cit., 363:6; *Ar. ha-Sh.*, op. cit., 363:15.

15. Tosafot, op. cit.; *Rosh*, op. cit.

16. *Machaneh Ephraim, Nizkei Mamon*, chap. 2; R. Chayyim Soloveichik, quoted by R. Baruch Ber Leibowitz (1866–1939) in *Birkat Shemue'el, Baba Metzia*, p. 54; R. Shimon Shkop (1860–1940), *Novelae R. Shimon, Baba Kamma*, chap. 19; R. Aharon Kotler (1892–1962), *Mishnat Rabbi Aharon*, vol. 1, pp. 56–66, 121.

17. *Novelae R. Shimon*, loc. cit.

18. R. Solomon b. Isaac (1040–1105), *Rashi, Baba Metzia* 101a; *Yad*, op. cit., X:4, on interpretation of R. Yom Tov Vidal ad loc.; *Beit Yosef, Tur*, op. cit., 375:2. For variant opinions, see R. Isaac b. Jacob Alfasi (1013–1103), *Rif, Baba Metzia* 101a; R. Zerachiah b. Isaac ha-Levi of Gerondi (1135–after 1186), *Ha-Ma'or ha- Gadol to Rif, Baba Metzia* 101a.

19. R. Abraham b. David of Posquières (1125–1198), quoted by R. Nissim Gerondi (1488–1575), in *Ran, Ketubbot* 80a.

20. R. Shabbetai b. Meir, *Siftei Kohen, Sh. Ar., Choshen Mishpat* 391:2.

21. R. Moshe Feinstein, *Dibberot Moshe, Baba Bathra*, vol. 1, p. 25.

22. *Baba Bathra* 4b.

23. *Rashi, Baba Bathra* 4b; see R. Menachem b. Solomon (1249–1316), *Meiri, Baba Bathra* 4b.

24. *Yad, Shekhenim* III:3–4.

25. R. Abraham b. David of Posquières, ad loc.

26. Nachmanides, *Ramban, Baba Bathra*, 4b.

27. *Maggid Mishneh, Yad, Shekhenim* III:3.

28. *Dibberot Moshe, Baba Bathra*, vol. 1, p. 29.

29. *Mishnat Rabbi Aharon*, vol. 1, pp. 56–66, 121.

30. Tosafot, *Baba Bathra* 4b; *Ramban*, op. cit.

31. R. Aryeh Loeb b. Joseph ha-Kohen (1745–1813), *K'tzot, Sh. Ar.*, op. cit., 158, note 6.

32. *Novelae R. Shimon*, loc. cit.

33. R. Meir Abulafia (1170–1244), quoted in *Tur*, op. cit., 158:14. The interpretation of R. Meir Abulafia's view presented in the text represents renditions of R. Moshe Sofer (1762–1839), *Chatam Sofer, Baba Bathra* 4b, and R. Abraham I. Karelitz, *Chazon Ish, Baba Bathra* 4b. For a variant interpretation of R. Meir Abulafia's view, see R. Joel Sirkes (1561–1640), *Bach, Tur, Sh. Ar.*, ad loc.

34. *Dibberot Moshe, Baba Bathra*, vol. 1, p. 25.

35. *Ramban*, loc. cit.

NOTES TO CHAPTER 7

1. R. Joshua b. Alexander ha-Kohen Falk (1555–1614), *Sma, Sh. Ar., Choshen Mishpat* 231, note 43.

2. *Baba Bathra* 90a; R. Isaac b. Jacob Alfasi (1013–1103), *Rif,* ad loc.; Maimonides (1135–1204), *Yad, Mekhirah* XIV:1; R. Asher b. Jechiel (1250–1327), *Rosh, Baba Bathra* V:2; R. Jacob b. Asher (1270–1343), *Tur, Choshen Mishpat* 231:27; R. Joseph Caro (1488–1575), *Shulchan Arukh, Choshen Mishpat* 231:20; R. Jechiel Michael Epstein (1829–1908), *Arukh ha-Shulchan, Choshen Mishpat* 231:20.

3. R. Vidal Yom Tov (fl. 14th cent.), *Maggid Mishneh, Yad,* loc. cit.

4. R. Joseph Caro, *Beit Yosef, Tur,* op. cit., 231:28.

5. *Sma, Sh. Ar.,* op. cit., 231, note 36.

6. Ibid., note 43.

7. Baraita, *Baba Metzia* 51b; *Rif,* ad loc.; *Yad,* op. cit., XIII:6; *Rosh, Baba Metzia* IV:19; *Tur,* op. cit., 227:39; *Sh. Ar.,* op. cit. 227:28; *Ar. ha-Sh.,* op. cit., 227:32.

8. R. Menachem b. Solomon (1249–1316), *Beit ha-Bechirah, Baba Metzia* 40b; *Rosh, Baba Metzia* III:16; *Tur,* op. cit., 231:26, and comment of *Perishah* ad loc. The implicit wage element of the cost base is presumably limited to the competitive rate for the type of work performed.

9. *Rosh,* loc. cit.; *Tur,* loc. cit.

10. *Baba Bathra* 9a; *Yoma* 9a; *Yad,* op. cit., XIV:1; *Tur,* op. cit., 231:26; *Sh. Ar.,* op. cit., 231:20; *Ar. ha-Sh.,* op. cit., 231:20.

11. *Yad, Genevah* VIII:20; *Tur,* op. cit., 231:27; *Sh. Ar.,* op. cit., 231:21.

12. *Yad,* loc. cit. The import of Maimonides' phrase "and they are compelled to sell at the *market* price," in our view, is that vendors in the Necessity Sector may sell their wares at the current market price, notwithstanding any windfall above the one-sixth profit-rate constraint they may realize thereby. This interpretation places Maimonides in agreement with R. Jacob b. Asher (*Tur,* op. cit., 231:26) and R. Joseph Caro (*Sh. Ar.,* op. cit., 231:20) on this point.

13. R. Meir b. Todros Abulafia (1170–1244), quoted in *Tur,* op. cit., 231:26; *Sh. Ar.,* op. cit., 231:20; *Ar. ha-Sh.,* loc. cit.

14. R. Meir b. Todros Abulafia, loc. cit.

15. R. Simeon b. Samuel of Joinville (12th–13th cent.), quoted in Tosafot, *Baba Bathra* 91a.

16. *Tur,* loc. cit.; *Sh. Ar.,* loc. cit. See also note 12.

17. *Yad, Mekhirah* XIV:9.

18. Exodus 22:24, Leviticus 25:35–37, Deuteronomy 23:20–21.

19. R. Abraham Danzig, *Chokhmat Adam Ribbit* 131:1.

20. R. Abraham b. David of Posquières (1125–1198), *Hassagot Rabad* on *Yad, Malveh* VI:3, quoted in *Sh. Ar., Yoreh De'ah* 166:2; R. Shabbetai b. Meir ha-Kohen (1621–1662), *Siftei Kohen, Sh. Ar.,* ad loc., n. 8; *Chokhmat Adam,* op. cit., 131:2. R. Menachem b. Solomon (*Beit ha-Bechirah, Kiddushin* 6b) posits that should the offer of extending the maturity date of the loan in exchange for a *ribbit* premium be made *before* the maturity date, the *ribbit ketzuzah* interdict is not violated. The conduct is, however, prohibited by force of the *avak ribbit* interdict. See also R. Jacob Y. Blau, *B'rit Yehuda* (Jerusalem: Akiva Yosef, 1976), pp. 51–52.

21. *Mishnah, Baba Metzia* 75b; *Rif,* ad loc.; *Yad, Malveh* IV:2; *Rosh, Baba Metzia* V:80; *Tur,* op. cit., 160:2; *Sh. Ar.,* op. cit., 160:1; *Chokhmat Adam* 130:1.

22. R. Moses Isserles (1525–1572), *Rema, Sh. Ar.,* op. cit., 160:5, on in-

terpretation of *Sha'ar De'ah*; R. Jacob Lorberbaum, *Chavvot Da'at, Yoreh De'ah* 166:5.

23. *Baba Metzia* 61b; *Rif*, ad loc.; *Yad*, op. cit., IV:3; *Tur*, op. cit., 161:5; *Sh. Ar.*, op. cit., 161:5; *Chokhmat Adam* 133:1.

24. *Rosh*, quoted in *Tur*, op. cit., 160:7–8; Maimonides, on interpretation of *Beit Yosef* ad loc.; *Sh. Ar.*, op. cit., 160:5.

25. *Tur, Sh. Ar.*, op. cit., 161:17; *Sh. Ar.*, op. cit., 161:11; *Chokhmat Adam*, loc. cit.

26. *Ar. ha-Sh.*, *Choshen Mishpat* 52:1; *Tur, Yoreh De'ah* 161:17; *Sh. Ar.*, loc. cit.

27. *Chokhmat Adam*, loc. cit.; *Ar. ha-Sh.*, loc. cit.

28. *Ar. ha-Sh.*, loc. cit.; *Chokhmat Adam*, loc. cit.

29. *Tur*, op. cit., 160:11; *Sh. Ar.*, op. cit., 160:7; *Chokhmat Adam* 131:10.

30. *Tur*, loc. cit.; *Chokhmat Adam*, loc. cit.

31. *Tur*, op. cit., 160:12; *Sh. Ar.*, loc. cit.; *Chokhmat Adam*, loc. cit.

32. *Tur*, loc. cit.; *Sh. Ar.*, loc. cit.; *Chokhmat Adam*, loc. cit.

33. *Baba Metzia* 75b; *Rif*, ad loc.; *Yad*, op. cit., V:12; *Rosh, Baba Metzia* V:79; *Tur*, op. cit., 160:18; *Sh. Ar.*, op. cit., 160:11; *Chokhmat Adam* 131:11.

34. *Baba Metzia* 75b; *Rif*, ad loc.; *Yad*, op. cit., V:13; *Rosh*, loc. cit.; *Tur*, op. cit., 160:19; *Sh. Ar.*, op. cit., 160:12; *Chokhmat Adam*, loc. cit.

35. Mishnah, *Baba Metzia*, 75a; *Rif*, ad loc.; *Yad*, op. cit., X:3; *Rosh*, op. cit., V:75; *Tur*, op. cit., 162:1; *Sh. Ar.*, op. cit., 162:1; *Chokhmat Adam* 134:1.

36. *Tur*, loc. cit.

37. Mishnah, *Baba Metzia* 75a; *Rif*, ad loc.; *Yad*, op. cit., VII:11; *Rosh*, op. cit., V:78; *Tur*, op. cit., 160:13–16; *Sh. Ar.*, op. cit. 160:9; *Chokhmat Adam* 136:3.

38. R. Eliezer, *Baba Metzia* 61b; *Rif*, ad loc.; *Yad*, op. cit., VI:1; *Rosh*, op. cit., V:5; *Tur*, op. cit., 161:3; *Sh. Ar.*, 161:2; *Chokhmat Adam* 133:1.

39. *Rosh*, loc. cit; *Sh. Ar.*, loc. cit.; *Chokhmat Adam*, loc. cit.

40. *Rema, Sh. Ar.*, loc. cit.; *Chokhmat Adam*, loc. cit.

41. *Yad*, op. cit., IV:14; *Tur*, op. cit., 160:25; *Sh. Ar*, op. cit, 160:18; *Chokhmat Adam* 130:1.

42. *Tur*, loc. cit.; *Sh. Ar.*, loc. cit.; *Chokhmat Adam*, loc. cit. See, however, *Siftei Kohen Sh. Ar.*, op. cit., note 26.

43. *Baba Bathra* 8b; *Rif*, ad loc.; *Yad, Mekhirah* XIV:9; *Rosh, Baba Bathra* I:29; *Tur, Choshen Mishpat* 231:30; *Sh. Ar., Choshen Mishpat* 231:27; *Ar. ha-Sh., Choshen Mishpat* 231:27.

44. R. Moses b. Joseph de Trani, *Responsa MaBit* I:237.

45. *Baba Bathra* 90b; *Rif*, ad loc.; *Yad*, op. cit., XIV:5–6; *Tur*, op. cit., 231:29; *Sh. Ar.*, op. cit., 231:24; *Ar. ha-Sh.*, op. cit., 231:24. For an interesting glimpse into how the Sages viewed the effect of hoarding on market price, see *Baba Bathra* 90b.

46. R. Simeon b. Gamliel here relied on the principle, *et la'asot la'Shem, heferu toratecha* (see *Tiferet Yisroel* ad loc.).

47. *Baba Bathra* 91a; *Rif*, ad loc.; *Yad*, op. cit., XIV:4; *Sh. Ar.*, op. cit., 231:23; *Ar. ha-Sh.*, op. cit., 231:23.

48. R. Samuel b. Meir (ca. 1080–1174), *Rashbam, Baba Bathra* 91a; *Ar. ha-Sh.*, loc. cit.

49. *Baba Bathra* 90b; *Rif*, ad loc.; *Yad*, op. cit., XIV:8; *Sh. Ar.*, op. cit., 231:26; *Ar. ha-Sh.*, op. cit., 231:26.

50. *Sma, Sh. Ar.*, op. cit., 231, notes 42 and 44; *Ar. ha-Sh.*, op. cit., 231:23.

51. See *Sma*, op. cit., note 44.

52. M. Tamari, "Competition, Prices and Profits in Jewish Law," in *Memo-*

rial to H. M. Shapiro, ed. H. Z. Hirschberg (Ramat Gan: Bar-Ilan University, 1972), p. 133 [Hebrew].

53. *Baba Bathra* 91a; *Rif*, ad loc.; *Yad*, *Ta'anit* II:14; *Rosh*, op. cit., V:21; *Tur*, *Orach Chayyim* 576; *Sh. Ar*, *Orach Chayyim* 576:10; *Ar. ha-Sh*., *Orach Chayyim* 576:17.

54. See *Baba Metzia* 61a; *Tur*, *Choshen Mishpat* 227:1; *Sma*, *Sh. Ar*., *Choshen Mishpat*, op. cit., 227, note 1.

55. *Baba Metzia* 50b; *Rif*, ad loc.; *Yad*, *Mekhirah* XII:4; *Rosh*, *Baba Metzia* IV:15; *Tur*, op. cit., 227:6; *Sh. Ar*., *Choshen Mishpat* 227:4; *Ar. ha-Sh*., *Choshen Mishpat* 227:3.

56. *Yad*, loc. cit.; *Sh. Ar*., loc. cit, and *Sma*, ad loc., n. 6; R. Asher b. Jechiel (*Rosh*, *Baba Bathra* V:14) understands this to be the view of R. Isaac b. Jacob Alfasi.

57. R. Jonah b. Abraham Gerondi, quoted in *Tur*, loc. cit., in *Rema*, *Sh. Ar*., loc. cit, and in *Ar. ha-Sh*., op. cit., 227:4. Ruling in accordance with R. Jonah is R. Asher b. Jechiel (*Rosh*, *Baba Bathra* V:14).

58. *Baba Metzia* 50b; *Rif*, ad loc.; *Yad*, op. cit., XII:2; *Rosh*, op. cit., IV:15; *Tur*, op. cit., 227:3; *Sh. Ar*., op. cit., 227:2; *Ar. ha-Sh*., loc. cit.

59. *Baba Metzia* 50b; *Rif*, ad loc.; *Yad*, op. cit., XII:3; *Tur*, op. cit., 227:4; *Sh. Ar*., loc. cit.; *Ar. ha-Sh*., loc. cit.

60. *Baba Bathra* 78a and *Rashi*, ad loc.; *Rif*, ad loc.; *Yad*, *Mekhirah* XXVII:5; *Rosh*, *Baba Bathra* V:7; *Tur*, op. cit., 220:5; *Sh. Ar*., op. cit., 220:8; *Ar. ha-Sh*., op. cit., 220:7.

61. *Tanna Kamma Mishnah Baba Metzia* 51a; *Rif*, ad loc.; *Yad*, op. cit., XII:8; *Rosh*, *Baba Metzia* IV:17; *Tur*, op. cit., 227:13; *Sh. Ar*., op. cit., 227:14; *Ar. ha-Sh*., op. cit., 227:15.

62. *Baba Metzia* 49b; *Rif*, ad loc.; *Yad*, op. cit., XII:5; *Rosh*, op. cit., IV:15; *Tur*, op. cit., 227:15; *Sh. Ar*., op. cit., 227:7; *Ar. ha-Sh*., op. cit., 227:8.

63. *Rashi*, *Baba Metzia* 49b.

64. *Ar. ha-Sh*., op. cit., 227:10.

65. *Baba Metzia* 50b; *Rif*, ad loc.; *Yad*, op. cit., XII:6; *Tur*, op. cit., 227:10; *Sh. Ar*., op. cit., 227:8; *Ar. ha-Sh*., 227:11.

66. R. Judah, *Kiddushin* 19b; *Yad*, *Ishut* VI:9; *Tur*, *Even ha-Ezer* 38:13; *Sh. Ar*., *Even ha-Ezer* 38:5; *Ar. ha-Sh*., *Even ha-Ezer* 38:9.

67. *Baba Metzia* 51b; *Rif*, ad loc.; *Yad*, *Mekhirah* XIII:3–4; *Tur*, *Choshen Mishpat* 227:26; *Sh. Ar*., *Choshen Mishpat* 227:21; *Ar. ha-Sh*., *Choshen Mishpat* 227:22.

68. *Baba Metzia* 51b; *Rif*, ad loc.; *Yad*, op. cit., XIII:5; *Rosh*, op. cit., IV:17; *Tur*, op. cit., 227:37; *Sh. Ar*., op. cit., 227:27; *Ar. ha-Sh*., op. cit., 227:28.

69. *Yad*, loc. cit. For a variant view of what constitutes selling on trust, see R. Israel Krems, *Haggahot Asheri*, *Baba Metzia* IV:17.

70. *Ar. ha-Sh*., loc. cit.

71. *Yad*, op. cit., XIII:1; *Tur*, op. cit., 227:22–23; *Sh. Ar*., op. cit., 227:20; *Ar. ha-Sh*., op. cit., 227:21. For a variant view, see R. Abraham b. David of Posquières, *Hassagot Rabad*, *Yad*, ad loc.

72. *Ar. ha-Sh*., loc. cit.

73. *Rava*, *Kiddushin* 42b; *Rif*, ad loc.; *Yad*, op. cit., XIII:9; *Tur*, op. cit., 227:48; *Sh. Ar*., op. cit., 227:30; *Ar. ha-Sh*., op. cit., 227:36.

74. R. Chisda, *Baba Metzia* 51a; *Rif*, ad loc.; *Yad*, op. cit., XIII:2; *Rosh*, op. cit., IV:16; *Tur*, op. cit., 227:23; *Sh. Ar*., op. cit., 227:23; *Ar. ha-Sh*., op. cit., 227:24.

75. R. Joseph Ibn Chabib (15th cent.), *Nimmukei Yosef, Rif, Baba Metzia* 51a; *Sh. Ar.*, op. cit., 227:24.

76. *Shittah M'kubbetzet* 51a; "some authorities" quoted in *Sh. Ar.*, op. cit., 227:24.

77. *Yad*, loc. cit.; *Tur*, loc. cit.; *Sh. Ar.*, loc. cit.

78. *Responsa Rosh*, quoted in *Tur*, op. cit., 227:34; *Ar. ha-Sh.*, loc. cit.

79. *Responsa Rosh K'lal* 102, quoted in *Tur*, op. cit., 227:27, and in *Sh. Ar.*, op. cit., 227:23.

80. *Sma, Sh. Ar.*, op. cit., 227, n. 42.

81. R. David b. Samual ha-Levi, *Turei Zahav, Sh. Ar.*, op. cit., 227:23.

82. Mishnah, *Baba Metzia* 56a and *Gemara* 56b; *Rif*, ad loc.; *Yad*, op. cit., XIII:8; *Tur*, op. cit., 227:40; *Sh. Ar.*, op. cit., 227:29; *Ar. ha-Sh.*, op. cit., 227:34.

83. *Ramban*, commentary on Leviticus 25:14.

84. *Rif*, loc. cit., *Yad*, loc. cit.

85. *Siftei Kohen, Sh. Ar.*, op. cit., 227, note 17.

86. *Rosh*, loc. cit; *Tur*, loc. cit.; *Sma, Sh. Ar.*, op. cit., 227, note 49.

87. *Siftei Kohen*, loc. cit.

88. Mishnah, *Baba Metzia* 56a and *Gemara* 56b; *Rif*, loc. cit; *Yad*, loc. cit; *Tur*, loc. cit.; *Sh. Ar.*, loc. cit.; *Ar. ha-Sh.*, loc. cit.

89. *Yad*, op. cit., XIII:15; *Tur*, op. cit., 227:45–46; *Sh. Ar.*, op. cit., 227:33; *Ar. ha-Sh.*, op. cit., 227:37.

90. *Yad*, op. cit., XIII:18; *Tur*, op. cit., 227:47; *Sh. Ar.*, op. cit., 227:36; *Ar. ha-Sh.*, loc. cit. R. Moses b. Nachman (*Ramban, Baba Metzia* 56b), however, quotes "some authorities" who assimilate the piece-worker to the day-laborer in regard to the *ona'ah* exemption.

91. Mishnah, *Baba Metzia* 56a and *Gemara* 56b; *Rif*, ad loc.; *Yad*, op. cit., XIII:8; *Rosh*, op. cit., IV:21; *Tur*, op. cit., 227:40; *Sh. Ar.*, op. cit., 227:29; *Ar. ha-Sh.*, op. cit., 227:34.

92. Viewing the above presumption as being universally descriptive of human nature, R. Joshua ha-Kohen Falk (*Sma, Sh. Ar.*, op. cit., 227, note 14) rules that even if the plaintiff had not yet made payment, consummation of the transaction by means of *kinyan* obligates him to make payment in full, including the *ona'ah* component of the sale price. The plaintiff's protest that he does not waive his claim against third-degree *ona'ah* is received incredulously, as *everyone* is presumed to waive his claims against third-degree *ona'ah* (*batlah da'ato eitzel kol adam*).

The above presumption is viewed in a different light by R. Ephraim Nabon (*Machaneh Efraim, Hilkhot Ona'ah* 13). In his view the presumption is merely descriptive of majority behavior. Viewing the presumption in this attentuated form effectively places the claimant at a disadvantage. Hence, in the event payment had already been made, the plaintiff's demand for restoration of the third-degree *ona'ah* is denied, as we presume he is of the majority that waives such claims. On the other hand, in the event payment was not yet made, the buyer need not pay the *ona'ah* component of the purchase price, as he may insist that he is of the minority that does not waive such claims.

93. *Rosh, Baba Metzia* IV:20.

94. R. Moses b. Nachman, *Ramban*, commentary on Leviticus 25:14; R. Ezra Basri, *Dinei Mamonot*, vol. 2 (Jerusalem: Sucath David, 1976), p. 160. For a variant view, see R. Aaron ha-Levi of Barcelona (1235–1300), *Sefer ha-Chinnukh, mitzvah* 337.

95. *Ar., ha-Sh.*, op. cit., 227:21.

96. R. Moses Isserles, *Darkhei Moshe, Tur*, op. cit., 209. This view is advanced to dispute R. Joseph Caro's position on this matter.

97. R. Eliezer b. Joel ha-Levi, quoted in *Mordechai, Baba Metzia* IV:307, and in *Rema, Sh. Ar.*, op. cit., 227:7.

98. R. Jacob Lorberbaum, *N'tivot ha-Mishpat, Sh. Ar.*, op. cit., 227, note 4; *Ar. ha-Sh.*, op. cit., 227:9. For a variant interpretation of R. Eliezer b. Joel ha-Levi's position, see *Sma, Sh. Ar.*, op. cit., 227, note 18; and R. Aryeh Loeb b. Joseph ha-Kohen (1745–1813), *K'tzot, Sh. Ar.*, op. cit., 227, note 5.

99. R. Yom Tov Ishbili, *Ritva, Kiddushin* 8a. A difficulty against R. Ishbili's position is raised by R. Aryeh Loeb b. Joseph ha-Kohen (see *K'tzot, Sh. Ar.*, op. cit., 227, note 1).

100. *Baba Metzia* 65a; *Rif*, ad loc.; *Yad, Malveh* VIII:1; *Tur, Yoreh De'ah* 173:1; *Sh. Ar., Yoreh De'ah* 173:1; *Chokhmat Adam, Ribbit* 139:1.

101. Tosafot, *Baba Metzia* 63b; *Rashba* and *Ha-Ma'or*, quoted in *Maggid Mishneh, Yad, Malveh*, loc. cit.; *Tur*, loc. cit; *Sh. Ar.*, loc. cit.; *Chokhmat Adam*, op. cit., 139 n. 2–3.

102. R. Ezra Basri, *Dinei Mamonot*, vol. 1 (Jerusalem: Reuben Mass, 1973), p. 127.

103. *Mordechai* and *Nimmukei Yosef*, quoted in *Beit Yosef, Tur*, loc. cit.; *Rema, Sh. Ar.*, op. cit., 173:3; *Chokhmat Adam* 139:7.

104. R. Nachman, *Baba Metzia* 63b; *Rif*, ad loc.; *Yad*, op. cit., IX:6; *Rosh*, op. cit., V:11; *Tur*, op. cit., 173:7; *Sh. Ar.*, op. cit., 173:7.

105. *B'rit Yehuda*, op. cit., p. 395.

106. *Rema, Sh. Ar.*, op. cit., 173:7; *Chokhmat Adam* 139:14. For a variant view, see *Turei Zahav, Sh. Ar.*, loc. cit., note 12.

107. R. Moses b. Naphtali Hirsch Rivkes (d. ca. 1671–72), *Be'er ha-Golah, Sh. Ar.*, op. cit., 173, note 18.

108. *B'rit Yehuda*, op. cit., p. 396.

109. *Rema*, loc. cit.; *Chokhmat Adam*, loc. cit.

110. R. Nachman, *Baba Metzia* 63b; *Rif*, ad loc.; *Yad*, loc. cit.; *Rosh*, loc. cit.; *Tur*, loc. cit.; *Sh. Ar.*, loc. cit.; *Brit Yehuda*, loc. cit.

111. *Responsa RiBash*, quoted in *Beit Yosef, Tur*, loc. cit.

112. *B'rit Yehuda*, op. cit., p. 401.

113. Mishnah, *Baba Metzia* 65a; *Rif*, ad loc.; *Yad*, op. cit., VII:8; *Rosh*, op. cit., V:21; *Tur*, op. cit., 176:6; *Sh. Ar.*, op. cit., 176:6; *Chokhmat Adam* 136:10.

114. *Rema, Sh. Ar.*, loc. cit.; *Chokhmat Adam*, loc. cit.

115. *Maggid Mishneh, Yad*, op. cit., VII:10; *Sh. Ar.*, loc. cit.

116. *Novelae Rashba, Baba Bathra* 86b.

117. *Tur*, op. cit., 173:21; *Sh. Ar.*, op. cit., 173:12; R. Joel Sirkes, *Bach, Tur*, op. cit., 161; *B'rit Yehuda*, op. cit., p. 37.

118. Leviticus 19:13.

119. *Bach*, op. cit.

120. R. Eliezer of Toul, quoted in Meir ha-Kohen, *Teshuvot Maimuniyyot, Sefer Mishpatim* 16; R. Meir b. Baruch of Rothenburg, quoted in R. Jerocham b. Meshullam, *Toledot Adam ve-Chavvah, n'tiv* 29, pt. 3; *Bach*, op. cit.; R. Moshe Sofer, *Novellae Chatam Sofer, Baba Metzia* 73a; R. Isaac Yehuda Schmelkes, *Beit Yitzchak, Yoreh De'ah* 11:2 at 2.

121. R. Isaac b. Moses of Vienna, *Or Zaru'a, Baba Metzia* V:21; R. Israel of Krems, *Haggahot Asheri, Baba Metzia* V:21; R. Joseph Caro, *Beit Yosef, Tur*, op. cit. 160.

122. *Bach*, op. cit. For alternative rationalizations of R. Eliezer of Toul's

view, see *Novellae Chatam Sofer, Baba Metzia* 73a, and *Beit Yitzchak, Yoreh De'ah* 11:2 at 2.

123. R. Judah Rosanes, *Mishneh le-Melekh, malveh* VII–II.

124. R. Nachum Rakover, "Pitzuyim al Ikkuv Kesafim," in I. Raphael, ed., *Torah she-be'al Peh* (Jerusalem: Mosad Harav Kook, 1977), p. 216.

125. *B'rit Yehuda,* op. cit., p. 36.

NOTES TO CHAPTER 8

1. Maimonides (1135–1204), *Yad, Genevah* VII:7, VIII:4–5, 8–11, 17; R. Jacob b. Asher (1270–1343), *Tur, Choshen Mishpat* 231:4–5, 11–14, 17–18, 22; R. Joseph Caro (1488–1575), *Shulchan Arukh, Choshen Mishpat* 231:4–5, 9–10, 13, 15; R. Jechiel Michael Epstein (1829–1908), *Arukh ha-Shulchan, Choshen Mishpat* 231:4–5; 9–10, 12–13.

2. *Baba Bathra* 89a and *Rashi,* ad loc.; R. Isaac b. Jacob Alfasi (1012–1103), *Rif,* ad loc.; *Yad,* op. cit., VIII:8–11; R. Asher b. Jechiel (1250–1327), *Rosh, Baba Bathra* V:24; *Tur,* op. cit., 231:17; *Sh. Ar.,* op. cit., 231:13; *Ar. ha-Sh.,* op. cit., 231:12–13.

3. *Baba Bathra* 90a; *Yad,* op. cit., VII:7; *Tur,* op. cit., 231:4; *Sh. Ar.,* op. cit., 231:4; *Ar. ha-Sh.,* op. cit., 231:4.

4. *Baba Bathra* 89b; *Rif,* ad loc.; *Yad,* op. cit., VIII:7; *Rosh,* op. cit., V:27; *Tur,* op. cit., 231:15; *Sh. Ar.,* op. cit., 231:11; *Ar. ha-Sh.,* op. cit., 231:12.

5. Tosafot, *Baba Bathra* 89b; *Yad,* loc. cit.; *Tur,* loc. cit.; *Ar. ha-Sh.,* loc. cit. For a variant rationalization of the interdict, see R. Solomon b. Isaac, *Rashi, Baba Bathra* 89b.

6. *Baba Bathra* 89b; *Rif,* ad loc.; *Yad,* loc. cit.; *Rosh,* loc. cit.; *Tur,* op. cit., 231:7; *Sh. Ar.,* op. cit., 231:6; *Ar. ha-Sh.,* op. cit., 231:6.

7. *Rashi, Baba Bathra* 89b; *Yad,* loc. cit.; *Tur,* loc. cit., *Sh. Ar.,* loc. cit.; *Ar. ha-Sh.,* loc. cit.

8. Mishnah, *Baba Bathra* 89a; *Rif,* ad loc.; *Yad,* op. cit., VIII:18; *Rosh,* op. cit., V:22; *Tur,* op. cit., 231:16; *Sh. Ar.,* op. cit., 231:7; *Ar. ha-Sh.,* op. cit., 231:7.

9. *Yad,* op. cit., VII:3; *Tur,* op. cit., 231:3; *Sh. Ar.,* op. cit., 231:3; *Ar. ha-Sh.,* op. cit., 231:2.

10. R. Yehuda, reporting in the name of Rav, *Baba Bathra* 89b; *Rif,* ad loc.; *Yad,* loc. cit.; *Rosh,* loc. cit.; *Tur,* loc. cit.; *Sh. Ar.,* loc. cit.; *Ar. ha-Sh.,* loc. cit.

11. R. Pappa, *Baba Bathra* 89b; *Rif,* ad loc.; *Yad,* loc. cit.; *Rosh,* loc. cit.; *Tur,* loc. cit.; *Sh. Ar.,* loc. cit.; *Ar. ha-Sh.,* loc. cit.

12. Rami b. Chamma, reporting in the name of R. Yitzchak, *Baba Bathra* 89a; *Rif,* ad loc.; *Yad,* op. cit., VIII:20; *Rosh,* op. cit., V:22; *Tur,* op. cit., 231:2; *Sh. Ar.,* op. cit., 231:2; *Ar. ha-Sh.,* op. cit., 231:3.

13. *Yad,* loc. cit.; *Tur,* loc. cit.; *Sh. Ar.,* loc. cit.; *Ar. ha-Sh.,* loc. cit.

14. *Yad,* op. cit., XVIII:1; *Tur,* op. cit., 228:5; *Sh. Ar.,* op. cit., 228:6; *Ar. ha-Sh.,* op. cit., 228:3.

15. R. Joshua ha-Kohen Falk (1555–1614), *Sma, Sh. Ar.,* op. cit., 228, note 7; *Ar. ha-Sh.,* loc. cit.

16. See *Sma,* loc. cit.

17. *Yad,* op. cit., XV:7–9.

18. *Tur,* op. cit., 232:8; *Sh. Ar.,* op. cit., 232:8, both on the interpretation of R. Jechiel Michael Epstein (*Ar. ha-Sh.,* op. cit., 232:13).

19. *Yad*, op. cit., XV:5, quoted in *Tur*, op. cit., 232:6; *Sh. Ar.*, op. cit., 232:6; *Ar. ha-Sh.*, 232:7.

20. *Yad*, op. cit., XV:3; *Tur*, op. cit., 232:4; *Sh. Ar.*, op. cit., 232:3; *Ar. ha-Sh.*, op. cit., 232:4.

21. Use, according to R. Jacob Lorberbaum (ca. 1760–1832), *N'tivot ha-Mishpat, Sh. Ar.*, op. cit., 232, note 5, does not generate a presumption that the recision right is waived when the article of sale is an animal. Here, the complainant must make use of the animal in the pursuit of his livelihood until he returns it.

22. *Yad*, loc. cit.; *Tur*, loc. cit.; *Sh. Ar.*, loc. cit.; *Ar. ha-Sh.*, loc. cit.

23. *Yad*, op. cit., XV:4; *Tur*, loc. cit.; *Sh. Ar.*, op. cit., 232:4; *Ar. ha-Sh.*, op. cit., 232:6.

24. R. Ezra Basri, *Dinei Mamonot*, vol. 2 (Jerusalem: Sukkat David, 1976), p. 205.

25. *Yad*, op. cit., XV:5, quoted in *Tur*, op. cit., 232:6; *Sh. Ar.*, op. cit., 232:6; *Ar. ha-Sh.*, op. cit., 232:7.

26. *Yad*, op. cit., XV:6; *Tur*, op. cit., 232:7; *Sh. Ar.*, op. cit., 232:6; *Ar. ha-Sh.*, op. cit., 232:11.

27. *Rif, Baba Metzia* 58b; *Yad*, op. cit., XIV:12; *Rosh, Baba Metzia* IV:22; *Tur*, op. cit., 228:1; *Sh. Ar.*, op. cit., 228:1; *Ar. ha-Sh.*, op. cit., 228:1.

28. Examples of behavior in a noncommercial context that are interdicted on the basis of *ona'at devarim* include reminding a repentant person of his past misdeeds, soliciting technical advice from someone whom the inquirer knows lacks the necessary expertise, and telling someone that his suffering is due to his evil deeds. In all these instances the behavior causes needless pain and is therefore prohibited.

29. R. Yehuda, *Baba Metzia* 58b; *Rif*, ad loc.; *Rosh*, loc. cit.; *Tur*, op. cit., 228:3; *Sh. Ar.*, op. cit., 228:4; *Ar. ha-Sh.*, op. cit., 228:2.

30. R. Menachem b. Solomon, *Beit ha-Bechirah, Baba Metzia* 59a. Pricing an article with no intention to buy it is prohibited, according to R. Samuel b. Meir (ca. 1080–1174), *Rashbam, Pesachim* 114b, on account of the possible financial loss this behavior might cause the vendor. While the vendor is preoccupied with the insincere inquiry, serious customers may turn elsewhere.

31. See commentary of R. Solomon b. Isaac on Leviticus 25:17.

32. R. Judah b. Samuel He-Chasid, *Sefer Chasidim, siman* 1069.

33. *Baba Metzia* 49a and *Rashi*, ad loc.

34. *Torat Kohanim*, Leviticus 19:14; *Yad, Rotzeach* XII:14.

35. *Yad*, loc. cit., on interpretation of R. Jerucham Fishel Perlow, commentary on *Sefer ha-Mitzvot* of R. Saadiah Gaon, p. 104.

36. *Halakhot Gedolot* on the interpretation of R. Jerucham Fishel Perlow, loc. cit. The authorship of this work is disputed, but it is generally dated to the geonic period. See *Encyclopaedia Judaica*, vol. 7, col. 1169.

37. *Rashi*, Leviticus 25:17.

38. R. Yom Tov Ishbili, *Ritva, Chullin* 94a.

39. R. Jonah b. Abraham Gerondi, *Sha'arei Teshuvah, sha'ar* 3, *ot* 184.

40. *Ar. ha-Sh.*, op. cit., 228:3.

41. Samuel, *Chullin* 94a; *Rif*, ad loc.; *Yad*, op. cit., XVIII:3; *Rosh, Chullin* VII:18; *Tur*, op. cit., 228:6; *Sh. Ar.*, op. cit., 228:6; *Ar. ha-Sh.*, loc. cit.

42. Generating undeserved good will in the gift case is permitted, according to R. Asher b. Jechiel (*Rosh*, loc. cit.) and Tosafot, *Chullin* 94a, on the interpretation of R. Joel Sirkes (*Bach, Tur*, loc. cit.).

Members of the school of thought prohibiting such action include R. Jacob Tam (quoted in *Rosh, Chullin* VII:18), R. Solomon Adret (*Rashba, Chullin* 94a), R. Isaac b. Jacob Alfasi, Maimonides, and R. Moses of Coucy on the interpretation of R. Solomon b. Jechiel Luria (see *Yam shel Shelomo, Chullin, siman* 19).

43. R. Joseph David Epstein, *Mitzvot ha-Shalom* (New York: Torat ha-Adam, 1969), p. 243.

44. *Rosh*, loc. cit.; *Tur*, op. cit., 228:7; *Sh. Ar.*, op. cit., 228:6; *Ar. ha-Sh.*, op. cit., 228:3.

45. *Kiddushin* 59a; *Rif*, ad loc.; *Rosh, Kiddushin* III:2; *Tur*, op. cit., 237; *Sh. Ar.*, op. cit., 237:1–2; *Ar. ha-Sh.*, op. cit., 237:1–5.

46. R. Meir b. Baruch, quoted in *Mordechai, Baba Bathra* III:551; *Rema, Sh. Ar.*, op. cit., 237:1; *Ar. ha-Sh.*, op. cit., 237:1.

47. R. Samuel b. Moses de Medina, *Responsa MaHarashdam, Choshen Mishpat* 259.

48. R. Isaiah b. Mali di Trani (ca. 1200–1260), *Tosafot Ri haZaken, Kiddushin* 59a; R. Joseph Chabib (fl. 15th cent.), *Nimmukei Yosef, Rif, Kiddushin* 59a; R. Joseph b. Solomon Colon (ca. 1420–1480), *Maharik* 192; R. Solomon Luria, *Responsa Maharshal* 36.

49. R. Joshua ha-Kohen Falk, *Perisha, Tur*, op. cit., 237, note 1.

50. *Pesak Din Rabbaniyim*, vol. VI, p. 202; R. Nachum Rakover, *Halikhut ha-Mischar*, no. 41 (Jerusalem: Misrad ha-Mishpatim, 1976), p. 39.

51. R. Elijah b. Chayyim, *Responsa Ranach* 125.

52. R. Moshe Feinstein, *Iggerot Moshe, Choshen Mishpat* 60.

53. R. Jacob Tam, quoted in Tosafot, *Kiddushin* 59a, and in *Tur*, loc. cit.; *Ar. ha-Sh.*, op. cit., 237:1.

54. R. Isaac, quoted in Tosafot, *Kiddushin* 59a.

55. *Responsa Maharshal* 36.

56. *Masat Binyamin* 27.

57. *Responsa Maharik* 20, *ot* 8, 9.

58. R. Jacob Tam, quoted in Tosafot, *Kiddushin* 59a; *Rema, Sh. Ar.*, loc. cit. R. Solomon b. Isaac (*Rashi, Kiddushin* 59a) interprets the interference interdict to apply to the acquisition of ownerless property as well.

59. *Iggerot Moshe*, loc. cit.

60. See R. Jacob Lorberbaum, *N'tivot ha-Mishpat, Sh. Ar.*, op. cit., 237, note 5.

61. R. Isaac, quoted in Tosafot, *Kiddushin* 59a; *Sh. Ar.*, op. cit., 237:2; *Ar. ha-Sh.*, op. cit., 237:5.

62. *Ar. ha-Sh.*, loc. cit.

63. *Ramban*, quoted in *Siftei Kohen, Sh. Ar.*, op. cit., 237, note 3; *Ar. ha-Sh.*, op. cit., 237:2. R. Moses Isserles (*Rema, Sh. Ar.*, op. cit., 237:1), however, assimilates the bargain-sale case with the acquisition of ownerless property and suspends the interference interdict.

64. *Rashi, Baba Bathra* 21b.

65. *Ramban, Baba Bathra* 21b.

66. Tosafot, *Gittin* 59b; Tosafot, *Kiddushin* 59a; Tosafot, *Baba Bathra* 21b.

67. Cf. R. Mordechai Jacob Breisch (contemporary), *Responsa Chelkat Yaakov* II:65; R. Isaac Arieli (contemporary), *Enayim le-Mishpat, Baba Bathra* 21b.

68. Cf. R. Binyamin Aharon Slonick, *Responsa Masat Binyamin* 27; R. Moshe Sofer, *Responsa Chatam Sofer, Choshen Mishpat* 78.

69. Harvesting the *shikcha* olives at the top of the tree by first collecting them in his hand and then throwing the olives down to the ground entitles A to the fruit by virtue of pentateuchal law. If the interloper snatches away the

fruit before A takes possession of them, he is required by judicial decree, to return the fruit to A (*Yad, Gezelah* VI:13; *Tur,* op. cit., 370:10; *Rema, Sh. Ar.,* op. cit., 370:5; *Ar ha-Sh.,* op. cit., 370:8).

70. *Rif, Gittin* 59b; *Yad,* loc. cit.; *Rosh, Gittin* V:20; *Tur,* loc. cit.; *Sh. Ar.,* op. cit., 370:5; *Ar. ha-Sh.,* loc. cit.

71. *Responsa Masat Binyamin* 27.

72. R. Elezar derives the warning against slander from Leviticus 19:16. R. Nathan derives the admonishment from Deuteronomy 23:11 (see *Ketubbot* 46a).

73. Leviticus 19:11.

74. R. Yisroel Meir ha-Kohen (1838–1933), *Chofetz Chayyim, Hilkhot Issurei Rekhilut, K'lal* 9:1, *Be'er Mayim Chayyim,* note 1.

75. Leviticus 19:16. Talebearing, depending upon the circumstances, may involve violation of a total of thirty-one pentateuchal positive commandments and prohibitions (see *Chofetez Chayyim Lavin* 1–17, *Essin* 1–14).

76. *Chofetz Chayyim,* op. cit., *Hilkhot Issurei Leshon ha-Ra k'lal* 10:1–17; *Hilkhot Rekhilut K'lal* 9:1–15.

77. *Chofetz Chayyim,* op. cit., *Hilkhot Issurei Leshon ha-Ra, Haggahot, ha-Mechaber* on *k'lal* 4:11.

NOTES TO CHAPTER 9

1. H. M. Hochman and J. D. Rodgers, "Pareto-Optimal Redistribution," *American Economic Review* 59, no. 4 (September 1969): 542–57.

2. E. J. Mishan, "The Futility of Pareto-Efficient Distributions," *American Economic Review* 62, no. 5 (December 1972): 971–76.

3. Daniel Bell, "Meritocracy and Equality," *Public Interest,* no. 29 (Fall 1972): 29–69.

4. For a discussion of the role the economic-efficiency criterion would assign the public sector, see Bernard P. Herber, *Modern Public Finance,* 3d ed. Homewood, Ill.: Richard D. Irwin, 1975), pp. 3–84.

5. R. Solomon b. Abraham Adret (1235–1310), *Responsa Rashba,* vol. 1, no. 729; vol. 3, no. 411, vol. 5, no. 126.

6. *Responsa Rashba,* vol. 3, no. 411; R. Isaac b. Sheshet Perfet (1326–1408), *Responsa Ribash,* no. 399; R. Simeon b. Tzemach Duran (1361–1444), *Tashbez* 2:132; R. Moses b. Isaac Alashkar (1466–1542), *Responsa Maharam Alashkar,* no. 49.

7. R. Meir b. Baruch of Rothenburg (1215–1293), quoted by R. Mordechai b. Hillel (d. 1298), *Mordechai, Baba Bathra* I:482.

8. R. Asher b. Jechiel (1250–1327), *Responsa Rosh* VI:5, 7.

9. R. Joshua ha-Kohen Falk, *Sma, Shulchan Arukh, Choshen Mishpat,* 163, note 13; see R. Jechiel Michael Epstein (1829–1908), *Arukh ha-Shulchan, Choshen Mishpat* 163:7.

10. *Responsa Rashba,* vol. 3, no. 411; *Tashbez* 2:132 and 239.

11. *Responsa Ribash,* no. 305.

12. *Responsa Rashba,* vol. I:788; see also *Responsa Rashba,* vol. I:399.

13. *Responsa Rashba,* vol. 1, no. 26; vol. 4, no. 185; R. Asher b. Jechiel, *Piskei ha-Rosh, Baba Bathra* 1:33; R. Joseph Caro (1488–1575), *Shulchan Arukh, Choshen Mishpat* 231:28—*Rema, Sma,* and *Siftei Kohen,* ad loc.

For a precise definition of *adam chashuv,* see Maimonides (1135–1204), *Yad,*

Mekhirah XIV:11; *Piskei ha-Rosh* 1:33; R. Jacob b. Asher (d. 1340), *Tur, Choshen Mishpat* 231:30; *Sh. Ar.,* op. cit., 231:28.

A minority opinion held the approval of the "Distinguished Person" to be necessary only with reference to agreements enacted by a restricted section of the public, such as professional associations. See R. Moses b. Nachman (1194–1270), *Novelae Ramban, Baba Bathra* 9a; R. Nissim b. Reuben Gerondi (1310–1375), *Novelae Ran, Baba Bathra,* loc. cit.; *Responsa RiBash,* no. 399; *Responsa Maharam Alashkar,* no. 49.

14. R. Meir Abulafia (1170–1244), *Ramah, Baba Bathra* I:103; R. Vidal Yom Tov (fl. 14th cent.), *Maggid Mishneh, Yad, Mekhirah* XIV:11.

15. The term Tanna (pl. Tannaim) designates scholars who were active in the first and second centuries c.e.

16. Mishnah, *Baba Bathra* 7b and commentary of Maimonides, ad loc.

17. Maimonides' commentary on Mishnah, *Baba Bathra* I:4; R. Nissim b. Reuben Gerondi, quoted by R. Joseph Chabib (fl. 15th cent.), *Baba Bathra* 7b; R. Jerocham b. Meshullam (1290–1350), *Toledot Adam ve-Chavvah, n'tiv* 31, *chelek* 6; *Maggid Mishneh, Yad, Shekhenim* VI:1; R. Joseph Caro, *Beit Yosef, Tur, Choshen Mishpat* 163:1; R. Joshua ha-Kohen Falk, *Perishah, Tur, Choshen Mishpat* 163, note 1; R. Joshua ha-Kohen Falk, *Sma, Sh. Ar., Choshen Mishpat* 163:1.

18. *Baba Bathra* 24b.

19. R. Solomon b. Isaac, *Rashi, Baba Bathra* 24b.

20. R. Meir b. Baruch of Rothenburg, *Responsa Maharam,* no. 39.

21. See *Sukkah* 26a: *pirsah kore'ah le-ganav.*

22. Mishnah, *Baba Bathra* I:4; *Yad,* op. cit., VI:5; *Rosh, Baba Bathra* I:27; *Tur,* op. cit, 163:3–4. For the requirement that the inhabitant actually *live* in the home, see *Nimmukei Yosef, Baba Bathra* 8b, and *Ar. ha-Sh.,* op. cit., 163:3.

23. R. Mordechai b. Hillel (1240–1298), *Mordechai, Baba Bathra* I:477; *Responsa Ribash* 475; *Beit Yosef,* op. cit., 163:2; *Ar. ha-Sh.,* op. cit., 163:3.

R. Isaac b. Sheshet Perfet (*Ribash,* loc. cit.) maintains that *rental* of a home for a period of twelve months provides sufficient grounds to include the inhabitant in the security levy. Disagreeing with this view, R. Mordechai b. Hillel (loc. cit.) posits that such action does not unequivocally communicate an intent on the part of the inhabitant to remain in the town on a permanent basis. Both views are quoted in *Rema* (*Sh. Ar.,* op. cit., 163:2).

24. *Baba Bathra* 7b. Codifiers invoking the rabbinical-scholar exemption in connection with the security tax levy include R. Asher ben Jechiel (*Rosh, Baba Bathra* I:25); R. Isaac Alfasi (1013–1103; *Rif, Baba Bathra* 7b); Maimonides (*Yad, Shekkenim* VI:6); R. Jacob b. Asher (*Tur,* op. cit., 163(10); R. Joseph Caro (*Sh. Ar.,* op. cit., 163:5); and R. Jechiel Michael Epstein (*Ar. ha-Sh.,* op. cit., 163:15).

25. The term Amora (pl. Amoraim) designates scholars active from the second century to the close of the fifth century.

26. R. Gershon b. Judah Me'or ha-Golah (960–1028), *Rabbenu Gershon, Baba Bathra* 7b. See R. Isaac Arieli (contemporary), *Enayim le-Mishpat, Baba Bathra* 7b.

27. R. Abraham Yeshayahu Karelitz (1878–1953) understands this to be the basis of the rabbinical-scholar exemption (see *Chazon Ish, Baba Bathra* IV). In a different context, R. Meir Loeb b. Jechiel Michael Malbim (1809–1879) makes a similar statement (see *Malbim, parshat Vayishlach*).

28. *Rif, Baba Bathra* I; *Rosh, Baba Bathra* I:22; *Tur,* op. cit., 163:5–10; *Sh. Ar.,* op. cit., 163:3; *Ar. ha-Sh.,* op. cit., 163:6.

29. *Rashi, Baba Bathra* 7b.

30. *Rif, Baba Bathra* I; *Rosh,* loc. cit.; *Tur,* loc. cit.; *Sh. Ar.,* loc. cit.; *Ar. ha-Sh.,* loc. cit.

31. Tosafot, *Baba Bathra* 7b.

32. See *Mordechai, Baba Bathra* I:475.

33. Ibid., I:481.

34. See *Ar. ha-Sh.,* op. cit., 163:8. Disputing this view, R. Jacob Tam (quoted in *Mordechai, Baba Kamma* X:179) refused to increase the tax liability of an individual on account of the business transactions he carried out with other people's capital. The contention that these transactions increase the revenue demands made on the community by creating a false impression of affluence is rejected outright by R. Tam. Quite to the contrary, maintains R. Tam, the weight of circumstantial evidence could easily persuade the authorities that certain transactions conducted in the town are carried out with capital not belonging to anyone in the community. Quoting both these views, R. Moses Isserles (*Rema, Sh. Ar.,* op. cit., 163:3) records that the prevailing practice is in accordance with the first opinion.

35. R. Elijah b. Solomon Zalman (1720–1797), *ha-Gra, Sh. Ar.,* op. cit., 163, ot 43.

36. R. Reuvan Grozovsky, *Novelae R. Reuven, Baba Bathra, siman* 6.

37. R. Vidal Yom Tov of Tolosa, *Maggid Mishneh, Chovel ve-Mazzik* XVIII:15.

38. Jerusalem Talmud, *Baba Kamma* III:1.

39. *Beit Yosef, Tur,* op. cit., 157:5; R. Shabbetai b. Meir ha-Kohen, *Siftei Kohen, Sh. Ar.,* op. cit., 155:22; R. Jacob Lorberbaum, *N'tivot ha-Mishpat, Sh. Ar.,* op. cit., 155, ot 22.

40. R. Meir Abulafia, quoted in *Tur,* op. cit., 157:5.

41. R. Moshe Gaon, quoted in *Toledot Adam ve-Chavvah, n'tiv* 31, *chelek* 5.

42. *Tur,* loc. cit.; R. Joel Sirkes (1561–1640), *Bach, Tur,* op. cit., 157:5–6.

43. *Maggid Mishneh,* loc. cit.

44. *Rema,* op. cit., 163:3.

45. See *Rema,* op. cit., 163:1; see *Ar. ha-Sh.,* op. cit., 163:1.

46. *Baba Bathra* 8a and commentary of R. Solomon b. Isaac ad loc.; R. Gershon, *Baba Bathra* 8a; R. Joseph Ibn Chabib, *Nimmukei Yosef, Baba Bathra* 8a; *Tur,* op. cit., 163:15; R. Joseph Caro, *Sh. Ar., Yoreh, De'ah* 243:1–2.

47. *Nimmukei Yosef, Baba Metzia* 108a; *Sh. Ar.,* op. cit., 243:1; *Ar. ha-Sh., Yoreh De'ah* 243:2. For a minority opposing view, see *Sefer Toledot Adam ve-Chavvah, n'tiv* 32, *chelek* 2.

48. *Baba Bathra* 8a; *Rif, Baba Bathra,* ad. loc.; *Yad, Shekhenim* VI:7; *Rosh, Baba Bathra* I:26; *Tur,* op. cit., 163:16; *Sh. Ar., Choshen Mishpat* 163:4; *Ar. ha-Sh. Choshen Mishpat* 163:15.

49. *Responsa Rashba* III:381.

50. R. Jacob ben Judah Weil (d. ca. 1456), *Responsa Maharyu,* no. 84.

51. R. Nissim ben Reuben Gerondi (1310–1375), *Responsa Ran,* no. 2:21.

52. *Responsa Rashba,* vol. 1, no. 1074.

53. R. Joseph b. Samuel Bonfils (11th cent.), quoted in *Responsa R. Meir of Rothenburg* (Prague ed.), no. 941.
  R. Israel b. Petachiah Isserlein (1390–1460) posits that mature debt obligations, despite fears of default on the part of the creditor, are assessed at their value at maturity. Should the asset-holder find the above arrangement unacceptable, he can have the debt obligation removed temporarily from his property base by transferring ownership of it to the community. In the event the debt is eventually paid off, the community retains one third of the proceeds, while the remaining two thirds revert to the creditor.
  An alternative method of assessment is cited by R. Isserlein. This proce-

dure would allow the asset-holder himself to determine the value of his debt obligation. Once he attaches a value to his promissory note, however, he is obliged to sell it to any member of the community wishing to purchase it at the set price. This latter provision apparently provides the creditor with a disincentive to underassess the value of his asset.

R. Isserlein, however, rejects the above assessment procedure on the grounds that it would not adequately safeguard against underassessment. This follows from the assumption that the value the creditor attaches to his promissory note will always exceed its market valuation. The creditor valuates his note on the basis of the probability that he will realize payment from it. Given a liquidity preference, the market will, however, assign a value to the asset below the price that it would have on the basis of this probability alone. No one would exchange purchasing power for a nonliquid asset unless he could obtain it at a considerable discount (*Responsa Terumat ha-Deshen*, no. 342).

The argument obviously presupposes that the current asset-holder shares no such intense preference for liquidity and is aware of this discrepancy. Should the liquidity preferences of the current note-holder and the potential investors converge, self-assessment would not lead to underassessment. The reluctance on the part of would-be investors to surrender their liquidity for a nonliquid asset would be matched by the eagerness on the part of the current asset-holder to exchange his nonliquid asset for cash. No divergence between the current asset-holder's valuation of the note and the market's valuation of it would thus occur on account of the liquidity-preference phenomenon.

Ascribing identical liquidity preferences to all participants in the market does not, however, preclude the possibility that self-assessment would lead to underassessment. Underassessment would occur when the current asset-holder either attaches a lower probability to the prospect of default than the market consensus or is more favorably disposed toward risk bearing than investors in general. Under these conditions, the current note-holder, assuming he is aware of these discrepancies, can fix the value of his asset below its true value to him with assurance that no one would exercise his option to purchase it at that price.

54. *Responsa Terumat ha-Deshen*, no. 342.

55. *Responsa Ran*, no. 2.

56. R. Menachem Mendel b. Abraham Krochmal, *Responsa Tzemach Tzedek*, no. 34.

57. *Yad, Shekhenim* V:1.

58. *P'sachim* 6b.

59. *Baba Kamma* 50a; *Rif*, ad. loc.; *Tur*, op. cit., 410:3; *Sh. Ar.*, op. cit., 410:7; *Ar. ha-Sh.*, op. cit., 410:7.

60. R. Chananel b. Hushi'el of Rome (d. 1055/56), *Rabbenu Chananel, Baba Bathra* 8a; *Rosh, Baba Bathra* I:26; *Rif, Baba Bathra* 8a; *Yad*, op. cit., VI:6; *Tur*, op. cit., 163:15; *Sh. Ar.*, op. cit., 163:4; *Ar. ha-Sh.*, op. cit., 163:15.

61. Tosefta, *Baba Metzia* XI:12; *Rif, Baba Bathra* 7b; *Yad, Shekhenim* VI:1; *Rosh, Baba Bathra* 1:24; *Tur*, op. cit., 163:1; *Sh. Ar.*, op. cit., 163:1; *Ar. ha-Sh.*, op. cit., 163:1.

62. R. Joseph Caro, *Sh. Ar., Orach Chayyim* 55:22; *Ar. ha-Sh.*, op. cit., 163:1.

63. *Sh. Ar.*, op. cit., 54:21.

64. R. Moses Sofer, *Responsa Chatam Sofer, Choshen Mishpat*, no. 159.

65. R. Hai b. Sherira of Pumbedita (939–1038), quoted in *Beit Yosef, Tur, Orach Chayyim* 53.

66. R. Meir b. Isaac Katzenellenbogen, *Responsa Maharam of Padua*, no. 42.

67. *Sh. Ar., Orach Chayyim* 55:21–22; *Ar. ha-Sh., Orach Chayyim* 55:25–26.

68. R. Meir ha-Kohen, *Haggahot Maimuniyyot* (fl. 13th cent.), *Yad, Tefillah* XI.

69. R. David b. Samuel ha-Levi (1586–1667), *Turei Zahav, Sh. Ar.,* op. cit., 55, *ot* 6; R. David Solomon Eybeschuetz (d. 1810), *Levushei Sered, Sh. Ar.,* loc. cit.

70. *Ar. ha-Sh., Choshen Mishpat,* 163:1.

71. R. Moses Alshekh of Adrianople (d. ca. 1593), quoted in *K'nesset ha-Gedolah, Choshen Mishpat,* 163, comments on *Tur, ot* 5.

72. *Baba Bathra* 21a; *Yad, Talmud Torah* 11:1; *Tur, Yoreh De'ah* 245:1; *Sh. Ar., Yoreh De'ah* 245:7; *Ar. ha-Sh., Yoreh De'ah* 245:9.

73. *Ar. haSh.,* op. cit., 245:9, 27.

74. *Tosafot, Baba Kamma* 21a; *Rosh, Baba Bathra* 11:7. This view is quoted in *Rema, Sh. Ar., Yoreh De'ah* 245:15.

75. *Yad, Talmud Torah* 11:5; R. Jonah b. Abraham Gerondi (ca. 1200–1263), quoted in *Nimmukei Yosef, Baba Bathra* 21a. This view is quoted in *Rema,* loc. cit.

76. *Rema, Sh. Ar., Choshen Mishpat* 163:1; *Ar. ha-Sh., Choshen Mishpat* 163:1.

77. *Baraita, Baba Bathra* 8a; *Rif, Baba Bathra* 8a; *Yad, Mattenot Aniyim* IX:1–3; *Rosh, Baba Bathra* I:27; *Tur, Yoreh De'ah* 256:1–2; *Sh. Ar., Yoreh De'ah* 256:1 *Ar. ha-Sh., Yoreh De'ah* 256:1–2.

78. Jerusalem Talmud, *Baba Bathra* 1:4; *Mordechai, Baba Bathra* I:477; R. Isaac b. Moses of Vienna (ca. 1180–ca. 1250), *Or Zaru'a, Hilkhot Pesachim, ot* 255.

79. *Rema, Choshen Mishpat* 163:1; *Ar. ha-Sh., Choshen Mishpat* 163:1.

80. *Or Zaru'a* quoted in *Rema, Sh. Ar. Orach Chayyim* 429:1.

81. *Baraita, Baba Bathra* 8a; *Rif, Baba Bathra* 8a; *Yad, Mattenot Aniyim* IX:12 *Rosh, Baba Bathra* I:27; *Tur, Yoreh De'ah* 256:5; *Sh. Ar., Yoreh De'ah* 256:5; *Ar. ha-Sh, Yoreh De'ah* 256:15.

82. *Rif,* loc. cit; *Yad,* loc. cit.

83. *Rosh,* loc. cit.; *Tur,* loc. cit.

84. *Responsa Rashba,* vol. III:381.

85. *Yad,* op. cit., VII:10; *Tur,* op. cit., 248:1–2; *Sh. Ar.,* op. cit., 248:1–2; *Ar. ha-Sh.,* op. cit., 248:4–5. For a minority view regarding the nature of the coercion the recalcitrant may be subject to, see the opinions quoted in *Tosafot, Baba Bathra* 8b.

86. *Ar. ha-Sh., Yoreh De'ah* 250:12.

87. Deuteronomy 15:8; *Ketubbot* 67b; *Rif,* ad loc.; *Sh. Ar., Yoreh De'ah* 249:1; *Ar. ha-Sh., Yoreh De'ah* 249:1–2.

88. For a complete ordering of assistance requests on a priority basis, see *Tur,* op. cit., 251; *Sh. Ar.,* op. cit., 251:7–11, 13; *Ar. ha-Sh.,* op. cit., 251:10–12.

89. *Baba Bathra* 9a; *Rif,* ad loc.; *Rosh,* op. cit., 11:34; *Yad,* op. cit., VII:6 *Tur,* op. cit., 251–11; *Sh. Ar.,* op. cit., 251:7 *Ar. ha-Sh.,* op. cit., 251:10.

90. *Ketubbot* 67b; *Rif,* ad loc.; *Yad,* op. cit., VII:1–4; *Rosh, Ketubbot* VI:8; *Tur,* op. cit., 249:1–2; *Sh. Ar.,* op. cit., 249:1; *Ar. ha-Sh.,* op. cit., 249:1–2.

91. *Baba Bathra* 9b; *Yad,* op. cit., X:4–6, 7–15; *Tur,* op. cit., 249:4–13; *Sh. Ar.,* op. cit., 249:3–4, 6–13; *Ar. ha-Sh.,* op. cit., 249:13, 15–17.

92. Jerusalem Talmud, *Ketubbot* VI:5; *Sh. Ar.,* op. cit., 257:5.

93. *Ar. ha-Sh,* op. cit., 250:5.

94. *Yad,* op. cit., VII:5; *Tur,* op. cit., 249:1; *Sh. Ar.* op. cit., 249:1; *Ar. ha-Sh.* 249:1. R. Ezra Basri's survey of the responsa literature concludes that the majority of the talmudic decisors regard the 10 percent level as an obligation by rabbinical, as opposed to pentateuchal, decree. See R. Ezra Basri, *Dinei Mamonot,* vol. 1 (Jerusalem: Rubin Mass, 1974), p. 403.

95. *Ketubbot* 50a; *Rif*, ad loc.; *Yad, Arakhin* VIII:13; *Ketubbot* IV:15; *Rema Sh. Ar.*, op. cit., 249:1; *Ar. ha-Sh.*, op. cit., 249:1.

96. Basri, *Dinei Mamonot*, p. 405.

97. Ibid.

98. R. Moses Feinstein (b. 1895), *Iggerot Moshe, Yoreh De'ah* 143.

99. *Tur*, op. cit., 253:6; *Sh. Ar.*, op. cit., 253: 1–2; *Ar. ha-Sh.*, op. cit., 253:2.

100. *Yad, Mattenot Aniyim* IX:14; *Tur*, op. cit., 253:4–5; *Sh. Ar.*, op. cit., 253:1; *Ar. ha-Sh.*, op. cit., 253:5.

101. Tosafot, *Baba Kamma* 7b, claim that the realty market in general is subject to the same fluctuation.

102. Tosafot, *Baba Kamma* 7a; *Rif*, ad loc.; *Tur*, op. cit., 253:8–9, quoted in *Rema*, op. cit., 253:3. For a different view, see *Yad*, op. cit., IX:16, and *Sh. Ar.*, op. cit., 253:3.

103. *Baba Kamma* 7a; *Yad*, op. cit., IX:17; *Tur*, op. cit., 253:8; *Sh. Ar.*, op. cit., 253:3; *Ar. ha-Sh.*, op. cit., 253:8.

104. R. Joseph Caro, *Kesef Mishneh, Yad*, op. cit., IX:17; *Tur*, loc. cit.; *Ar. Sh.*, loc. cit.

105. *Pe'ah* V:4; *Yad*, op. cit., IX:15; *Tur*, op. cit., 253:9; *Sh. Ar.*, op. cit., 253:4.

106. *Torat Kohanim, B'har; Yad*, op. cit., 249:7; *Sh. Ar.*, 249:6; *Ar. ha-Sh.*, op. cit., 249:15.

107. *Ar. ha-Sh., Choshen Mishpat* 163:1.

108. Laws regulating family life are discussed in the rabbinic literature under the rubric of *hilkhot niddah*. For a discussion of these laws, see *Sh. Ar., Yoreh De'ah* 184–200. For laws relating to mikveh, see *Sh. Ar.*, op. cit., 201–202.

109. In the time of the First and Second Commonwealths, the practice of immersing in a mikveh on the eve of Festivals was a definite pentateuchal obligation. See *Rosh ha-Shana* 16b and references cited in *Rosh, Yoma* VIII:24; *S'fat Emet, Rosh ha-Shana* 16b.

110. *Rosh, Yoma* VIII:24; *S'fat Emet Rosh ha-Shana* 16b.

111. *Iggerot Moshe, Choshen Mishpat* 41.

112. *K'nesset ha-Gedolah* 163; notes on *Tur, ot* 5.

113. *Yad, Gittin* 11:20.

114. *Avot* 1:2.

115. *Yad, Talmud Torah* 11:1.

116. Cf. Leviticus 7:12–17, 26:27; Deuteronomy 11:13–22; *Avot* V:10, 11, 12.

NOTES TO CHAPTER 10

1. See *Tur, Yoreh De'ah* 159–77; *Sh. Ar., Yoreh De'ah* 159–77; R. Abraham Danzig (1748–1820), *Chokhmat Adam* 130–42.

2. Tosafot, *Baba Metzia* 70b; *Yad, Malveh* V:1; *Rosh, Baba Metzia* V:52; *Tur*, op. cit., 159:1; *Sh. Ar.*, op. cit., 159:1; *Chokhmat Adam*, op. cit., 130:6; R. Ezra Basri, *Dinei Mamonot*, vol. 1 (Jerusalem: Reuben Mass, 1974), pp. 170–71. The Jew is, however, obligated to extend an interest-free loan to a non-Jew who demonstrated kindness and conferred him favors in the past—see R. Solomon Eger (1786–1852), *Gilyon Maharsha; Sh. Ar.*, op. cit., 159:1.

3. R. Isaac b. Sheshet Perfet, quoted in *Sh. Ar.*, op. cit., 173:5.

4. R. Isaac Lewin, "Responsa of R. Abraham son of the Masat Binyamin," *Talpiot* 9 (1970): 570–74.

5. *Tur,* op. cit., 173:4; *Sh. Ar.,* op. cit., 173:4; *Yad, Malveh* XIV:14; *Chokhmat Adam* 139:8; R. Jacob Y. Blau, *B'rit Yehuda* (Jerusalem, 1975), p. 281.

6. R. Shabbetai b. Meir ha-Kohen (1621–1662), *Siftei Kohen, Sh. Ar.,* op. cit., 173, note 8.

7. *Dinei Mamonot,* vol. 1, p. 136.

8. See *B'rit Yehuda,* p. 279.

9. R. Joshua ha-Kohen Falk (1555–1614), *Kunteres ha-Sma Arukha, ot* 26, *Ketzorah, ot* 7.

10. R. Moshe Sofer (1762–1839), *Responsa Chatam Sofer, Yoreh De'ah,* no. 135.

11. Cf. R. Israel Bari, "Milveh Memshaltet Mahu be-Issur Ribbit," *Ha-Torah ve-ha-Medina* 5–6 (1953–54): 296–301.

12. R. Isaac b. Jacob Alfasi (1013–1103) and R. Moshe b. Jacob of Coucy (13th cent.), quoted by R. Joseph Caro (*Beit Yosef, Tur,* op. cit., 177); R. Moses Isserles (1525–1572), *Rema, Sh. Ar.,* op. cit., 177:3; *Chokhmat Adam* 142:5; *Dinei Mamonot,* vol. 1, pp. 146–47. For a variant view, see *Yad, Sheluchin* VI:1.

13. *Baba Metzia* 70a; *Rif,* ad loc.; *Yad,* op. cit., V:8; *Rosh, Baba Metzia* V:50; *Tur,* op. cit., 177:1; *Sh. Ar., op. cit.,* 177:1; *Chokhmat Adam* 131:4, 142:1.

13a. *Baba Metzia* 104b; *Rif,* ad loc.; *Yad,* op. cit. VI:2; *Rosh, Baba Metzia* IX:9; *Tur,* op. cit. 177:2; *Sh. Ar.,* op. cit. 177:2; *B'rit Yehuda,* op. cit., p. 542.

14. *Baba Metzia* 68a, 104b; *Yad,* op. cit., VI:2; *Rosh, Baba Metzia* IX:9; *Tur,* op. cit., 177:1–2; *Sh. Ar.* op. cit., 177:2; *Chokhmat Adam* 142:2.

15. R. David b. Samuel ha-Levi (1586–1667), *Turei Zahav, Sh. Ar.,* op. cit., 177, note 5; *Siftei Kohen, Sh. Ar.,* op. cit., 177, note 9; *Chokhmat Adam,* loc. cit.; for the monetary requirements of the nominal fee, see *Dinei Mamonot,* vol 1, pp. 144–45.

16. Tosafot, *Baba Kamma* 102a; R. Baruch (ca. 1150–1221), quoted in *Mordechai, Baba Kamma* IX:122; *Tur,* op. cit., 177:14; *Sh. Ar.,* op. cit., 177:5; *Rema,* op. cit., 177:5; *Chokhmat Adam* 142:26. Limiting the protective force of the devolvement clause, R. Abraham Y. Karelitz (1878–1953), *Yoreh De'ah* 76:1 posits that the *iska* agreement may only call for B to assume full responsibility for loss when the losses occur as a result of B's failure to adhere to A's conditions. Should the realized loss be unrelated to B's departure from A's conditions, the loss must be divided according to the profit-loss stipulation of the *iska* agreement. R. Shneur Zalman of Lyady (1745–1813), *Shulchan Arukh of the Rav, Hilkhot Ribbit, sief* 44, however, validates the devolvement clause even for losses not caused by B's departure from A's conditions.

17. R. Abraham b. Mordechai ha-Levi (late 17th cent.), *Ginnat Veradim, Yoreh De'ah* VI:9.

18. *Chazon Ish,* loc. cit.

19. *Rema,* loc. cit.; *Chokhmat Adam* 142:6.

20. R. Israel b. Petachiah Isserlein (1390–1460), quoted in *Turei Zahav, Sh. Ar.,* op. cit., 167, note 1, and in *Siftei Kohen, Sh. Ar.,* op. cit., 167, note 1; *Chokhmat Adam,* loc. cit.

21. *Turei Zahav,* loc. cit.

22. *Turei Zahav,* loc. cit; *Siftei Kohen,* loc. cit.; *Chokhmat Adam,* loc. cit.

23. *Turei Zahav,* loc. cit.; *Kunteres ha-Sma Arukha ot* 9; see *B'rit Yehuda,* p. 588.

24. *Responsa Rema,* no. 80; R. Meir b. Gedaliah Lublin (1558–1616), *Responsa Maharam Lublin* 135; *Chokhmat Adam* 142:7.

25. R. Moses b. Joseph Trani (1500–1580), *Responsa MaBit* 43; *Ginnat Veradim, Yoreh De'ah* VI:8–9; R. Joseph Saul Nathanson (1810–1875), *Sho'el*

u-Meshiv, vol. 3, part 1, siman 137; R. Shalom Mordechai Schwadron (1835–1911), Responsa Maharsham, vol. II:215.

26. Under circumstances of self-evident loss, A may not insist that B submit to a solemn oath in regard to the occurrence of the loss. Cf. B'rit Yehuda, p. 592.

27. Baba Metzia 104b; Yad, op. cit., VII:4; Tur, op. cit., 177:38; Sh. Ar., op. cit., 177:30; Chokhmat Adam 142:9.

28. R. Baruch (ca. 1150–1221), quoted in R. Mordechai b. Hillel (1240–1298), Mordechai, Baba Kamma IX:122, and in Rema, Sh. Ar., op. cit., 177:5.

29. Shulchan Arukh of the Rav, loc. cit., sief 42.

30. Responsa Sho'el u-Meshiv, vol. 1, part 3, siman 160; vol. 3, part 1, siman 133. Sharing the above broad definition of iska is R. Shalom Mordechai Schwadron (1835–1911), Responsa Maharsham, vol. II:215,252; and R. Mordechai Yaakov Breisch (contemporary), Responsa Chelkat Yaakov, vol. III:199,200.

31. R. Meir Arik (ca. 1925), Imrei Yosher I:108. R. Arik's position is articulated in various forms of elaboration in earlier rabbinic literature. Cf. Ginnat Veradim, op. cit., VI:4; Shulchan Arukh of the Rav, op. cit., sief 42; R. Solomon b. Joseph Ganzfried, Kitzur Shulchan Arukh 66:10; R. Solomon Leib Tabak (1832–1908), Erekh Shai 177:7.

32. See Imrei Yosher, loc. cit. Requiring a third party to take possession of this merchandise on behalf of A when B acquires it is, according to R. Arik, unnecessary. B's resolve, at the time he purchases and transacts with the requisite merchandise, that his actions are on behalf of A suffices to allow A to acquire part ownership in the merchandise. For an alternative hetter iska arrangement designed to accommodate the businessman desiring capital for personal use, see Kitzur Shulchan Arukh 66:10.

33. Appreciation in the market value of an iska asset is legitimately regarded as an iska profit. See R. Solomon Leib Tabak (1832–1908), Teshurat Shai, vol. I:23.

34. Manuscript of R. Shimon Greenfeld, published by courtesy of Rabbi M. Lemberger in No'am (1960), pp. 244–250.

35. R. Mordechai Yaakov Breisch, Chelkat Yaakov, vol. III:190.

36. Baba Metzia 69b; Rif, ad loc.; Yad op. cit., V:14; Rosh, Baba Metzia V:52; Ran, Baba Metzia 69b; Tur, op. cit., 160:14; Sh. Ar., op. cit., 160:13; Chokhmat Adam, op. cit., 132:1.

37. R. Nissim Gerondi (Ran, loc. cit.), R. Joseph Caro (Beit Yosef, Tur, op. cit.,), and R. Abraham Danzig (Chokhmat Adam, loc. cit.) legitimize the above procedure as long as C does not indicate a willingness to compensate A for influencing B to loan him money. R. Asher and R. Jacob, however, disallow C from instructing B to financially induce A to lend him money.

Subject Index

Name Index

Aaron ha-Levi of Barcelona, 220 n. 94
Abramsky, R. Jechezkiel, 192 n. 10, 193 n. 30
Adret, R. Solomon b. Abraham, 179 n. 6, n. 13, 180 n. 18, 41, 52, 54, 186 n. 26, n. 42, n. 53, 187 n. 59, n. 61, 188 n. 74, 189 n. 90, n. 102, 190 n. 121, n. 131, 64, 67, 192 n. 10, n. 15, 193 n. 20, n. 24, n. 27, n. 31, 195 n. 57, n. 66, n. 67, n. 69, 195 n. 3, 112–113, 201 n. 101, n. 116, 203–204 n. 42, 135, 148, 151, 205 n. 5, n. 6, n. 10, n. 12, n. 13, 207 n. 49, n. 52, 209 n. 84
Abraham b. David, 181 n. 36, 39, 186 n. 26, n. 39, n. 41, n. 42, 189 n. 102, 192 n. 17, 82, 85, 196 n. 19, n. 25, 197 n. 20, 199 n. 71
Abraham b. Mordechai ha-Levi, 190 n. 131, n. 132, 211 n. 17, n. 25, 212 n. 31
Abulafia, R. Meir, 180 n. 18, n. 20, 67, 191 n. 6, 192 n. 15, 195 n. 57, n. 66, 195 n. 3, 196 n. 33, 197 n. 13, n. 14, 145–146, 206 n. 14, 207 n. 40
Aharon b. Chayyim ha-Kohen, 179 n. 10
Alashkar, R. Moses b. Isaac, 205 n. 6, 205–206 n. 13
Albeck, R. Shalom, 184 n. 3
Alfasi, R. Isaac b. Jacob, 11, 180 n. 15, n. 16, n. 17, n. 21, n. 26, n. 30, 181 n. 36, 187 n. 45, n. 61, 31, 183 n. 4, 184 n. 4, n. 5, n. 6, 185 n. 9, n. 14, n. 19, 186 n. 27, n. 30, 187 n. 62, 188 n. 76, n. 77, 189 n. 95, 191 n. 146, n. 147, 192 n. 8, n. 9, n. 12, n. 16, n. 18, 193 n. 20, n. 21, n. 23, n. 36, 194 n. 42, n. 45, n. 48, n. 49, n. 51, n. 56, 195 n. 58, n. 60, n. 62, n. 66, 196 n. 18, 105, 197 n. 2, n. 7, n. 21, 198 n. 23, n. 33, n. 34, n. 35, n. 37, n. 38, n. 43, n. 45, n. 47, 199 n. 53, n. 55, n. 56, n. 58, n. 59, n. 60, n. 61, n. 62, n. 65, n. 67, n. 68, n. 73, 200 n. 82, n. 84, n. 88, n. 91, 201 n. 100, n. 104, n. 110, n. 113, n. 114, 127, 202 n. 2, n. 3, n. 5, n. 6, n. 8, n. 10, n. 11, n. 12, 203 n. 27, n. 29, n. 41, n. 42, 204 n. 45, 205 n. 70, 155, 206 n. 24, n. 28, 207 n. 30, n. 48, 208 n. 59, n. 60, n. 61, 209 n. 77, n. 81, n. 82, 209 n. 89, n. 90, 210 n. 95, n. 102, 211 n. 12, n. 13, 13a, 212 n. 36

Alshekh, R. Moses, 154, 207 n. 41, 209 n. 71
Alter, R. Judah Aryeh Loeb, 210 n. 109, n. 110
Areeda, Phillip, 183 n. 1
Arieli, R. Isaac, 183 n. 67, 184 n. 18, 204 n. 67, 206 n. 26
Arik, R. Meir, 179 n. 13, 169–170, 212 n. 31, n. 32
Arukh ha-Shulchan, see Epstein, R. Jechiel Michael
Aryeh Loeb b. Joseph ha-Kohen, 42, 46, 186 n. 49, 187 n. 58, 189 n. 87, n. 90, n. 91, 192 n. 15, 195 n. 62, 87, 196 n. 31, 201 n. 98, n. 99
Asher b. Jechiel, 16, 179 n. 3, n. 6, n. 7, 180 n. 15, 181 n. 36, 182 n. 45, n. 47, n. 54, n. 56, n. 58, n. 59, 183 n. 4, 184 n. 4, n. 5, n. 6, 185 n. 7, n. 14, n. 19, 186 n. 27, n. 30, 187 n. 60, n. 61, n. 62, n. 65, n. 66, 188 n. 76, 189 n. 90, n. 100, n. 102, n. 104, 191 n. 146, n. 147, 73, 191 n. 6, 192 n. 8, n. 16, 193 n. 20, n. 21, n. 23, n. 24, n. 31, n. 36, 194 n. 42, n. 45, 194 n. 48, n. 50, n. 56, 195 n. 58, n. 60, n. 63, n. 66, 195 n. 3, 196 n. 7, n. 13, n. 14, n. 15, 92, 104–109, 197 n. 2, n. 7, n. 8, n. 9, n. 21, 198 n. 24, n. 33, n. 35, n. 37, n. 38, n. 39, n. 43, 199 n. 53, n. 55, n. 56, n. 57, n. 58, n. 60, n. 61, n. 62, n. 68, n. 74, 202 n. 2, n. 4, n. 6, n. 8, n. 10, n. 11, n. 12, 203 n. 27, n. 29, n. 41, n. 42, 204 n. 44, 205 n. 70, 135, 154–155, 205 n. 8, n. 13, 206 n. 22, n. 24, n. 28, 207 n. 30, n. 48, 208 n. 60, n. 61, 209 n. 74, n. 77, n. 81, n. 83, n. 89, n. 90, 210 n. 95, n. 109, n. 110, 210 n. 2, 211 n. 13, 13a, n. 14, 212 n. 36
Ashkenazi, R. Bezalel, 186 n. 26, n. 39, n. 40, 187 n. 59, 189 n. 97, n. 99, n. 102, 180 n. 32, 192 n. 10, n. 15, 193 n. 27, n. 28, n. 31, 195 n. 57, n. 66, 200 n. 76

Bacharach, R. Jair Chayyim, 40, 186 n. 46
Bari, R. Israel, 211 n. 11
Baruch, R., 212 n. 28
Baruch b. Samuel, 168–169, 211 n. 16
Basri, R. Ezra, 180 n. 33, 181 n. 36, 200 n. 94, 201 n. 102, 203 n. 24, 209 n. 94,